Rise
of the
Tyrant

Volume 2

of

*Change to Chains-The 6,000
Year Quest for Global Power*

William J. Federer

Rise of the Tyrant
Volume 2 of Change to Chains-the 6,000 Year Quest for Global Power
by William J. Federer

This book is a part of a multi-volume project in which thousands of books,
articles and reference works were researched, with effort made to credit
sources. Cover design by DustinMyersDesign.com 573-308-6060

Library of Congress HISTORY / POLITICAL / EDUCATION

paperback book   ISBN13 978-0-9827101-7-3

FREE EBOOK
For a limited time, as owner of this book, you may receive an ebook of
this title. Email **wjfederer@gmail.com** with subject line **"ebook Rise of
the Tyrant."** It will be emailed as a pdf attachment.

Amerisearch, Inc.
www.AmericanMinute.com
1-888-USA-WORD, 314-502-8924
wjfederer@gmail.com

Special thanks for valuable assistance in editing this volume is given to
Thomas A. Federer, Esq., Dr. Jerry Newcombe, Judge Darrell White,
and my wife, Susie Federer.

CONTENTS

"The story of the future
is written in the past."

-Lord Acton, 1877

"Those who cannot remember the past are condemned to repeat it."
-George Santayana, 1905

"When the past no longer
illuminates the future,
the spirit walks in darkness."
-Alexis de Tocqueville

"I know of no way of judging
the future but by the past."
-Patrick Henry

"The farther back you can look,
the farther forward you are
likely to see."
-Winston Churchill

"Live both in the future and the past. Who does not
live in the past
does not live in the future."
-Lord Acton

"When a nation goes down... one condition may
always be found; they forgot where they came
from."
-Poet Carl Sandburg

INTRODUCTORY QUOTES

George Washington warned in his Farewell Address, 1796:

A small but artful and enterprising minority... are likely, in the course of time ... to become potent engines, by which cunning, ambitious, and unprincipled men will be enabled to subvert the power of the people and to usurp for themselves the reins of government ...

Let there be no change by usurpation; for though this, in one instance, may be the instrument of good, it is the customary weapon by which free governments are destroyed ...

This leads at length to a more formal and permanent despotism ... Disorders and miseries ... gradually incline the minds of men to seek security and repose in the absolute power of an Individual ... [who] turns this disposition to the purposes of his own elevation, on the ruins of public liberty ...

The spirit of encroachment tends to consolidate the powers of all the departments in one, and thus to create, whatever the form of government, a real despotism.

A little over 40 years later, President Andrew Jackson remarked in his Farewell Address, 1837:

Washington ... seemed to be ... the voice of prophecy, foretelling events and warning us of the evil to come ... There have always been those amongst us who wish to enlarge the powers of the General Government ... to overstep the boundaries marked out for it by the Constitution ...

Government ... passed from the hands of the many to the hands of the few, and this organized money power from its secret conclave would have dictated the choice of your highest officers and compelled you to make peace or war, as best suited their own wishes ...

It is from within, among yourselves – from cupidity (excessive desire), from corruption, from disappointed ambition and inordinate thirst for power – that factions will be formed and liberty endangered.

Benjamin Franklin stated at the Constitutional Convention, June 2, 1787:

> And of what kind are the men that will strive for this profitable preeminence, through all the bustle of cabal, the heat of contention, the infinite mutual abuse of parties, tearing to pieces the best of characters?
>
> It will not be the wise and moderate, the lovers of peace and good order, the men fittest for the trust. It will be the bold and the violent, the men of strong passions and indefatigable activity in their selfish pursuits. These will thrust themselves into your government and be your rulers.

President William Henry Harrison stated in his Inaugural Address, March 4, 1841:

> The tendency of power to increase itself, particularly when exercised by a single individual... would terminate in virtual monarchy ... Not only will the State authorities be overshadowed by the great increase of power in the Executive department ... but the character of that government ... will be essentially and radically changed ...
>
> This is the old trick of those who would usurp the government of their country. In the name of democracy they speak, warning the people against the influence of wealth and the danger of aristocracy...
>
> The tendencies of all such governments in their decline is to monarchy ... and, like the false Christs whose coming was foretold by the Savior, seeks to, and were it possible would, impose upon the true and most faithful disciples of liberty ...
>
> A dangerous accession to the Executive power introduced and established amidst unusual professions of devotion to democracy.

Jefferson wrote in his *Notes on Virginia*, 1782:

> Our Assembly ... should look forward to a time, and that not a distant one, when corruption in this as in the country from which we derive our origin, will have seized the heads of government, and be spread by them through the body of the people ... The time

to guard against corruption and tyranny is before they shall have gotten hold of us.

HISTORY IS THE MEMORY OF A NATION

"Evil is stirring in Mordor. The Ring has awakened. It's heard its master's call ... Always remember, Frodo, the Ring is trying to get back to its master. It wants to be found." – warned Gandalf, in J.R.R. Tolken's *The Lord of the Rings.*

A digital photo greatly magnified on a computer screen appears as square colored pixels – it is unrecognizable. But by clicking "zoom out" the photo comes into focus and the image is recognizable.

In the same way, if one only sees the day-to-day news headlines, it can be unrecognizable what is happening in the world. But by zooming out and seeing trends over several centuries, it begins to come into focus what is happening. Winston Churchill stated:

> The farther back you can look, the farther forward you are likely to see.

This volume is an in-depth review of the rise and fall of great republics, kings and tyrants, with profound quotes from notable philosophers, statesmen and historians, allowing the reader to gain powerful insights from the past into what is happening in the world today. By the end of this book, you will be one step closer to answering the question, "is history repeating itself?"

Pulitzer Prize winning historian Arthur M. Schlesinger, Jr., wrote in an op-ed titled "Folly's Antidote" (*The New York Times*, Jan. 1, 2007):

> History is to the nation as memory is to the individual. As persons deprived of memory become disoriented and lost, not knowing where they have been and where they are going, so a nation denied a conception of the past will be disabled in dealing with its present and its future.

"The longer you look back," said Winston Churchill, "the farther you can look forward" ... I believe a consciousness of history is a moral necessity for a nation.

Lord John Dalberg-Acton served in Britain's Parliament and was friends with many influential leaders of his day, including Alexis de Tocqueville and British Prime Minister William Ewart Gladstone. Lord Acton stated in his address "The History of Freedom in Christianity" (Bridgnorth Institute, May 28, 1877):

The story of the future is written in the past.

John F. Kennedy wrote in the Introduction to *The American Heritage New Illustrated History of the United States*, 16 volumes (Dell Publishing Company, 1960):

History, after all, is the memory of a nation. Just as memory enables the individual to learn, to choose goals and stick to them, to avoid making the same mistake twice – in short, to grow – so history is the means by which a nation establishes its sense of identity and purpose ...

Knowledge of history is ... responsibility to those who came before us and struggled and sacrificed to pass on to us our precious inheritance of freedom ... and ... responsibility to those who will come after us and to whom we must pass on that inheritance with what new strength and substance it is within our power to add.

Justice Oliver Wendell Holmes wrote in *New York Trust Co. v. Eisner* (256 U.S. 345, 349, 1921, Holmes, J.):

A page of history is worth a volume of logic.

Lord Acton wrote:

The value of history is CERTAINTY – against which opinion is broken up.

Harvard professor George Santayana wrote in "Reason in Common Sense" (*The Life of Reason*, Vol. 1, 1905):

Those who cannot remember the past are condemned to repeat it.

Alexander Solzhenitsyn stated:

If we don't know our own history, we will simply have to endure all the same mistakes, sacrifices, and absurdities all over again.

Ronald Reagan stated:

Freedom is never more than one generation away from extinction. We didn't pass it to our children in the bloodstream. It must be fought for, protected, and handed on for them to do the same, or one day we will spend our sunset years telling our children and our children's children what it was once like in the United States where men were free.

Poet Carl Sandburg wrote:

When a nation goes down, or a society perishes, one condition may always be found; they forgot where they came from. They lost sight of what had brought them along.

Karl Marx stated:

Take away the heritage of a people and they are easily destroyed.

George Orwell wrote in *Nineteen Eighty-Four*:

"Who controls the past," ran the Party slogan, "controls the future: who controls the present controls the past."

George Orwell added:

The Party could thrust its hand into the past and say of this or that event, it never happened ...

Past events, it is argued, have no objective existence, but survive only in written records and in human memories. The past is whatever the records and the memories agree upon. And since the Party is in full control of all records, and in equally full control of the minds of its members, it follows that the past is whatever the Party chooses to make it ...

The past, he reflected, had not merely been altered, it had been actually destroyed ... Everything faded into mist. The past was erased, the erasure was forgotten, the lie became truth.

Lord Acton wrote:

> Government rules the present. Literature rules the future.

Adolph Hitler threatened Nov. 6, 1933 (William Shirer, *Rise and Fall of the Third Reich,* NY: Simon and Schuster, 1960, p, 249):

> When an opponent declares, "I will not come over to your side," I calmly say, "Your child belongs to us already ... What are you? You will pass on. Your descendants, however, now stand in the new camp. In a short time they will know nothing else but this new community."

Dr. James Dobson addressed the National Religious Broadcasters, Feb. 16, 2002:

> If they can get control of children ... they can change the whole culture in one generation ... There is a concerted effort to manipulate the minds of kids ... A stem cell is a cell in the human being ... that in the very early stages of development it is undifferentiated. In other words, it's not yet other kinds of tissue, but it can go any direction depending on the environment that it's in ... Do you understand that children are the stem cells for the culture?

In America:

–The COUNTRY is controlled by LAWS

–LAWS are controlled by POLITICIANS

–POLITICIANS are controlled by VOTERS

–VOTERS are controlled by PUBLIC OPINION

–PUBLIC OPINION is controlled by MEDIA
   & EDUCATION.

So whoever controls MEDIA & EDUCATION
   controls the COUNTRY!

Testifying before the U.S. Senate in June of 2005, historian David McCullough quoted former Librarian of Congress Daniel J. Boorstin:

> Trying to plan for the future without a sense of the past is like trying to plant cut flowers.

McCullough continued:

> If we raise generation after generation of young Americans who are historically illiterate, we running a terrible risk for this country ... Will knowing history make one a better citizen? Absolutely. Will knowing history give us a sense of who we are and how we got to be where we are and why we are the way we are? Absolutely.

Judge Learned Hand wrote:

> The use of history is to tell us ... past themes, else we should have to repeat, each in his own experience, the successes and the failures of our forebears.

Roman historian Livy (59 BC–17 AD) stated:

> What chiefly makes the study of history beneficial and fruitful is this, that you behold the lessons of every kind of experience as upon a famous monument; from these you may choose for your own state what to imitate, and mark for avoidance what is shameful.

Patrick Henry told the Second Virginia Convention at St. John's Church in Richmond, Virginia, March 23, 1775:

> I have but one lamp by which my feet are guided, and that is the lamp of experience. I know of no way of judging the future but by the past.

C.S. Lewis wrote in *Mere Christianity*, 1952:

> All that we call human history – money, poverty, ambition, war, prostitution, classes, empires, slavery – is the long terrible story of man trying to find something other than God which will make him happy.

Ben Franklin addressed delegates at Constitutional Convention, June 28, 1787:

> We have gone **back to ancient history** for models of government, and examined the different forms of those **republics** which, having been formed with **the seeds of their own dissolution**, now no longer exist.

Readers of this book will embark on journey to retrace Franklin's steps, in hopes that by looking "back to ancient history" and by examining "the different forms of those

Republics," we may be able to identify what were "the seeds of their own dissolution," and thereby gain insight to help our Republic continue to exist.

BACK TO ANCIENT HISTORY

There have been approximately 6,000 years of recorded human history, that is, human beings writing down human records. Initial attempt of humans to leave records was the piling up of stones or bricks to mark significant places, events or agreements.

Genesis 11:4:

> And they said, Go to, let us build us a city and a tower, whose top may reach unto heaven; and let us make us a name, lest we be scattered abroad upon the face of the whole earth.

The earliest "written" records appeared around 3,300 BC, namely, Sumerian cuneiform on clay tablets in the Mesopotamia Valley, the land between the Tigris and Euphrates Rivers. This was followed by Egyptian hieroglyphics around 3,000 BC written on papyrus and etched on monuments along the Nile River.

Around 2,600 BC, China's Yellow Emperor oversaw the creation of Chinese characters. Bamboo Annals recorded China's first dynasty, the Xia Dynasty, c.2,070 BC.

3,000 to 4,000 BC to the present time of just over 2,000 AD equals approximately 5,000 to 6,000 years of recorded history. Franklin D. Roosevelt stated in 1940:

> 5,000 years of recorded history have proven that mankind has always believed in God in spite of many abortive attempts to exile God.

Richard Overy, editor of *The Times Complete History of the World*, stated in "The 50 Key Dates of World History" (Oct. 19, 2007):

> No date appears before the start of human civilizations about 5,500 years ago and the beginning of a written or pictorial history.

Secretary of State William Jennings Bryan wrote in his address, "Prince of Peace," *New York Times*, Sept. 7, 1913:

> 6,000 years of recorded history and yet we know no more about the secret of life than they knew in the beginning.

Astronomer Johannes Kepler wrote in *The Harmonies of the World* (1619):

> The book is written ... It may be well to wait a century for a reader, as God has waited 6,000 years for an observer.

James Wilson was a signer of the Declaration of Independence and the U.S. Constitution, and was appointed a Supreme Court Justice by President George Washington. Wilson remarked at Pennsylvania's Ratifying Convention, Nov. 26, 1787:

> After a period of 6,000 years has elapsed since the creation, the United States exhibit to the world the first instance ... of a nation... assembling voluntarily... and deciding calmly concerning that system of government under which they would wish that they and their posterity should live.

Daniel Webster state in 1802:

> Miracles do not cluster, and what has happened once in 6,000 years, may not happen again. Hold on to the Constitution, for if the American Constitution should fail, there will be anarchy throughout the world.

In a sense, 6,000 years is not that long. It is only 60 people living 100 years each, back-to-back. Everyone has met someone who has lived 100 years, or close to it – maybe a grandmother. 6,000 years is just 60 grandmothers living 100 years each back-to-back.

During the past 6,000 years, written records are replete with stories of empires rising and falling, followed by more empires rising and falling. What the records reveal is that the most common form of government in recorded human history is a MONARCHY – the rule of a king.

Kings have had different titles: Caesar, Caliph,

Chairman, Chieftain, Communist Dictator, Czar, Despot, Dey, Dictator, Doge, Emir, Emperor, General Secretary, Grand Mughal, Kaiser, Khan, Maharajah, Monarch, Pasha, Pharaoh, Potentate, President, Prime Minister, Prince, Raja, Regent, Satrap, Shah, Sheikh, Shogun, Sovereign, Sultan, Tsar, Tyrant.

The name changes but the role remains the same – kings control the lives of those in their kingdoms. The selfish climb for one person to dominate others is the default setting for human government.

The first account in the Bible illustrates this. Just as an electric magnet can switch polarity from positive to negative in an instant, the Book of Genesis tells of the fall of Adam and Eve, and the subsequent polarity switch in human nature.

John Jay, the First Chief Justice of the Supreme Court, appointed by George Washington, stated May 13, 1824:

> Man was originally created and placed in a state of happiness, but, becoming disobedient, was subjected to the degradation and evils which he and his posterity have since experienced.

Instantly, human nature changed from "Creator focused" to "self-focused." This "self-focused" attitude became the dominant universal trait of human nature. Every child is born with the "default-setting" of selfishness: "Foolishness is bound in the heart of a child." (Proverbs 22:15)

British Prime Minister William Gladstone wrote:

> Selfishness is the greatest curse of the human race.

Lord Acton wrote:

> Self-preservation and self-denial — the basis of all political economy ...

> Everybody likes to get as much power as circumstances allow, and nobody will vote for a self-denying ordinance.

Sigmund Freud believed that human beings are irrational beings motivated primarily by selfish desires hidden in their unconscious. By understanding and acting upon these selfish desires, people can be manipulated. Ernest Dichter wrote: "Modern man...tries to work off his frustrations by spending on self-sought gratification." Edward L. Bernays was hired in 1928 by the America Tobacco Company to devise a media campaign to entice women to smoke cigarettes. Appealling to the selfish desire for power and gratificaion, his successful techniques were compiled in *The Engineering of Consent* (1947).

If a child is left to their own unrestrained selfish impulses, the child grows into a bully, bossing around others around, and inevitably breaking out into aggression. This was demonstrated in the biblical story of Cain killing Abel. To use a computer analogy, the fall of man allowed the software virus of selfishness to infect human behavior.

Sir Alexander Fraser Tytler wrote in *Universal History from the Creation of the World to the Beginning of the 18th Century* (Boston: Fetridge & Co., 1834; 1850):

> Man is a being instigated by the love of power – a passion visible in an infant, and common to us even with the inferior animals – he will seek personal superiority in preference to every matter.

Gaius Cornelius Tacitus (56–117AD) wrote in *Annals*, book 15.53:

> Lust of absolute power is more burning than all the passions.

Lord Acton wrote:

> Absolute power demoralizes.

Frederic Bastiat wrote in *The Law* (1850):

> But there is also another tendency that is common among people. When they can, they wish to live and prosper at the expense of others. This is no rash accusation. Nor does it come from a gloomy and uncharitable spirit.
>
> The annals of history bear witness to the truth of it: the incessant wars, mass migrations, religious persecutions, universal slavery, dishonesty in

commerce, and monopolies.

This fatal desire has its origin in the very nature of man — in that primitive, universal, and insuppressible instinct that impels him to satisfy his desires with the least possible pain.

Put babies in a playpen and one will grab the rattle from the others. Put boys on a playground and one will be the bully hogging the ball. Put girls at a school lunch table and one will be the diva of the clique. Put natives in the woods and one will be the Indian chief. Put politicians in a city and one will be the party boss. Put people in an inner-city hood and one will be the gang leader.

And, in a sense, a king is nothing more than a glorified gang leader. Thomas Paine wrote in his third edition of *Common Sense*, Philadelphia, Feb. 14, 1776:

> The present race of kings, ... could we take off the dark covering of antiquity and trace them to their first rise, we should find the first of them nothing better than the principal ruffian of some restless gang, whose savage manners of preeminence in subtlety obtained him the title of chief among plunderers ...

> Of more worth is one honest man to society and in the sight of God, than all the crowned ruffians that ever lived.

Alexander Hamilton stated at the Constitutional Convention, June 22, 1787:

> Take mankind as they are, and what are they governed by? Their passions ... One great error is that we suppose mankind is more honest than they are.

If a powerful person dies, another is quick to replace him, keeping the hierarchical structure in place. An analogy of this are the 20 foot high termite hills that rise from the African plains. Somewhere deep inside each termite's DNA is a blueprint of what the hill should look like. If one termite is removed, the others pick up where it left off and, without missing a beat, instinctively continue construction. Similarly, somewhere deep inside the human DNA is a "pecking-order" to dominate others, concentrating power in the building a human hill – Tower of Babel.

An allegory of this is a scene from the sci-fi movie, *Terminator 3: Rise of the Machines* (2003), where a killer robot T-X is sent from the future to assassinate John Connor. In a fight, the T-X robot is blown-up, but to the dismay of the audience, the scattered metal pieces melt into silvery balls that roll together into a molten pool, out of which the T-X rises again to chase John Connor.

In the same way, Nimrod's power at the Tower of Babel was scattered when God confused the languages. Tragically, in each generation, power tries to re-concentrate with a tyrant dominating his subjects. In this sense, death is a blessing, as often it is only when the tyrant dies that people get relief.

George Orwell wrote in *Nineteen Eighty-Four*:

> The Party seeks power entirely for its own sake. We are not interested in the good of others; we are interested solely in power. Not wealth or luxury or long life or happiness: only power, pure power.

David Horowitz wrote in *Rules for the Revolution–The Alinsky Model* (Freedom Center, PO Box 55089, Sherman Oaks, CA 91499, 2009, p. 8–9):

> An SDS (Students for a Democratic Society) radical once wrote: "The issue is never the issue ... but only an occasion to advance the real cause which is the accumulation of power" ... The *New Republic*'s Ryan Lizza nicely illustrates ... When Alinsky would ask new students why they wanted to organize, they would invariably respond with selfless bromides about wanting to help others. Alinsky would then scream back at them that there was a one-word answer: "You want to organize for POWER!"

Thomas Jefferson wrote in his *Notes on Virginia*, 1782:

> Nor should our Assembly be deluded by the integrity of their own purposes, and conclude that these unlimited powers will never be abused, because themselves are not disposed to abuse them.
>
> They should look forward to a time, and that not a

distant one, when corruption in this as in the country from which we derive our origin, will have seized the heads of government, and be spread by them through the body of the people; when they will purchase the voices of the people and make them pay the price.

Human nature is the same on each side of the Atlantic, and will be alike influenced by the same causes. The time to guard against corruption and tyranny is before they shall have gotten hold of us. It is better keep the wolf out of the fold, than to trust to drawing his teeth and talons after he shall have entered.

SPECTRUM OF POWER

J.R.R. Tolken wrote in *Lord of the Rings*:

One Ring to rule them all, One Ring to find them, One Ring to bring them all and in the darkness bind them.

There is a spectrum of power. On one side of the spectrum is TOTAL GOVERNMENT and the other side is NO GOVERNMENT.

On the TOTAL GOVERNMENT side, power concentrates into the hands of a king with the irresistible gravitational pull of a black hole. Newton's Law of Gravity states that objects of lesser mass are attracted to objects of greater mass.

Once power concentrates, fawning subjects, like groupies, are magnetically drawn into a personality-cult of loyalty to a self-absorbed king, who rules with an obsession of staying in power and expanding his power.

The king's state is supreme over all, as he has an insatiable appetite to regulate and control every aspect of everyone's life. King David was tempted with this when he took a national census, though he later repented. Augustus Caesar instituted an empire-wide census in the same spirit of modern-day NSA tracking of citizens' emails, web searches, and credit card purchases, where, under the guise of safety, control is usurped.

Harvard President Samuel Langdon stated, June 5, 1788:

> Where kings reigned their will was a law.

France's "Sun King" Louis XIV commented:

> It is legal because I wish it.

PATRONAGE SYSTEM

> Luke 22:25: The kings of the Gentiles exercise lordship over them, and they that exercise authority upon them are called benefactors.

Wherever there is a King, he is the "benefactor" of a "patronage system":

–if you are friends with the king, you are more equal;

–if you are not friends with the king, you are less equal; and

–if you are an enemy of the king, you are dead – it is called "treason."

George Orwell wrote in *Animal Farm*, 1945:

> All animals are equal, but some animals are more equal than others.

For most of history "EQUALITY" was how close of an orbit can one get to the KING. Kings claimed to be divinely appointed and those close to them enjoyed favoritism. Those at the bottom of the social ladder were slaves, condemned to obey the King's will, as in Egypt where they built cities of the dead, such as Pharaoh's Memphis.

George Mason wrote August 22, 1787:

> Every master of slaves is born a petty tyrant.

TOTAL GOVERNMENT - NO GOVERNMENT

On the other side of the power spectrum is NO GOVERNMENT. Power is separated into the hands of the people – where each individual is supreme unto themselves. NO GOVERNMENT is the classic definition of anarchy and chaos, except in one rare circumstance.

America's founders sought this rare circumstance. The founders' genius was in identifying the secret ingredient that allowed the country to get closest to the NO GOVERNMENT side of the spectrum, but still maintain order. What was the secret ingredient?

VIRTUE – where each individual is taught to exercise self-restraint, following an internal moral law.

The first instance in recorded history of a nation attempting a government based on virtue was the Hebrew nation. A significant part of the Hebrew Law is the teaching that individuals should exercise self-restraint – to treat others the way they would like to be treated – "The Golden Rule." In Matthew 2:37–40, Jesus said: "On these two commandments hang ALL THE LAW and the prophets." What were these two commandments?

> "Love the Lord thy God with all thy heart, and with all thy soul, and with all thy mind. This is the first and great commandment.
>
> And the second is like unto it, THOU SHALT LOVE THY NEIGHBOR AS THYSELF."

Accountability to God, in the first commandment, provided the motivation to keep His second commandment. This system gives to each individual maximum liberty, but at the same time, it is dependent on each individual personally practicing self-restraint and charity.

E.C. Wines wrote in *Commentaries on the Laws of the Ancient Hebrews, with an Introductory Essay on Civil Society & Government* (NY: Geo. P. Putnam & Co., 1853):

> Another of those great ideas, which constituted the basis of the Hebrew state, was liberty ... Liberty is a right of doing what the laws permit. If one citizen might do what they forbid, all might do it, which would be anarchy. True liberty would expire in such a state of things ...
>
> The learned Claude Fleury (*The Manners of the*

Ancient Israelites, 1681, c. 20) has declared his opinion on this point in unequivocal terms. "The Israelites," he says, "were perfectly free. They enjoyed the liberty cherished by Greece and Rome. Such was the purpose of God" ...

The Hebrew people enjoyed as great a degree of personal liberty, as can ever be combined with an efficient and stable government.

In other words, for there to be order in society with **less external government**, the people needed **more internal self-government**. To use a math concept, there is an inverse relationship: the decrease in one condition results in a proportional increase of another. Ben Franklin wrote:

Only a virtuous people are capable of freedom.

MONTESQUIEU

Different political philosophers categorized governments in different ways. French political philosopher Montesquieu (1689–1755) divided governments into 3 categories: 1) Republics; 2) Monarchs; and 3) Despots.

Montesquieu's *The Spirit of the Laws*, 1748, had a significant impact on America's founders, especially in introducting the idea that the power of a king could be divided into three branches: judicial, legislative, and executive. Each branch would selfishly attempt to pull power from the other two, thus preventing any one branch from usurping power.

Montesquieu listed in *The Spirit of the Laws*, Book 3:

A **republican** government ... the COLLECTIVE BODY OF THE PEOPLE ... should be possessed of THE SUPREME POWER ...

A **monarchy**, that the PRINCE should have THIS POWER, but in the execution of it should be DIRECTED BY ESTABLISHED LAWS ...

A **despotic** government, that A SINGLE PERSON should rule according to HIS OWN WILL AND CAPRICE.

Montesquieu described the three forms of government:

–A **Republic**: the PEOPLE rule through their REPRESENTATIVES.

–A **Monarchy**: a king rules, but Montesquieu considered it *a king with a conscience;* a king with strings attached; A KING LIMITED by established customs and traditions. The king has his hands tied by barons, noblemen, and parliaments. The king is limited by religious leaders who remind him to be fair as he will be ultimately be held accountable before the Eternal Judge of All.

–A **Despot**: a king rules *without a conscience*, a king with no strings attached; a king who yields to his passions and lusts, ruling by his whims and caprices; A KING WITH NO LIMITATIONS.

Montesquieu described these three forms of government and what makes them work. Like a wind-up clock relies on the power of a spring, each form of government has a different motivating force.

The motivating "spring" upon which a Republic relies is VIRTUE; the "spring" of Monarchy is HONOR; and the "spring" of Despotism is FEAR.

REPUBLIC

Montesquieu explained that "VIRTUE is necessary in a REPUBLIC." But since it is rare for people to have virtue, Republican governments are rare and of limited duration.

For a Republic to function, the mass of people need to have internal self-control causing them to treat others fairly. A government where "people" rule themselves is termed a "popular" government.

Montesquieu wrote in *The Spirit of the Laws*, 1748, that virtue is the *spring* or motivating force – the key ingredient, necessary for a people to rule themselves:

> It is the nature of a republican government that... the collective body of the people ... should be

possessed of the supreme power ...

In a *popular* state, one *spring* more is necessary, namely, virtue ... The politic Greeks, who lived under a *popular* government, knew no other support than virtue ...

When virtue is banished, ambition invades the minds of those who are disposed to receive it, and avarice possesses the whole community ...

When, in a *popular* government, there is a suspension of the laws, as this can proceed only from the corruption of the republic, the state is certainly undone.

A republic must be supported by virtue, and virtue is greatly empowered by the Judeo-Christian beliefs. British Prime Minister David Cameron stated in his Easter message, April 2015:

The values of the Bible, the values of Christianity are the values that we need – values of compassion, of respect, of responsibility, of tolerance.

Now ... you don't have to be a Christian ... to have strong values, to believe in strong values or to pass those values on to your children, but the point I always make is that it helps.

We're always trying to tell our children not to be selfish, but is there a better way of putting it than "love thy neighbor"?

We're always telling our children to be tolerant... but is there a better way of explaining tolerance than saying, "do to others as you would be done by"? It's the simplest encapsulation of an absolutely vital value and the Christian church and the teaching of the Bible has put it so clearly.

We're always telling our children that they must make the most of what they have; they must not waste what they have been given, and is there a better way of putting that than "don't hide your light under a bushel, make the most of your talents"?

Noah Webster wrote to James Madison, Oct. 16, 1829:

The Christian religion, in its purity, is the basis or rather the source of all genuine freedom in government

... No civil government of a republican form can exist and be durable, in which the principles of that religion have not a controlling influence.

English author G.K. Chesterton twice visited America, in 1921 and 1930. He wrote "What I Saw in America" (*The Collected Works of G.K. Chesterton*, Volume 21):

America is the only nation in the world that is founded on a creed. That creed is set forth with dogmatic and even theological lucidity in the Declaration of Independence; perhaps the only piece of practical politics that is also theoretical politics and also great literature.

It enunciates that all men are equal in their claim to justice, that governments exist to give them that justice, and that their authority is for that reason just.

It certainly does ... condemn atheism, since it clearly names the Creator as the ultimate authority from whom these equal rights are derived.

H.G. Wells wrote in *The Pocket History of the World* (1941):

Ideas of human solidarity, thanks to Christianity, were far more widely diffused in the newer European world, political power was not so concentrated, and the man of energy anxious to get rich turned his mind, therefore, very willingly from the ideas of the slave and of gang labor to the idea of mechanical power and the machine.

In *Outlines of History*, (NY: MacMillian Co., 1920), H.G. Wells commented of the U.S. Constitution:

Its spirit is indubitably Christian.

During the French Revolution, 40,000 were beheaded in Paris and 300,000 were killed in the Vendée, a western part of France. Noah Webster wrote "Political Fanaticism, No. III," published in *The American Minerva*, Sept. 21, 1796:

The reason why severe laws are necessary in France, is, that the people have not been educated republicans – they do not know how to govern themselves [and so] must be governed by severe laws and penalties, and a most rigid administration.

Lord Acton added:

> On France: The country that had been so proud of its kings, of its nobles, and of its chains, could not learn without teaching that *popular* power may be tainted with the same poison as personal power.

Lord Acton wrote:

> The danger is not that a particular class is unfit to govern. Every class is unfit to govern.

A parent may give their responsible teenager the car keys and let them drive whenever they want. But if the teenager becomes irresponsible, hangs around the wrong kids, drinks, parties, and drives, they will end up getting pulled over by the police, arrested, and jailed behind bars.

The teenager is either going to be voluntarily controlled from the inside or forcibly controlled from the outside. A puppy may have freedom to go into any room in the house, but if it cannot control itself, its owner restricts its freedom, confining it to the backyard or to a cage.

As people give up their virtue and give into to their passions and lusts, there is more crime. This causes a clamor to arise for more government to restore order, necessitating a loss of freedom and ultimately a "cage." With more government, power concentrates, and as power concentrates, it gets more corrupt. Lord Acton wrote:

> Power tends to corrupt and absolute power corrupts absolutely. Great men are almost always bad men, even when they exercise influence and not authority; still more when you superadd the tendency of the certainty of corruption by authority.

It is hard to visualize corruption, but a similar word is "favoritism." You may say, "If I were king, I would be fair." True, but what if you had a sister with a teenage son who partied with the wrong friends, drank, drove, and hit someone with his car on the way home.

As he sits in jail facing manslaughter charges, your sister comes begging to you to spare her son. What would you be tempted to say? "OK, I will let little Johnnie off the hook this time, but don't let it happen again."

As soon as you say that, you have just become the corrupt dictator. You sent ripples through your kingdom, that if someone is your family member or friend, they will get "favorite" treatment, being "more equal" than others.

Secretary of State Daniel Webster stated at the Bicentennial Celebration of the landing of the Pilgrims at Plymouth Rock, Dec. 22, 1820:

> Our ancestors established their system of government on morality and religious sentiment ... Whatever makes men good Christians, makes them good citizens ...
>
> We are bound ... to convince the world that order and law, religion and morality, the rights of conscience, the rights of persons, and the rights of property, may all be preserved and secured, in the most perfect manner, by a government entirely and purely elective.
>
> If we fail in this, our disaster will be signal, and will furnish an argument ... in support of those opinions which maintain that government can rest safely on nothing but power and coercion.

Since the moral virtue necessary for a republic is rare, Thomas Paine wrote in his third edition of *Common Sense* (Philadelphia, Feb. 14, 1776):

> Here then is the origin and rise of government; namely, a mode rendered necessary by the inability of moral virtue to govern the world.

MONARCHY

Montesquieu's distinction between a despot and a monarch is a matter of the degree of limitations. As already mentioned, it can be summed up by saying the monarch is a king with a conscience – a king with strings attached.

The king is reminded by religious leaders that he will be held accountable to the Judge of All as to whether he treated his subjects fairly. The king maintains traditions and ancestral laws, and may be held accountable to nobles or a parliament.

The king rules by motivating his subjects through the positive and negative motivations of honor and dishonor: conferring titles and ranks those who are loyal to them and shaming and disgracing those who are not.

Montesquieu explained:

> Virtue is necessary in a republic, and in a monarchy – honor.

The positive and negative motivations used by a monarch are primarily mental, social and emotional appeals – akin to peer pressure. Monarchs reward and promote those who are loyal to them, dispensing positions, titles, and honors. This appeals to the human pride of reputation. Monarchs dishonor and punish those who are disloyal to them with demotions, embarrassments, and public shame.

Every pre-school child knows the honor of being accepted and the dishonor of being rejected. All want to be in the "IN" clique, and cringe at the thought of being shunned; avoided; made fun of; ridiculed; not picked as a friend; passed over to join a team; or not invited to a party.

Similar to the diva of a school girl clique, those who please the monarch are publicly honored and those who displease the monarch are publicly shamed.

The political unit historically progressed toward a king:

–Fathers ruled their families;

–Extended families formed a village, hamlet or band, ruled by a respected elder or "the big man";

–Several bands formed a clan ruled by a patriarch;

–Several clans formed a tribe ruled by a chief;

–Several tribes formed a chiefdom ruled by a paramount chief;

–Several chiefdoms formed a kingdom ruled by a king;

–And finally, several kingdoms formed an empire ruled by an emperor.

Woodrow Wilson wrote in *The State: Elements of Historical & Practical Politics* (Boston: Heath & Co., 1889):

The original bond of union and the original sanction for magisterial authority were one and the same thing, namely, real or feigned blood relationship. In other words, families were the primitive states. The original State was a family. Historically the State of today may be regarded as in an important sense only an enlarged family: "State" is "family"; writ large ...

That the patriarchal family, to which the early history of the greater races runs back, and with which that history seems to begin, was the family in its original estate, the original, the true archaic family. The patriarchal family is that in which descent is traced to a common male ancestor, through a direct male line, and in which the authority of rule vests in the eldest living male ascendant ...

We have, as clearer evidence still, the undoubted social beginnings of Greek and Roman politics. They too originated, if history is to be taken at its most plainly written word, in the patriarchal family. Roman law, that prolific mother of modern legal idea and practice, has this descent from the time when the father of the family ruled as the king and high priest of his little state impressed upon every feature of it ...

The patriarchal family being taken, then, as the original political unit of these races, we have a sufficiently clear picture of the infancy of government.

First there is the family ruled by the father as king and priest. There is no majority for the sons so long as their father lives. They may marry and have children, but they can have no entirely separate and independent authority during their father's life save such as he suffers them to exercise. All that they possess, their lives even and the lives of those dependent upon them, are at the disposal of this absolute father–sovereign.

The family broadens in time into the House, the gens, and over this too the chiefest kinsman rules. There are common religious rites and observances which the gens regards as symbolic of its unity as a composite family; and heads of houses exercise high representative and probably certain imperative magisterial functions by virtue of their position.

Houses at length unite into tribes; and the chieftain is still hedged about by the sanctity of common kinship with the tribesmen whom he rules. He is, in theory at least, the chief kinsman, the kinsman in authority. Finally, tribes unite, and the ancient state emerges, with its king, the father and priest of his people.

Woodrow Wilson continued in *The State*, 1889:

How is it possible ... for the modern mind to conceive distinctly a traveling political organization, a state without territorial boundaries or the need of them, composed of persons, but associated with no fixed or certain habitat?

And yet such were the early states, – nomadic groups, now and again hunting, fishing, or tending their herds by this or that particular river or upon this or that familiar mountain slope or in-land seashore, but never regarding themselves or regarded by their neighbors as finally identified with any definite territory.

In the history of Europe no further back than the fifth century of our own era ... the Franks came pouring into the Roman empire just because they had no idea ... being confined to any particular Frank-land.

They left no France behind them at the sources of the Rhine; and their kings quitted those earlier seats of their race, not as kings of France, but as kings of the Franks. There were kings of the Franks when the territory now called Germany, as well as that now known as France, was in the possession of that imperious race ...

They became kings of France only when, some centuries later, they had settled down to the unaccustomed habit of confining themselves to a single land. Drawn by the processes of feudalization, sovereignty then found at last a local habitation and a new name ... The same was true of the other Germanic nations. They also had chiefs who were their chiefs, not the chiefs of their lands.

As an individual rules over more people, their style of judgment moves from personal to impersonal, from a wise and caring counselor to that of an authoritarian enforcer.

In small societal settings, maintenance of order is due to offended individuals being persuaded to reconcile by peer pressure from intertwined family relationships.

In larger societal settings, maintenance of order is due to offended individuals being afraid of external police punishment and the hiring of lawyers to sue and defend in courts administered by impersonal judges.

Monarchs set the standard of what would be the socially accepted values. Chuck Colson described what German sociologist Elisabeth Noelle-Neumann called the "spiral of silence." In a controlled experiment it was found that individuals denied their privately held values in order to conform to perceived publicly held values, thus avoiding "a negative social judgment." Chuck Colson concluded:

> Simply stated, out of a desire to avoid reprisal or isolation, people go along with what they think is the popular opinion — even if they object to that opinion personally. Instead of voicing their objections, they remain silent. (Chuck Colson, *BreakPoint*, Nov. 2, 2011, Breaking the Spiral of Silence.)

The Washington Post article "Mass surveillance silences minority opinions according to study," by Karen Turner, March 28, 2016, revealed:

> A new study shows that knowledge of government surveillance causes people to self-censor their dissenting opinions online ... The study, published in *Journalism and Mass Communication Quarterly*, studied the effects of subtle reminders of mass surveillance on its subjects ... Participants reacted by suppressing opinions that they perceived to be in the minority ... The "spiral of silence" is a well-researched phenomenon in which people suppress unpopular opinions to fit in and avoid social isolation.

Monarchs set the standard of dress, speech, and behavior in the society. The innate desire of acceptance by a group outside of one's immediate family is observable in every child and teenager. A person succumbs to peer pressure by self-modifying their behavior to fit in, to be accepted by the clique, the team, or the brotherhood.

Saul Alinsky wrote about ridicule being one of the most powerful negative motivators: "Ridicule is man's most potent weapon"; and "Pick the target, freeze it, personalize it, and polarize it."

Hollywood, media, and late-night comedy shows have encroached into the traditional role of the king by fixing in the minds of their viewers what is the current acceptable style and behavior. Banishment, ostracizing and public humiliation are tools to bring citizens into compliance.

French philosopher Claude-Adrien Helvétius wrote:

> The tyrant no longer excites to the pursuits of ... virtue; it is not talents, it is baseness and servility that he cherishes, and the weight of arbitrary power destroys the spring of emulation (desire to excel).

George Orwell wrote in *Nineteen Eighty-Four*:

> Power is in inflicting pain and humiliation.

In an irony, just as kings use honor to control subjects, kings themselves crave honor from their subjects and will adjust his behavior accordingly. King Herod had John the Baptist's head cut off because he was afraid of those at his party saying he did not keep his word, thus dishonoring him.

Matthew 14:76–9:

> Whereupon he promised with an oath to give her whatsoever she would ask. And she, being before instructed of her mother, said, Give me here John Baptist's head in a platter. And the king was sorry: nevertheless for the oath's sake, and them which sat with him at dinner, he commanded it to be given her.

Jerusalem would have been spared being burned by the Babylonians in 586 BC if Judah's King Zedekiah had not been afraid of being ridiculed.

Jeremiah 38:17–19:

> Then said Jeremiah unto Zedekiah, Thus saith the LORD, the God of hosts, the God of Israel; If thou wilt assuredly go forth unto the king of Babylon's princes, then thy soul shall live, and this city shall not be burned with fire; and thou shalt live, and thine house:

But if thou wilt not go forth to the king of Babylon's princes, then shall this city be given into the hand of the Chaldeans, and they shall burn it with fire, and thou shalt not escape out of their hand. And Zedekiah the king said unto Jeremiah, I am afraid of the Jews that are fallen to the Chaldeans, lest they deliver me into their hand, AND THEY MOCK ME."

~

GAME OF THRONES

Thomas Paine wrote in his third edition of *Common Sense*, Philadelphia, Feb. 14, 1776:

Yet I should be glad to ask how they suppose kings came at first? The question admits but of three answers, namely, either by LOT, by ELECTION, or by USURPATION.

If the first king was taken by LOT, it establishes a precedent for the next, which excludes hereditary succession. Saul was by lot, yet the succession was not hereditary, neither does it appear from that transaction that there was any intention it ever should.

If the first king of any country was by ELECTION, that likewise establishes a precedent for the next; for to say, that the right of all future generations is taken away, by the act of the first electors, in their choice not only of a king but of a family of kings forever, hath no parallel in or out of scripture but the doctrine of original sin, which supposes the free will of all men lost in Adam;

and from such comparison, and it will admit of no other, hereditary succession can derive no glory, for as in Adam all sinned, and as in the first electors all men obeyed; as in the one all mankind were subjected to Satan, and in the other to sovereignty;

as our innocence was lost in the first, and our authority in the last; and as both disable us from reassuming some former state and privilege, it unanswerably follows that original sin and hereditary succession are parallels ... The most subtle sophist cannot produce a juster simile.

As to USURPATION, no man will be so hardy as to defend it; and that William the Conqueror was an usurper is a fact not to be contradicted.

Thomas Paine continued:

The plain truth is, that the antiquity of English monarchy will not bear looking into. But it is not so much the absurdity as the evil of hereditary succession which concerns mankind.

Did it ensure a race of good and wise men it would have the seal of divine authority, but as it opens a door to the foolish, the wicked, and the improper, it hath in it the nature of oppression.

Men who look upon themselves born to reign, and others to obey, soon grow insolent. Selected from the rest of mankind, their minds are early poisoned by importance; and the world they act in differs so materially from the world at large, that they have but little opportunity of knowing its true interests, and when they succeed in the government are frequently the most ignorant and unfit of any throughout the dominions.

Paine added:

Another evil which attends hereditary succession is, that the throne is subject to be possessed by a minor at any age; all which time the regency acting under the cover of a king have every opportunity and inducement to betray their trust.

The same national misfortune happens when a king worn out with age and infirmity enters the last stage of human weakness.

In both these cases the public becomes a prey to every miscreant (depraved villain) who can tamper successfully with the follies either of age or infancy.

Thomas Paine concluded:

The most plausible plea which hath ever been offered in favor of hereditary succession is, that it preserves a nation from civil wars; and were this true, it would be weighty; whereas it is the most bare-faced falsity ever imposed upon mankind.

The whole history of England disowns the fact. Thirty kings and two minors have reigned in that distracted kingdom since the conquest, in which time there has been (including the revolution) no less than eight civil wars and nineteen Rebellions.

Wherefore instead of making for peace, it makes against it, and destroys the very foundation it seems to stand upon. The contest for monarchy and succession, between the houses of York and Lancaster, laid England in a scene of blood for many years.

Twelve pitched battles besides skirmishes and sieges were fought between Henry and Edward. Twice was Henry prisoner to Edward, who in his turn was prisoner to Henry.

And so uncertain is the fate of war and the temper of a nation, when nothing but personal matters are the ground of a quarrel, that Henry was taken in triumph from a prison to a palace, and Edward obliged to fly from a palace to a foreign land; yet, as sudden transitions of temper are seldom lasting, Henry in his turn was driven from the throne, and Edward recalled to succeed him.

The parliament always following the strongest side. This contest began in the reign of Henry the Sixth, and was not entirely extinguished till Henry the Seventh, in whom the families were united. Including a period of 67 years, namely, from 1422 to 1489.

In short, monarchy and succession have laid (not this or that kingdom only) but the world in blood and ashes. 'Tis a form of government which the word of God bears testimony against, and blood will attend it.

At the time the United States came into being, nearly the entire world was ruled by kings, from China's Qing (Ch'ing) Emperor Qianlong (Ch'ien Lung) to Spain's King Carlos III to Russia's Catherine the Great to France's King Louis XVI to Hawaii's King Kamehameha I to India's Mughal Emperor Shah Alam II, who fought the British.

Dr. Pat Robertson wrote in *America's Dates with Destiny*, 1986:

On September 17, 1787, the day our Constitution was signed, the absolute monarch Ch'ien Lung, emperor of the Manchu (or Ch'ing) Dynasty, reigned supreme over the people of China. To guard against revolt, Chinese officials could not hold office in their home provinces, and ... revolts were put down by ruthless military force.

In Japan the shogun (warriors) of the corrupt Tokugawa chamberlain Tanuma Okitsugu exercised corrupt and totalitarian authority over the Japanese.

In India, Warren Hastings, the British Governor of Bengal, had successfully defeated the influence of the fragmented Mogul dynasties that ruled India since 1600.

Catherine II was the enlightened despot of All the Russias.

Joseph II was the emperor of Austria, Bohemia and Hungary.

For almost half a century, Frederick the Great had ruled Prussia.

Louis XVI sat uneasily on his throne in France just years away from revolution, a bloody experiment in democracy, and the new tyranny of Napoleon Bonaparte.

A kind of a constitutional government had been created in the Netherlands in 1579 by the Protestant Union of Utrecht, but that constitution was really a loose federation of the northern provinces for a defense against Catholic Spain ...

What was happening in America had no real precedent, even as far back as the city-states of Greece. The only real precedent was established thousands of years before by the tribes of Israel in the covenant with God and with each other.

DESPOT

A despot is a king without a conscience, with no limitations, who rules by whims and caprices. A despot has absolute and arbitrary power: absolute, in that the moment he says something it is the law; and arbitrary, in that no one knows what he will say next.

Despots use positive motivations of physical pleasure and negative motivations of physical punishment – the bribe or the bullet, the silver or the lead. A despot rewards those who unhesitatingly obey him, without concern for conscience, by enticing them with lustful physical gratification, sensual booty, and financial rewards. He strikes terror into those who fail to obey him by public punishment, torture, dismemberment and death.

A despot is either irreligious or follows a religion which does not value fairness. He rules as a warlord, a gang leader.

Thomas Paine wrote in his third edition of *Common Sense*, Philadelphia, Feb. 14, 1776:

> A thirst for absolute power is the natural disease of monarchy.

In 1788, Mercy Otis Warren wrote: "Observations on the new Constitution, and on the Federal and State Conventions":

> Despotism usually while it is gaining ground, will suffer men to think, say, or write what they please; but when once established, if it is thought necessary to subserve the purposes, of arbitrary power, the most unjust restrictions may take place in the first instance, and an imprimatur on the Press in the next, may silence the complaints, and forbid the most decent remonstrances of an injured and oppressed people.

Absolute and arbitrary rule appeals to the most base and carnal aspects of human nature. Montesquieu wrote:

> As virtue is necessary in a republic, and in a monarchy – honor, so FEAR is necessary in a DESPOTIC GOVERNMENT: with regard to virtue, there is no occasion for it, and honor would be extremely dangerous.

Ghiyas ud din Balban, the Muslim Mamluk Sultan of Dehli, 1266–1286, according to the Muslim historian Ziauddin Barani, insisted on instilling:

Fear of the governing power, which is the basis of all good government.

Machiavelli wrote:

It is much more secure to be feared than to be loved.

Robespierre's despotic use of terror to bring France's population into compliance resulted in the Reign of Terror with over 40,000 beheadings.

Blaise Pascal wrote in *Thoughts of M. Pascal on religion, and on some other subjects*, 1670:

If they (Plato and Aristotle) wrote about politics it was as if to lay down rules for a madhouse. And if they pretended to treat it as something really important it was because they knew that the madmen they were talking to believed themselves to be kings and emperors. They humored these beliefs in order to calm down their madness with as little harm as possible.

Lord Acton described bureaucracy as a despot's weapon:

Bureaucracy is undoubtedly the weapon and sign of a despotic government, inasmuch as it gives whatever government it serves, despotic power.

Lord Acton added:

Bureaucracy tries to establish so many administrative maxims that the minister is as narrowly controlled and guided as the judge.

In an ironic twist, just as a despot controls his subjects through fear, the despot himself is always suspicious and in constant fear of being poisoned, betrayed, plotted against or overthrown.

LIMITS ON KINGS & DESPOTS

Throughout history, various attempts have been made to limit the power of a king or despot:

1) by holding a king to HIS OWN WORD, as with accounts of King Ahasuerus and King Darius the Median.

Esther 1:19:

If it please the king, let there go a royal commandment from him, and let it be written among the laws of the Persians and the Medes, that it be not altered.

Daniel 6:15:

Then these men assembled unto the king, and said unto the king, "Know, O king, that the law of the Medes and Persians is, That no decree nor statute which the king establisheth may be changed."

Montesquieu wrote in *The Spirit of the Laws*:

In Persia, when the king has condemned a person... even if the prince were intoxicated, or non compos (Latin: not of sound mind), the decree must be executed; otherwise he would contradict himself, and the law admits of no contradiction. This has been the way of thinking in that country in all ages; as the order which Ahasuerus gave, to exterminate the Jews, could not be revoked, they were allowed the liberty of defending themselves.

2) by reminding a king of the WORD OF PAST KINGS, as when the children of Israel were told to stop rebuilding the temple but then.

Ezra 6:1–7:

Then Darius the king made a decree, and search was made in the house of the rolls, where the treasures were laid up in Babylon. And there was found at Achmetha, in the palace that is in the province of the Medes, a roll, and therein was a record thus written: "In the first year of Cyrus the king the same Cyrus the king made a decree concerning the house of God at Jerusalem, Let the house be builded ... " Now therefore, Tatnai, governor beyond the river, Shethar-boznai, and your companions the Apharsachites ... Let the work of this house of God alone; let the governor of the Jews and the elders of the Jews build this house of God in his place.

3) by kings writing down their laws for the public to view, as with King Hammurabi or King Draco of Athens.

4) by Traditions and Customs, such as the people of

England who always tried to limit the "superior" power of kings by reminding them of their ancient Common Law of England. U.S. Supreme Court Justice James Wilson wrote in his *Lectures on Law*, 1790–91, on the:

> Now that the will of a superior is discarded ... What principle shall be introduced in its place?... The consent of those whose obedience the law requires. This I conceive to be the true origin of the obligation of human laws ... Let us ascend to the first ages of societies. Customs, for a long time, were the only laws known among them. The Lycians had no written laws; they were governed entirely by customs.
>
> Among the ancient Britons also, no written laws were known: they were ruled by the traditionary ... customary—laws of the Druids. Now custom is ... evidence of consent. How was a custom introduced? By voluntary adoption. How did it become general? By the instances of voluntary adoption being increased. How did it become lasting? By voluntary and satisfactory experience, which ratified and confirmed what voluntary adoption had introduced.
>
> In the introduction, in the extension, in the continuance of customary law, we find the operations of consent universally predominant. "Customs," in the striking and picturesque language of my Lord Bacon, "are laws written in living Tables (tablets)." In regulations of justice and of government, they have been more effectual than the best written laws. The Romans, in their happy periods of liberty, paid great regard to customary law.
>
> Let me mention, in one word, every thing that can enforce my sentiments: the common law of England is a customary law.

5) by Public Opinion. Even kings prefer public acceptance over public resistance to their decrees.

6) by Barons, Nobles, Princes, and Parliaments, who together can combine their strength to oppose a king.

7) by Charters and Constitutions whereby the king is pressured to agreed to his power being permanently

limited, such as when the 25 barons of England surrounded King John on the fields of Runnymeade in 1215 and forced him to sign the Magna Carta. This began the process of limiting a king with written constitutions.

Patrick Henry stated June 5, 1788:

> If we make a king, we may prescribe the rules by which he shall rule his people, and interpose such checks as shall prevent him from infringing them.

8) by Religious Beliefs. Since kings ruled by claiming they were the authorized representatives of heaven, they needed the religious class to validate their superior status, but in the same token, the religious class exercised some influence on the King by convicting his conscience or through superstitious omens and oracles.

The most profound religious statement limiting a king's power was given by Jesus in Matthew 22: 15–22:

> Then went the Pharisees, and took counsel how they might entangle him in his talk. And they sent out unto him their disciples with the Herodians, saying,
>
> Master, we know that thou art true, and teachest the way of God in truth, neither carest thou for any man: for thou regardest not the person of men. Tell us therefore, What thinkest thou? Is it lawful to give tribute unto Caesar, or not?
>
> But Jesus perceived their wickedness, and said, Why tempt ye me, ye hypocrites? Show me the tribute money. And they brought unto him a penny.
>
> And he saith unto them, Whose is this image and superscription? They say unto him, Caesar's.
>
> Then saith he unto them, Render therefore unto Caesar the things which are Caesar's; and unto God the things that are God's.
>
> When they had heard these words, they marveled, and left him, and went their way.

The United States was an experiment not just limit a king, but to break away from a king altogether.

The King of Great Britain was the most powerful king

in history. The sun never set on the British Empire. The Declaration of Independence, July 4, 1776, stated:

> The history of the present King of Great Britain is a history of repeated injuries and usurpations all having in direct object the establishment of an absolute Tyranny over these states ...
>
> He has refused to pass other Laws for the accommodation of large districts of people, unless those people would relinquish the right of Representation in the Legislature, a right inestimable to them and formidable to tyrants only ...
>
> A Prince, whose character is thus marked by every act which may define a Tyrant, is unfit to be the ruler of a free people.

The United States was founded with the intention of the government being as far away from a king as possible. The Constitution divided the king's power in a cross: horizontally, into three branches, and vertically, from Federal to State levels. This new Federal Frankenstein was tied up with "ten handcuffs" — the First Ten Amendments.

President Eisenhower told the Governors' Conference, June 24, 1957, Williamsbug, VA:

> The national government was itself ... the creature, of the States acting together. Yet today it is often made to appear that the creature, Frankenstein-like, is determined to destroy the creators ...
>
> Too often we have seen tendencies develop that transgress our most cherished principles of government, and tend to undermine the structure so painstakingly built by those who preceded us.
>
> Of those principles, I refer especially to one drawn from the colonists' bitter struggle against tyranny and from man's experiences throughout the ages. That principle is this: those who would be and would stay free must stand eternal watch against excessive concentration of power in government ...
>
> In faithful application of that principle, governmental power in our newborn nation was diffused – counterbalanced – checked, hedged about

and restrained – to preclude even the possibility of its abuse. Ever since, that principle, and those precautions have been ... the anchor of freedom ...

Our Constitutional checks and balances, our State and Territorial governments, our multiplicity of county and municipal governing bodies, our emphasis upon individual initiative and community responsibility, encourage unlimited experimentation in the solving of America's problems.

Through this diversified approach, the effect of errors is restrained, calamitous mistakes are avoided, the general good is more surely determined, and the self-governing genius of our people is perpetually renewed.

Being long accustomed to decentralized authority, we are all too inclined to accept it as a convenient, even ordinary, fact of life, to expect it as our right, and to presume that it will always endure.

Lord Acton wrote:

Divided ... authorities are the foundation of good government.

The Bill of Rights, ratified Dec. 15, 1791, contained "restrictive clauses" on the Federal Government, to prevent an "abuse of its powers," as stated in its Preamble:

The States, having at the time of their adopting the Constitution, expressed a desire, in order to prevent misconstruction or **abuse of its powers**, that further declaratory and **restrictive clauses** should be added.

Eisenhower concluded his address, June 24, 1957:

But in other lands over the centuries millions, helpless before concentrated power, have been born, have lived and have died all in slavery, or they have lost their lives and their liberty to despots.

Today, against the dark background of Eastern Europe, we see spotlighted once again the results of extreme and dictatorial concentration of power. There man's rightful aspirations are cruelly repressed by a despotism more far-reaching than the world has ever before known.

There, power is free, the people in chains ... A

nation cannot be enslaved by diffused power but only by strong centralized government.

The U.S. Constitution is essentially a collection of road blocks to prevent power from re-concentrating back into the hands of a king.

As the United States became an international success story, its unique form of government — a democratically elected constitutional republic — became renown.

This put pressure on kings and dictators around the world to hide their selfish monarchical ambitions by using democratic sounding titles, such as Chairman, Premier, General Secretary, Chancellor, Primier, Prime Minister, The Dear Leader, or El Presidente.

Nevertheless, as Lenin explained: "The goal of socialism is communism." Socialism and communism are essentially monarchy with a makeover. Every Communist country is ruled by a dictator, such as: Mao Zedung in China; Castro in Cuba; Pol Pot in Cambodia; Ho Chi Minh in Vietnam; and Kim Jong-un in North Korea.

Adolf Hitler was the Chancellor of the National *Socialist* German Workers' Party. Joseph Stalin was the General Secretary of the Union of Soviet *Socialist* Republics.

Franklin Roosevelt admitted, Feb. 10, 1940:

The Soviet Union ... is run by a dictatorship as absolute as any other dictatorship in the world.

"Communist party members" enjoy the position of the new royalty, with special shops to shop in, special neighborhoods, special lanes of traffic, and special treatment before the law.

"Citizens" are actually peasant-subjects, whose fate is determined by the State.

Some college students may naively entertain the view that in communism everybody owns everything equally. One simply has to ask: who decides who lives in the nice house and who lives in the dumpy house? The answer is: "Someone in the government dictates those things." Well, whoever ultimately dictates those things is THE DICTATOR!

Lord Acton wrote:

> Socialism easily accepts despotism. It requires the strongest execution of power – power sufficient to interfere with property.

President Gerald Ford stated at the annual Senate-House Fundraising Dinner, April 15, 1975:

> Never forget, a government big enough to give us everything we want is a government big enough to take from us everything we have.

What any particular nation labels itself is no longer an accurate description of what form of government that nation actually has. For example, the Democratic People's Republic of North Korea is neither Democratic, nor a Republic, nor do "The People" have any say. It is a dictatorship, pure and simple.

Christopher Hitchens wrote in his article "Worse Than 1984: North Korea, slave state" (*Slate*. May 2, 2005):

> In North Korea, every person is property and is owned by a small and mad family with hereditary power. Every minute of every day, as far as regimentation can assure the fact, is spent in absolute subjection and serfdom. The private life has been entirely abolished.
>
> One tries to avoid cliché, and I did my best on a visit to this terrifying country in the year 2000, but George Orwell's *1984* was published at about the time that Kim Il-sung set up his system, and it really is as if he got hold of an early copy of the novel and used it as a blueprint.

America was the ultimate departure from a king, as its government was set up to make "the people" the king, and politicians were made the public servants. They could be hired or fired, voted in or voted out.

Instead of the law being the ruler's will which the people had to carry out, in America the law is the people's will which their "public servants" – elected politicians –

had to carry out. Senator Robert M. La Follette Sr., stated:

> The Will of the People Shall Be the LAW of the Land

Theodore Roosevelt stated Oct. 24, 1903:

> In no other place and at no other time has the experiment of government of THE PEOPLE, by THE PEOPLE, for THE PEOPLE, been tried on so vast a scale as here in our own country.

The Political Debates Between Lincoln and Douglas (published 1897), has Abraham Lincoln's statement:

> THE PEOPLE of these United States are THE RIGHTFUL MASTERS of both Congresses and Courts.

REPUBLIC: ALTERNATIVE TO KINGS

"A republic, if you can keep it," answered Ben Franklin, when asked what form of government was created in Philadelphia.

Benjamin Franklin wrote to the Editor of the *Federal Gazette,* April 8, 1788 (*The Records of the Federal Convention of 1787, Farrand's Records,* Vol. 3, CXCV, pp. 296-297; *Documentary History of the Constitution,* IV, 567-571):

> I must own I have so much faith in the general government of the world by Providence, that I can hardly conceive a transaction of such momentous importance to the welfare of millions now existing, and to exist in the posterity of a great nation, should be suffered to pass without being in some degree influenc'd, guided and governed by that omnipotent, omnipresent beneficent Ruler, in whom all inferior spirits live & move and have their being. (Acts 17:28)

As noted earlier, Franklin addressed the Constitutional Convention, June 28, 1787:

> We have gone back to ancient history for models of government, and examined the different forms of those republics which, having been formed with the seeds of their own dissolution, now no longer exist.

Let us follow Franklin's example and go "back to

ancient history for models of government" and examine "the different forms of those republics" to identify what were "the seeds of their own dissolution" which caused those republics to "no longer exist."

The term "republic" is used in a general sense to mean a government where people rule themselves without a king. There are relatively few examples of republics in history, with most being city-states or regional confederations, though some were actually nations.

The specifics of how each operated varied, but each had qualities which America's founders found instructional:

–Israel under the Judges

–Phoenician Islands

–Democracy of Athens

–Doric city-states of Crete

–India city-states: Kuru of Hastinapur; Licchavi of Vaishali

–Republic of early Rome

–Carthage of North Africa

–Burma city-state of Pyu

–Icelandic Commonwealth

–Russian city-states of Novgorod and Pskov

–Italian city-states: Republics of Genoa; Venice; Pisa;
      Ragusa; Amalfi; Gaeta; Ancona; Noli.

–India's small republics

–Swiss Cantons

–Free German Cities

–Croatian city-state of Dubrovnik

–Republic of the Seven United Netherlands

–Batavian Republic

–Polish-Lithuanian Commonwealth: Nobleman's Republic

–French city-state of Goust

–English Commonwealth

–Iroquois Confederacy

America's founders were keenly aware of the journey they were embarking on as they sought to separate powers. After also studying States in Europe, Franklin continued:

> We have viewed Modern States all round Europe, but find none of their Constitutions suitable to our circumstances ... We have been assured, Sir, in the Sacred Writings, that "except the Lord build the House, they labor in vain that build it."

> I firmly believe this; and I also believe that without His concurring aid we shall succeed in this political building no better than the Builders of Babel.

AN IMPOSSIBILITY TO TAME A MONARCH

President Harry S Truman wrote in a personal memorandum, April 16, 1950:

> There is a lure in power. It can get into a man's blood just as gambling and lust for money have been known to do.

Lord Acton wrote:

> Everybody likes to get as much power as circumstances allow, and nobody will vote for a self-denying ordinance.

Lord Acton added:

> Liberty consists in the division of power. Absolutism, in concentration of power.

From Nimrod and the Tower of Babel, monarchs accumulated power, and resisted attempts to have their power limited. Yale President Ezra Stiles addressed Connecticut's General Assembly, May 8, 1783:

> Monarchy and aristocracy, when they become hereditary, terminate in the prostration of liberty. The greater part of the governments on earth may be termed monarchical aristocracies, or hereditary dominions independent of the people.

> The nobles and nabobs (Muslim officials in Mogul India), being hereditary, will at first have great power;

but the royal factions have not failed to intrigue this away from the nobles to the prince: the assembly of even hereditary nobles then become ciphers and nullities (unimportant persons) in dominion.

The once glorious Cortes (Court) of Spain experienced this loss of power. IT IS NEXT TO AN IMPOSSIBILITY TO TAME A MONARCH; and few have ruled without ferocity.

Scarcely shall we find in royal dynasties, in long line of princes, a few singularly good sovereigns – a few Cyruses, Antonini, Alfreds, Boroihmeses.

In Ezra Stiles' last sentence, "a few Cyruses, Antonini, Alfreds, Boroihmeses," he was referring to Cyrus of Persia, who helped the Jews resettle Jerusalem; Antony, who was the last champion of Roman Republic before Augustus Caesar ruled as emperor; Alfred the Great of England who fought off Viking invasions and codified English law acknowledging God-given individual rights; and Bryan Boroihmi who was credited with uniting Ireland in defense of Viking attacks.) Another was King Louis IX of France–"Saint Louis," who led the 7th and 8th Crusades.

Ezra Stiles continued to describe the few "enlightened" monarchs who ruled as KINGS WITH A CONSCIENCE:

If we look over the present sovereigns of Europe, we behold with pleasure two young princes, the emperor (Habsburg's Joseph II), and the monarch of France (King Louis XVI), who seem to be raised up in Providence to make their people and mankind happy.

A Ganganelli (Pope Clement XIV) in the pontifical throne was a phoenix of ages, shone for his moment ...

We see enterprising literary and heroic talents in a Frederick III (last Holy Roman Emperor crowned in Rome), and wisdom in a Poniatowski (last King and Grand Duke of the Polish–Lithuanian Commonwealth who sought reforms to expand freedoms).

Of monarchy, Thomas Paine wrote in *Common Sense*, third edition, Philadelphia, Feb. 14, 1776:

Of Monarchy and Hereditary Succession: Mankind

being originally equals in the order of creation, the equality could only be destroyed by some subsequent circumstance ... and that is the distinction of men into KINGS and SUBJECTS.

Male and female are the distinctions of nature, good and bad the distinctions of Heaven; but how a race of men came into the world so exalted above the rest, and distinguished like some new species, is worth inquiring into ...

To the evil of monarchy we have added that of hereditary succession ... claimed as a matter of right, is an insult and imposition on posterity.

For all men being originally equals, no one by birth could have a right to set up his own family in perpetual preference to all others for ever, and tho' himself might deserve some decent degree of honors of his contemporaries, yet his descendants might be far too unworthy to inherit them.

One of the strongest natural proofs of the folly of hereditary right in Kings, is that nature disapproves it, otherwise she would not so frequently turn it into ridicule, by giving mankind an ass for a lion ...

As no man at first could possess any other public honors than were bestowed upon him, so the givers of those honors could have no power to give away the right of posterity, and though they might say "We choose you for our head," they could not without manifest injustice to their children say "that your children and your children's children shall reign over ours forever" ... such an unwise, unjust, unnatural compact might in the next succession put them under the government of a rogue or a fool.

Most wise men in their private sentiments have ever treated hereditary right with contempt; yet it is one of those evils which when once established is not easily removed: many submit from fear, others from superstition, and the more powerful part shares with the king the plunder of the rest ...

Kings ... who by increasing in power and extending his depredations, overawed the quiet and defenseless to purchase their safety by frequent contributions. Yet his electors could have no idea of giving hereditary right to his descendants, because such a perpetual exclusion of themselves was incompatible with the free and restrained principles they professed to live by.

Wherefore, hereditary succession in the early ages of monarchy could not take place as a matter of claim, but as something casual ... but as few or no records were extant in those days, the traditionary history stuffed with fables, it was very easy, after the lapse of a few generations, to trump up some superstitious tale conveniently timed, Mahomet-like, to cram hereditary right down the throats of the vulgar.

Perhaps the disorders which threatened, or seemed to threaten, on the decease of a leader and the choice of a new one (for elections among ruffians could not be very orderly) induced many at first to favor hereditary pretensions; by which means it happened, as it hath happened since, that what at first was submitted to as a convenience was afterwards claimed as a right.

Yale President Ezra Stiles continued, May 8, 1783:

But when we contemplate the other European and Asiatic pontentates, and especially the sovereigns of Delhi, Ispahaun, and Constantinople, one cannot but pity mankind whose lot is to be governed by despots ...

But in a world or region of the universe where God has imparted to none either this superior power or adequate wisdom beyond what falls to the common share of humanity, it is absurd to look for such qualities in one man – not even in the man Moses, who shared the government of Israel with the senate of seventy. Therefore there is no foundation for monarchical government from supposed hereditary superiority in knowledge.

If it be said that monarchs always have a council of state, consisting of the wisest personages, of whose wisdom they avail themselves in the government of empires – not to observe that this is a concession indicating a deficiency of knowledge in princes – it may be asked, Why not, then, consign and repose government into the hands of the national council, where always resides the superiority of wisdom?

The supposed advantage of having one public head for all to look up to, and to concentrate the attention, obedience, and affection of subjects, and to consolidate the empire, will not counterbalance the evils of arbitrary despotism and the usual want of wisdom in the sovereigns and potentates of the earth.

For the hereditary successions in the dynasties of kings ... seem to be marked and accursed by Providence with deficient wisdom. And where is the wisdom of consigning government into such hands? ...

Should we call forth and dignify some family, either from foreign nations or from among ourselves, and create a monarch, whether a hereditary prince or protector for life, and seat him in supremacy at the head of Congress, soon, with insidious dexterity, would he intrigue, and secure a venal majority even of new and annual members, and, by diffusing a complicated and variously modified influence, pursue an accretion of power till he became absolute.

The celebrated historian Mrs. Catherine MacCaulay, that ornament of the republic of letters, and the female Livy of the age, observes (Mrs. MacCaulay's letter to Ezra Stiles, 1771):

"The man who holds supreme power for life will have a great number of friends and adherents, who are attached by interest to his interest, and who will wish for continuance of power in the same family. This creates the worst of factions, a government faction, in the state.

"The desire of securing to ourselves a particular unshared privilege is the rankest vice which infests humanity; and a protector for life, instead of devoting his time and understanding to the great cares of government, will be scheming and plotting to secure the power, after his death, to his children, if he has any, if not, to the nearest of his kin.

"This principle in government has been productive of such bloodshed and oppression that it has inclined politicians to give preference to hereditary rather than elective monarchies; and, as the lesser evil, to consign the government of society to the increasing and at length unlimited sway of one family, whether the individuals of it should be idiots or madmen.

"It is an uncontroverted fact, that supreme power never can continue long in one family without becoming unlimited."

President Calvin Coolidge wrote in 1924:

The history of government on this earth has been almost entirely ... rule of force held in the HANDS OF A FEW. Under our Constitution, America committed itself to power in the HANDS OF THE PEOPLE.

Jefferson wrote to William Johnson, 1823 (ME 15:451):

But the Chief Justice says, "There must be an ultimate arbiter somewhere." True, there must; but does that prove it is either party? THE ULTIMATE ARBITER IS THE PEOPLE OF THE UNION, assembled by their deputies in convention, at the call of Congress or of two-thirds of the States.

Let them decide to which they mean to give an authority claimed by two of their organs.

And it has been the peculiar wisdom and felicity of our Constitution, to have provided this peaceable appeal, where that of other nations is at once to force.

America's founders studied how to take power away from a king and separate it into the hands of the people. Unfortunately, there have been nefarious political philosophers who have studied how to take power from the people and re-concentrate it back into the hands of a king.

To understand what is happening today, one must zoom out from the day-to-day headlines and examine the past.

KINGS–THE MOST COMMON GOVERNMENT

There have been approximately 60 centuries of recorded history, with the general categories being:

4000–3300 BC – History before writing, stone tools & weapons

3300–1200 BC – Writing invented, earliest recorded

kingdoms & dynasties, bronze tools & weapons

1200–600 BC – Ancient Antiquity, iron tools & weapons

600–27 BC – Classical Antiquity

27 BC–476 AD – Roman Empire

476–1300 – Middle Ages/Rise of Islam

1300–1500 – Renaissance

1500–1700 – Age of Discovery

1700–1900 – Early Modern

1900–Present – Industrial Revolution/Modern

During these 60 centuries, the default setting for human government has been POWER in the hands of monarchs. "Mono" means "one" and "arch" means "to rule."

Some monarchs were good, some indifferent, some bad and some very bad – tyrannical despots. Santa Anna told U.S. Minister to Mexico, Joel R. Poinsett, 1824:

> I threw up my cap for liberty with great ardor ... but very soon found the folly of it. A hundred years to come my people will not be fit for liberty. They do not know what it is, unenlightened as they are ...
>
> A despotism is the proper government for them, but there is no reason why it should not be a wise and virtuous one.

There were bad kings who were overthrown by good kings, who in turn were followed by bad kings. None can argue, though, that it was predominately kings who ruled.

Naturalists observe that in various animal species, a pecking order of dominance is established in the same way human nature tends toward a government by monarchy.

EARLIEST CIVILIZATIONS

Ancient dates cannot be determined with accuracy, but an attempted time-line is as follows:

c.4000 BC – Pre-written history. The earliest tools and weapons were made out stone, giving rise to the term stone age or Paleolithic.

The Bible tells about how Adam and Eve were gathers of food, with abundant fruit on trees. When they sinned "The LORD God sent him forth from the garden of Eden, to TILL THE GROUND" (Genesis 3:23).

Farming is considered the first profession, as reflected in Cain being a tiller of the soil. The plow is the first invention. The other early profession was the domestication of animals, reflected in Abel being a shepherd of a flock.

The Epic of Gilgamesh is considered the oldest work of literature ever written in any language. It tells of a "Great Deluge" in which a man called Utnapishtim built a giant ship with many rooms, covered it with tar, and brought onto it his wife, children and animals. When the ship rested on a mountain, he opened the hatch and sent out a dove, which returned. He then sent out a raven, which did not return. When the flood receded, he released the animals to replenish the earth. He and his family reintroduced farming and animal domesticaion into the Mesopotamian Valley.

Over 100 ancient civilizations around the globe contain flood stories, flood legends and flood myths in their distant past. Jared Diamond's Pulitzer Prize winning book, *Guns, Germs, and Steel: The Fates of Human Societies* (W.W. Norton, 1997) traces civilization's advancement as connected to the development of food production.

The majority of plants able to be domesticated were found in fertile crescent – Mesopotamia, the land between the Tigris and Euphrates Rivers. These plants contained high amounts of protein, fiber and oil, such as wheat, rye, barley, oats and flax, together with beans, peas, and almonds. Plant fiber was used for textiles items, such as clothes, ropes, rugs, bedding, curtains, and sails.

These plants spread east and west across the Eurasian Continent. Other areas of the world did not have such an abundant variety of crops, nor such a favorable a climate.

North Africa and Egypt had limited plants able to be domesticated and these did not spread south across equatorial Africa. Asia had mainly rice. The Americas had beans, squash, potatoes, and later corn, but these did not spread north or south across equatorial central America. As farming produced more food per acre than could be procured by hunting and gathering, the phenomenon occurred where societies more advanced in food production gradually displaced societies of hunter-gathers.

The America Indian and Aboriginal Australian were hunter-gathers unable to oppose the advancement of societies who had mastered food production.

As previously mentioned, after the domestication of plants came the domestication of animals. Chickens, sheep, goats, and other small animals provided food and materials for clothing.

Out of the over 140 large animals potentially able to be domesticated, only 14 were done so with any success, such as: donkeys, horses, camels, cattle and oxen. Most of these animals happened to be located in the Mesopotamian Valley, from which they spread across Eurasia, to Europe, Middle East, Central Asia, India and China.

These large domesticated animals pulled plows and wagons, turned irrigation water-wheels and grain-grinding mills, and provided manure for fertilizer. They also pulled chariots of war and siege machines.

Africa had large animals, but, other than camels and elephants, their wild dispositions rendered them untamable, i.e., water buffalo, rhino, giraffe, gazelle, and zebra. In Australia, varieties were scarce.

Domestication of large animals in the Americas met little success: llama, alpaca, buffalo, and dogs to pull sleds. The lack of large animals to pull wagons may be why the wheel was not developed in the Americas. China had a wheel-barrel as early as the Han Dynasty, first century BC.

Hunter-gatherers spent the majority of their day obtaining sustenance, living mostly in forests where game was abundant. There was little time or motivation to develop new technologies.

Mesopotamia's mastery of animal domestication and food production contributed to its development of the technologies needed to store food. More advanced tools and weapons were created made out of copper and bronze, thus the term "bronze age."

Once people were freed people from having to spend their day scavenging for food, they had the opportunity to pursue other non-food producing professions. This led to inventions, political classes, armies and bureaucracies.

The abundance of storable food provided sustenance for soldiers on conquering campaigns, leading to the creation of the first empires in Mesopotamia, Egypt, China, and Asia Minor (modern-day Turkey).

As land was cleared to plant more fields, the forests disappeared. Centuries of farming led to soil depletion and erosion. As food production declined, the empires depending on that food also declined. What used to be the "fertile crescent" area of the world became barren.

This caused civilization to move out of the fertile crescent into other areas, which were subsequently cleared of forests, such as Greece, Italy, Central Asia, and North Africa.

Thomas Paine proposed how necessity may have caused people to gravitate together, as he wrote in the third edition of *Common Sense* (Philadelphia, Feb. 14, 1776):

> Let us suppose a small number of persons settled in some sequestered part of the earth, unconnected with the rest; they will then represent the first peopling of any country, or of the world. In this state of natural liberty, society will be their first thought.
>
> A thousand motives will excite them thereto; the strength of one man is so unequal to his wants, and his mind so unfitted for perpetual solitude, that he is soon obliged to seek assistance and relief of another, who in his turn requires the same.
>
> Four or five united would be able to raise a

tolerable dwelling in the midst of a wilderness, but one man might labor out the common period of life without accomplishing anything; when he had felled his timber he could not remove it, nor erect it after it was removed; hunger in the meantime would urge him to quit his work, and every different want would call him a different way.

Disease, nay even misfortune, would be death; for, though neither might be mortal, yet either would disable him from living, and reduce him to a state in which he might rather be said to perish than to die.

Thus necessity, like a gravitating power, would soon form our newly arrived emigrants into society, the reciprocal blessings of which would supersede, and render the obligations of law and government unnecessary while they remained perfectly just to each other;

but as nothing but Heaven is impregnable to vice, it will unavoidably happen that in proportion as they surmount the first difficulties of emigration, which bound them together in a common cause, they will begin to relax in their duty and attachment to each other: and this remissness will point out the necessity of establishing some form of government to supply the defect of moral virtue.

Lord Acton wrote:

Inequality: the Basis of society. We combined and put things in common to protect the weak against the strong.

The technology to make farming tools was easily adapted to making weapons. As mankind's selfishness led to more violence, people gravitated together, forming communities for protection. This was the beginning of the very first cities, Eridu, Uruk and Ur.

When people get together, there is always someone with a "type A" take-charge personality who tells others what to do. This is good as they are able to organize and successfully defend themselves from attackers. The children of these leaders have an impulse to establish a pecking order. A clique develops, where the weaker-willed, insecure individuals crave the leader's approval, and obey him.

Initially, this leader provides benefit to others, as Plato described: "This ... is the root from which a tyrant springs; when he first appears above ground he is a PROTECTOR." His initial beneficial actions convince people to yield more of their independence to him. His influence gradually extends over more people, increasing his in power.

Though early leaders genuinely served their communities well, the temptation grows for them and their heirs to want to stay in power. They attempt to eliminate challengers, similar to how a gang leader or a political boss grows in power, then resorts to unsavory methods to stay in power. Over time, this turns into a hereditary monarchy.

In many cases, the leader who exerts his will is the most aggressive and most demanding, as Ben Franklin stated:

> And of what kind are the men that will strive for this profitable preeminence, through all the bustle of cabal (secret plots), the heat of contention ... It will be the bold and the violent, the men of strong passions and indefatigable activity in their selfish pursuits. These will thrust themselves into your government and be your rulers.

When a challenger successfully overthrows a tyrannical king, his desire to stay in power transforms him into the next tyrant, thus the saying, "Beware lest the dragon-slayer becomes the dragon," or as Friedrich Nietzsche warned "Battle not with monsters lest you become one."

Kings are, in a sense, glorified gang leaders. The king considers his will to be law of the land, and he needs bureaucracies and armies to implement his "law."

As inventions of the plow and irrigation produced more food per acre, methods and technologies developed to store the grain. Kings claimed to own everythings and needed scribes to keep track of their inventories. Scribes developed methods of accounting using rods and beads – an abacus, or as in China – the tying of knots in ropes.

In Sumeria came the invention of accounting using clay tokens to represent bushels of grain. Markings were made on these clay tokens with a pointed stick, similar to tallying, and they were baked. This developed into the very first writing method called Sumerian cuneiform.

c.3300 BC – Sumerian cuneiform in the Mesopotamian Valley (present-day Iraq) is considered the birthplace of writing. Sumerian kings then used writing to list their genealogies, which included exceptionally long reigns of antediluvian (before the flood) rulers. Scribes recorded the kings' decrees and astronomical observations.

A king typically rules by showing favoritism. He honors and rewards those who are loyal to him, and he strikes fear and punishes those who are disloyal to him.

If one is an inside member of the king's clique, they will likely receive privileges. If the king is short-tempered, he silences opposition by shaming, excluding or banishing them. Ultimately, the king punishes those who offend him, even hunting them down and killing them. The rest of the people see this, and since they do not want to be killed, they quickly submit and do what the king says, even to the extent of obeying his orders to kill others.

St. Thomas Aquinas described how an Arab leader motivated followers, writing in *Summa contra Gentiles*, 1258, (bk 1, ch. 6, translated by Anton C. Pegis, Univ. of Notre Dame Press, 1975, pp. 73–75):

> (He) ... seduced the people by promises of carnal pleasure ... (He) said that he was sent in the power of his arms – which are signs not lacking even to robbers and tyrants ... Those who believed in him were brutal men and desert wanderers, utterly ignorant ... (He) forced others to become his followers by the violence of his arms.

When people are gathered together, a dynamic occurs, namely: the more they are concentrated, the more likely there will be favoritism, corruption, intrigue and crime. One need simply ask, where is there more crime, drugs, and voter fraud – in rural areas? or in inner cities?

Indeed, it is an example of direct proportionality: that the increased size of the city, together with its greater concentration of people, is directly proportional to an increase in political favoritism and corruption.

Jefferson wrote:

> When we get piled upon one another in large cities, as in Europe, we shall become corrupt as in Europe.

Kings harnessed the power of their people for grand building projects and conquering armies. Those not wanting to be ruled by a king were compelled to migrate away, just as two magnets with facing sides of the same polarity repel each other.

Ironically, the same aspect of human nature that repels at being controlled by others also wants to control others. When the people who did not want to be ruled by a king migrated away from him, they ended up forming communities which, too, became ruled by kings. This, in turn, led others to migrate still further away, till humans migrated to the ends of the earth.

An interesting DNA study found that native Americans have genes sequences showing they are related to peoples in Mongolia and eastern Siberia, thus leading scientists to speculate that their ancient ancestors must have crossed the Bering Strait when it was frozen or at lower levels.

Geographical distance did not allow mankind to escape his own selfish human nature. Ronald Reagan stated:

> Every other revolution simply exchanged one set of rulers for another.

Illustrating how those who fled repeat the progression are the three classes: pioneers, settlers, and ruling class.

"Pioneers" courageously ventured into new lands and subdued the dangers of the wilderness.

"Settlers" then organized and developed the new land.

"Ruling Class" are the grandchildren of the pioneers and settlers. They jealously claimed superiority over others as a preferential hereditary upper tier of society, a type of nobleman's republic. This "ruling class" ironically does not like courageous people like pioneers.

This progression from pioneers to settlers to ruling class can be seen in America's early colonial history.

The Puritans were dissidents who did not like being controlled by the King of England. They courageously ventured to Massachusetts, where they pioneered living in the wilderness. Settlers organized the colony and put laws in place. After a generation, there arose a privileged "ruling class," who were intolerant of dissidents like the first pioneers, causing dissidents to flee further, where they founded Connecticut, New Hampshire and Rhode Island.

NIMROD

The ancient "Table of Nations" mentioned Nimrod as the son of Cush, grandson of Ham, and great-grandson of Noah. He is credited with building the Tower of Babel.

Nimrod's kingdom included the cities of Babel, Uruk, Akkad and Calneh in the land of Shinar in Mesopotamia. (Genesis 10:8–12; 1 Chronicles 1:10; Micah 5:6; Talmud; midrash of Genesis Rabba.)

Nimrod was "a mighty one on the earth" and "a mighty hunter before God" but Jewish interpreters such as Philo, Yochanan ben Zakai, Pseudo-Philo, and Symmachus, interpreted "a mighty hunter before the Lord" as "in the face of the Lord" or "in opposition to the Lord." The name "Nimrod" is associated with a Hebrew word for "rebel."

Flavius Josephus wrote in *Antiquities of the Jews* (c. 94):

> Now it was Nimrod who excited them to such an affront and contempt of God. He was the grandson of Ham, the son of Noah, a bold man, and of great strength of hand.

> He persuaded them not to ascribe it to God, as if it were through his means they were happy, but to believe that it was their own courage which procured that happiness.

He also gradually changed the government into tyranny, seeing no other way of turning men from the fear of God, but to bring them into a constant dependence on his power.

He also said he would be revenged on God, if he should have a mind to drown the world again; for that he would build a tower too high for the waters to reach. And that he would avenge himself on God for destroying their forefathers.

Now the multitude were very ready to follow the determination of Nimrod, and to esteem it a piece of cowardice to submit to God;

and they built a tower, neither sparing any pains, nor being in any degree negligent about the work: and, by reason of the multitude of hands employed in it, it grew very high, sooner than anyone could expect; but the thickness of it was so great, and it was so strongly built, that thereby its great height seemed, upon the view, to be less than it really was.

It was built of burnt brick, cemented together with mortar, made of bitumen, that it might not be liable to admit water.

When God saw that they acted so madly, he did not resolve to destroy them utterly, since they were not grown wiser by the destruction of the former sinners; but he caused a tumult among them, by producing in them diverse languages, and causing that, through the multitude of those languages, they should not be able to understand one another.

The place wherein they built the tower is now called Babylon, because of the confusion of that language which they readily understood before; for the Hebrews mean by the word Babel, confusion.

Lord Acton wrote:

The notion of sin and repentance waned with the belief in authority. Men thought they could make good the evil they did.

Sir Walter Raleigh mentioned Nimrod in his *History of the World* (c. 1616). Yale President Ezra Stiles addressed Connecticut's General Assembly, May 8, 1783:

The location of the respective territories to the first nations, was so of God as to give them a divine right defensively to resist the NIMRODS and Ninuses, THE FIRST INVADING TYRANTS of the ancient ages ...

But after the spirit of conquest had changed the first governments, ALL THE SUCCEEDING ones have, in general, proved one CONTINUED SERIES OF INJUSTICE, which has reigned in all countries for almost four thousand years ...

Almost all the polities may be reduced to hereditary dominion, in either a monarchy or aristocracy, and these supported by a standing army...

Monarchy and aristocracy, when they become hereditary, terminate in the prostration of liberty ... It is next to an impossibility to tame a monarch; and few have ruled without ferocity.

TIMELINE 3200–2250 BC

c.3200 BC – Egyptian hieroglyph writing began. Egypt was the most powerful nation in the world for many of its 33 major dynasties over the next 3,000 years. The Pharaoh claimed a status superior to the people as son of the god Horus. The biblical account of a severe crisis, seven years of famine, resulted in all power being concentrated into the hands of the Pharaoh.

At the Constitutional Convention, June 2, 1787, Ben Franklin gave an address "Dangers of a Salaried Bureaucracy":

There is scarce a king in a hundred who would not, if he could, follow the example of Pharaoh—get first all the people's money, then all their lands, and then make them and their children servants for ever.

It will be said that we do not propose to establish kings ... but there is a natural inclination in mankind to kingly government ... They would rather have one tyrant than five hundred. It gives more of the appearance of equality among citizens; and that they like. I am apprehensive ... that the government of the States may, in future times, end in a monarchy.

> But this catastrophe ... may be long delayed, if in our proposed system we do not sow the seeds of contention, faction, and tumult, by making our posts of honor places of profit. If we do, I fear that ... it will only nourish the fetus of a king ... and a king will the sooner be set over us.

Commenting on the longevity of Egyptian civilization, Yale President Ezra Stiles stated May 8, 1783:

> Nor was the policy of Egypt overthrown for a longer period from the days of Metzraim (upper and lower Nile kingdoms, c.3,200 BC) till the time of Cambyses (Persian King, son of Cyrus the Great, who conquered Egypt in 525 BC) and Amasis (the last great ruler of Egypt before the Persian conquest).

c.2700 BC – Yellow Emperor began Chinese writing. China had at 25 major dynasties over its 5,000 year history.

c.2500 BC – Gilgamesh of King of Uruk in Sumeria, Mesopotamia. As mentioned earlier, *The Epic of Gilgamesh* is considered the oldest story ever recorded in any language. Gilgamesh built the walls around his city of Uruk, and considered himself not only a king, but claimed the status of demigod (part god).

c.2500 BC – Djoser, Pharaoh of Egypt's 3rd Dynasty, Old Kingdom.

c.2250 BC – Sargon of Akkad, whose Akkadian Empire was the LARGEST EMPIRE IN THE WORLD TO THIS DATE, SURPASSING ALL PREVIOUS ONES. Sargon expanded ruling from just one city or several cities of the same ethnic group, to what is considered to be the first multi-ethnic, centrally ruled empire, stretching from the Persian Gulf to the Mediterranean Sea, with the capital city being Nineveh. Sargon claimed a status superior to the people, styling himself as "priest of the god Anu" and "ensi (representative) the god Enlil." The ruins of ancient Nineveh were destroyed by ISIS in January of 2015.

&

CHINESE DYNASTIES

Yale President Ezra Stiles addressed Connecticut's General Assembly, May 8, 1783:

The nine bowls engraved with the map of dominion established the policy of the Chinese empire for near twenty ages. (Du Halde, Hist. China.)

The ancient division of the empire subsisted by means of these symbols of dominion, which passed in succession to the nine principal mandarins, or supreme governors under the imperial sovereignty; and this for the long tract from their first institution by the Emperor Yu, who reigned two thousand two hundred years before Christ, to Chey-lie-vang, who was contemporary with the great philosopher Menzius, three hundred years before Christ.

Woodrow Wilson wrote in *The State*, 1889:

If we would understand primitive society ... in that society men were born into the station and the part they were to have throughout life, as they still are among the peoples who preserve their earliest conceptions of social order.

This is known as the law of status. It is not a matter of choice or of voluntary arrangement in what relations men shall stand towards each other as individuals. He who is born a slave, let him remain a slave; the artisan, an artisan; the priest, a priest, is the command of the law of status. Excellency cannot avail to raise any man above his parentage; aptitude may operate only within the sphere of each man's birthright.

No man may lose caste without losing respectability also and forfeiting the protection of the law. Or, to go back to a less developed society, no son, however gifted, may lawfully break away from the authority of his father, however cruel or incapable that father may be; or make any alliance which will in the least degree draw him away from the family alliance and duty into which he was born ...

Every man's career is determined for him before his birth. His blood makes his life. To break away from one's birth station, under such a system, is to make breach not only of social, but also of religious duty, and to bring upon oneself the curses of men and gods. Primitive society rested, not upon contract, but upon status ...

Change of the existing social order was the last thing of which the primitive state dreamed; and those races which allowed the rule of status to harden about their lives still stand where they stood a thousand years ago.

Chinese Emperors ruled by claiming to have a mandate from heaven. Dynasties regularly went through a rise and fall pattern which became known as the Dynastic Cycle:

–A new ruler unites China, founds a new dynasty, and gains the "mandate of heaven."

–The new dynasty, achieves prosperity.

–The population increases.

–Corruption becomes rampant in the imperial court and the empire experiences internal instability.

–Then a crisis, possibly a natural disaster, occurs which brings distress and wipes out farm land. Because the corrupt government is ill-prepared to respond, there is a famine.

–The famine causes the population to rebel into a civil war.

–The disasters convince the people that the ruler had lost the "mandate of heaven."

–The population decreases because of insecurity and gang violence.

–This leads to a warring states period of disorder, chaos and anarchy.

–A strong leader emerges and unifies country.

–He centralizes power, establishes an authoritarian government and claims to have a "mandate from heaven,"

–and cycle repeats.

Chinese philosopher Mencius, who lived during the Period of Warring States, identified 3 stages for a dynasty:

1. The dynasty begins with energy and patriotism.
2. The dynasty grows, becomes prosperous and peaks.
3. The dynasty is burdened with debt and declines economically, then politically, until it collapses.

Major Chinese Dynasties:

    Xia Dynasty (2100–1600 BC)

    Shang Dynasty (1600–1046 BC)

    Zhou Dynasty (1045–256 BC)

    Spring and Autumn Period (771–476 BC)

    Warring States Period (475–221 BC)

        Qin, Yan, Zhao, Zhou, Zou, Zhong Shan,
        Wei, Chu, Han, Qi, Song, Lu, Teng

    Qin Dynasty (221–206 BC)

    Han Dynasty (206 BC–220AD)

    Three Kingdoms Wei, Shu, Yu (220–280)

    Jin Dynasty (265–420)

    Sixteen Kingdoms (304–439)

    Southern and Northern Dynasties (420–589)

    Sui Dynasty, (581–618)

    Tang Dynasty (618–907)

    Second Zhou (690–705)

    Five Dynasties & Ten Kingdoms period (907–979)

    Liao Dynasty (907–1125)

    Song Dynasty (960–1276)

    Jin (1115–1234)

    Western Xia (1038–1227)

    Yuan Dynasty founded by Mongols (1271–1368)

    Ming Dynasty (1368–1644)

    Qing Dynasty founded by Manchus (1644–1911)

    Republic of China (1912)

    People's Republic of China (1949)

There is a famous Chinese proverb that says:

After a long split, a union will occur; after a long union, a split will occur.

TIMELINE 2200–1279 BC

c.2200 BC – Kutik-Inshushinak, King of the Old Elamite Dynasty (area of Persia/Iran)

c.2061 BC – Nebhepetre Mentuhotep II, Pharaoh of Egypt's 11th Dynasty, Middle Kingdom

c.1900 BC – Bel-kap-kapu, King of Assyria's Old Kingdom

Yale President Ezra Stiles addressed Connecticut's General Assembly, May 8, 1783:

> The Medo-Persian (550 to 330 BC) and Alexandrine (Alexander the Great, 323 to 311 BC) empires, and that of Timur (Tamerlane, 1370 to 1405 AD), who once reigned from Smyrna to the Ganges, were, for obvious reasons, of short and transitory duration; but that of the Assyrian endured, without mutation, through a tract of one thousand three hundred years, from Semiramis (legendary female ruler of Babylonian antiquity) to Sardanapalus (considered last king of Neo-Assyrian Empire, 605 BC).

c.1878 BC – Senusret III, Pharaoh of Egypt's 12th Dynasty, Middle Kingdom

c.1800 BC – Patriarch Abraham was born in Ur of the Chaldees, the son of Terah, tenth in descent from Noah.

c.1800 BC – Yu the Great, Emperor of China's Xia Dynasty

c.1728 BC – Hammurabi's Babylonian Empire. His 282 laws, referred to as Hammurabi's Code, was one of the first collection of written laws. It was hierarchical, with the king at the top, followed by the royal upper class, which were "more" equal, then the artisan-merchant class, then commoners and slaves. It contained civil and criminal laws with scaled punishments depending on the social status of the law-breaker. There was no concept of men and women made equal in the image of a Creator, no spiritual dimension of loving God, nor that breaking the law was a "sin" against God.

c.1650 BC – Nedjeh, King of African Kerma Kingdom

c.1556 BC – Mursilis I, King of the Old Hittite Kingdom

c.1508 BC – Hatshepsut of Egypt's 18th Dynasty, New Kingdom – LARGEST EMPIRE IN THE WORLD TO THIS DATE, SURPASSING ALL PREVIOUS ONES. Her name means "Foremost of Noble Ladies," she is regarded as one of the most successful pharaohs and "the first great woman in history."

c.1479 BC – Thutmose III, Pharaoh of Egypt's 18th Dynasty, New Kingdom

c.1450 BC – Artatama I, King of Hurrian Mitanni Empire

c.1353 BC – Akhenaten, Pharaoh, and his wife Nefertiti, of Egypt's 18th Dynasty, New Kingdom

c.1344 BC – Suppiluliumas I, King of the New Hittite Empire (modern day Turkey and northern Syria) was the ruler, military leader and supreme judge, being considered the earthly deputy of the storm god.

Upon a Hittite king's death, he was considered a god. In Hittite social structure, below the royalty was a feudal farming society where common people were either freemen, artisans, or slaves. The Hittites mined iron, which they used for iron weapons and chariots, giving them military superiority. This began the era called the Iron Age.

c.1341 BC – Tutankhamun, Pharaoh of Egypt's 18th Dynasty, New Kingdom

c.1279 BC – Ramesses the Great, Pharaoh of Egypt's 18th Dynasty, New Kingdom. He who ruled 67 years, fought in foreign conquests and built ambitious structures.

DIVINELY APPOINTED KING?

Ancient Civilizations had numerous features in common, among which are three prominent ones:

1) Fascination with stars, heavens

2) Buildings to observe stars, heavens

3) A King who ascended the building and claimed to be the divinely-appointed political intermediary between the heavens and the people, thus legitimizing his totalitarian rule, often demanding that lives be sacrificed for the state.

–**Babylonia, Assyrian Kings** – were "king–priests"

–**Mesopotamia Kings** – considered deities upon death

–**Egyptian Pharaohs** – claimed to be son of the god Osiris

–**Tyre King** – bridge between temporal & celestial world

–**Persian Kings** – had a privileged relationship with the divine to maintain his creation.

–**South Asian Kings** – were "agents of God" protecting the world like God did.

–**Chinese Emperors** – ruled by claiming they had a mandate from heaven

–**Roman Emperors** – cult of deifying Caesars. The name "August" means "sacred" or "divine."

–**India Rajas** – semi-divine caste of rulers, post-Brahminism in Tamilakam, a Thiruvalangadu inscription referred to Emperor Raja Raja Chola I: "Having noticed by the marks (on his body) that Arulmozhi was the very Vishnu."

–**Muslim Sultan of Dehli** – maintained that the Sultan was the "shadow of God."

–**Inca Emperors** – claimed to be delegates of the Sun god

–**Caliphs** – successors of the Messenger of Allah

–**Medieval Monarchs** – divine right of kings

–**Japanese Emperors** – descendant of Shinto god Amaterasu

E.C. Wines highlighted how Israel was different in *Commentaries on the Laws of the Ancient Hebrews, with an Introductory Essay on Civil Society & Government* (NY: Geo. P. Putnam & Co., 1853):

> Menes in Egypt; Minos in Crete; Cadmus in Thebes; Lycurgus in Sparta; Zaleucus in Locris; and Numa in Rome. But ... Moses differed fundamentally from ... these heathen legislators.
>
> They employed religion in establishing their political institutions, while he made use of a civil constitution as a means of perpetuating religion ...
>
> Moses' ... national unity ... was not that species of unity, which the world has since so often seen, in which vast multitudes of human beings are delivered up to the arbitrary will of one man.
>
> It was a unity, effected by the abolition of caste; a unity, founded on the principle of equal rights; a unity, in which the whole people formed the state ... contrary to the celebrated declaration of a French monarch, who avowed himself to be the state.

The French monarch referred to above was Louis XIV. He was called "The Sun King" as he considered his subects as planets revolving around him. He had the longest, most powerful reign of any European monarch, with an empire that stretched the globe. He reportedly exclaimed: "L'Etat, c'est moi" (I am the state).

THE STATE IS GOD?

Prior to Jesus delineating a limitation of Caesar's power, "Render unto Caesar the things that are Caesar's and unto God the things that are God's," there was no separation of religion and government. Kings claimed dominion over the lives and consciences of their subjects.

Author and attorney Kelly O'Connell wrote in the article "Pagan Government Theory Insures Tyranny Returns to the West" (*Canada Free Press*, June 18, 2012):

> Of the central core of ideas from socialism and Marxism, none is more important than erecting a government to operate as a kind of default god ...
>
> After God is removed ... a humanistic cult allows mankind to pursue all his desires unfettered ...
>
> This ... was one of the key insights of Eric Voegelin in his epic *Modernity Without Restraint: The Political Religions, The New Science of Politics, and Science, Politics, and Gnosticism.*
>
> The fury against religion endemic in all leftist ideologies can only be understood as a Procrustean commitment (forced compliance to arbitrary standards) to break and recast the fundamental order established in the farthest recesses of human history ...
>
> This struggle represents the battle between humanistic philosophy against revealed religion ... Marxism ... versus the biblical view of the cosmos ...
>
> In the ancient classical world of Greece and Rome there was no constitutional or natural law theory of government. Instead, a muscular legal system developed, as in Rome (or Hammurabi's Babylon or Draco's Greece) – yet the state did not have yet its modern functions.
>
> So, for example, permanent prosecutors had yet to be created – so all cases in court were waged by private lawyers. The great Cicero made his reputation on prosecuting Gaius Verres as a private citizen.
>
> In the classical pagan world, government was the preeminent organization of society without parallel. Since there was no Bill of Rights, people had no defenses against the state.
>
> The notion of God-given personal, natural rights as contemplated by church thinkers, like William of Ockham and Thomas Aquinas, would have been seen absurd, if not unintelligible ...
>
> If warfare broke out, and the state demanded more

wealth to wage war, for the citizen to refuse would be tantamount to treason. There was no absolute right to private property. Within this context, the government operated as a de facto god because there was no theory or body to oppose it.

During the French Revolution, 1789–1799, Robespierre created a pseudo-religious "cult of the goddess of reason" which, in a sense, deified the secular State. People of faith were compelled to abandon their beliefs and submit their consciences to the secular state. Lord Acton wrote:

> What the French took from the Americans was their theory of revolution, not their theory of government — their cutting, not their sewing.

The French Revolution became a model for subsequent communist revolutions where bloody overthrows were justifiable if the goal was establish the elusive utopian workers' paradise. G.K. Chesterton wrote:

> Once the government removes God the government then becomes god.

The German political philosopher Hegel stated:

> The State is god walking on earth ...
>
> In considering the idea of the State, one must not think of particular states, nor of particular institutions, but one must contemplate the idea, this actual god, by itself ...
>
> The State is the divine idea as it exists on earth.

Kelly O'Connell continued in "Pagan Government Theory Insures Tyranny Returns to the West":

> But Marx did get his idea of "government as god" from Hegel who borrowed it from the atheist Jewish philosopher Spinoza. He taught no God existed, but to the extent the divine was present He expressed himself through government. This was an idea Spinoza himself borrowed from the ancient Greeks and Romans.

Supporting the idea that the State is supreme, Chinese Revolutionary Sun Yat-sen (1866–1925) stated:

> An individual should not have too much freedom.

A nation should have absolute freedom.

This echoed Greek philosopher Aristotle (384–322 BC) who wrote in *Nichomachean Ethics*, Book I, Chapter 1:

> For even if the good of an individual is identical with the good of a state, yet the good of the state is evidently greater and more perfect to attain or to preserve. For though the good of an individual by himself is something worth working for, to ensure the good of a nation or a state is nobler and more divine."

The political philosopher Thomas Hobbes, in the *Leviathan*, 1651, described the State as "our mortal god."

In *The Social Contract*, 1762, Rousseau wrote:

> When the prince says to him: "It is expedient for the State that you should die," he ought to die, because it is only on that condition that he has been living in security up to the present, and because his life is no longer a mere bounty of nature, but a gift made conditionally by the State.

Woodrow Wilson wrote in *The State*, 1889:

> The defects of the social compact theory are too plain to need more than brief mention ...

> Status was the basis of primitive society: the individual counted for nothing; society–the family, the tribe–counted for everything.

> Government came before the individual ... Man was merged in society ... Authority did not rest upon mutual agreement, but upon mutual subordination.

Political philosopher Carl Friedrich wrote in 1939:

> In a slow process that lasted several generations, the modern concept of the State was ... forged by political theorists as a tool of propaganda for absolute monarchs. They wished to give the king's government a corporate halo roughly equivalent to that of the Church.

With the exaltation of the secular State, the leaders of the State hold a superior position similar to the position previously held by kings who claimed "divine right."

ISRAEL: FIRST NATION WITHOUT A KING

Few instances exist in history where people had the opportunity to experiment in ruling themselves WITHOUT a KING. Ancient Israel is the first well recorded instance of this during their first 400 years in the Promised Land. When Moses came down the mountain, possibly around 1,400 BC, the Law he carried did not establish a monarchical hierarchy. If it had, Moses would have likely made himself king and entered the Promised Land on a red carpet. Instead, Moses was not allowed to enter the Promised Land, as he had struck the rock with his rod instead of speaking to it when the Lord wanted to perform a miracle of water coming forth for the thirsting Israelites.

Numbers 20:2, 7-12:

> And there was no water for the congregation: and they gathered themselves together against Moses and against Aaron ... And the LORD spake unto Moses, saying, Take the rod, and gather thou the assembly together ... and **speak ye unto the rock** before their eyes; and it shall give forth his water ...

> And Moses and Aaron gathered the congregation together before the rock, and he said unto them, Hear now, ye rebels; must we fetch you water out of this rock? And Moses lifted up his hand, and **with his rod he smote the rock twice**: and the water came out abundantly, and the congregation drank ...

> And the LORD spake unto Moses and Aaron, Because ye believed me not, to sanctify me in the eyes of the children of Israel, therefore **ye shall not bring this congregation into the land which I have given them.**

Numbers 27:12-14:

> And the LORD said unto Moses ... For ye rebelled against my commandment in the desert of Zin, in the strife of the congregation, to sanctify me at the water before their eyes: that is the water of Meribah in Kadesh in the wilderness of Zin.

Deuteronomy 3:23-27:

> And I besought the LORD at that time, saying... I pray thee, let me go over, and see the good land that is beyond Jordan, that goodly mountain, and Lebanon.
>
> But the LORD was wroth with me for your sakes, and would not hear me: and the LORD said unto me, Let it suffice thee; speak no more unto me of this matter. Get thee up into the top of Pisgah, and lift up thine eyes westward, and northward, and southward, and eastward, and behold it with thine eyes: **for thou shalt not go over this Jordan.**

If Moses made up the Law, he would have done as other leaders, placing himself in a superior status. Hammurabi did this, being exempt from obeying his own code. The fact that Moses was not allowed to enter the Promised Land is evidence he did not create the Law himself.

If Israel were to have an elite class, it most certainly would have been the High Priest Aaron's family. This was not the case. After the Lord had given Moses pages of details as to how He was to be approached, two of Aaron's sons decided to approach God as they wanted. Fire flashed out from the altar of the Lord and burned them to death.

Leviticus 10:1-2:

> And Nadab and Abihu, the sons of Aaron, took either of them his censer, and put fire therein, and put incense thereon, and offered strange fire before the LORD, which he commanded them not. And there went out fire from the LORD, and devoured them, and they died before the LORD.

The God of Israel made it clear that neither Moses nor the High Priest's family was above the law. In Israel, everyone was equal and equally had to follow the word of the Lord.

Enoch Cobb Wines (1806–1879) was Professor of Ancient Languages at Washington College, in Washington, Pennsylvania, and president of City University of St. Louis in the mid-19th century. He wrote in the Preface of his *Commentaries on the Laws of the Ancient Hebrews, with an Introductory Essay on Civil Society & Government* (NY: Geo. P. Putnam & Co., 1853):

The civil government of the ancient Hebrews was the government of a free people; it was a government of laws; it was a system of self-government. It was not only the first, but the only government of antiquity, to which this description is fully applicable...

In an age of barbarism and tyranny, Moses solved the problem how a people could be self-governed, and yet well governed; how men could be kept in order, and still be free; how the liberty of the individual could be reconciled with the welfare of the community.

Woodrow Wilson wrote in *The State*, 1889:

Influence of Mosaic Institutions: It would be a mistake, however, to ascribe to Roman legal conceptions an undivided sway over the development of law and institutions during the Middle Ages. The Teuton came under the influence, not or Rome only, buy also of Christianity; and through the Church there entered into Europe a potent leaven of Judaic thought.

The Laws of Moses as well as the laws of Rome contributed suggestions ... to the men and institutions which were to prepare the modern world; and if we could have but eyes to see ... we should easily discover how very much besides religion we owe to the Jew.

The first design for the official seal of the United States, recommended in 1776 by Franklin, Adams, and Jefferson depicted the Jews crossing the Red Sea with the motto: "Resistance to Tyrants is Obedience to God."

In denouncing the Tea Act, Dr. Benjamin Rush, who signed the Declaration of Independence, wrote:

What did not Moses forsake and suffer for his countrymen! What shining examples of patriotism do we behold in Joshua, Samuel, Maccabees and all the illustrious princes, captains & prophets among the Jews.

Dr. Benjamin Rush explained in *Essays, Literary, Moral, and Philosophical*, 1798:

In contemplating the political institutions of the United States, I lament that we waste so much time and money in punishing crimes and take so little pains to prevent them.

We profess to be republicans, and yet we neglect the only means of establishing and perpetuating our republican forms of government, that is, the universal education of our youth in the principles of Christianity by the means of the Bible.

For this Divine book, above all others, favors that equality among mankind, that respect for just laws, and those sober and frugal virtues, which constitute the soul of republicanism.

LANGUAGES

The United Nations Educational, Scientific, and Cultural Organization (UNESCO), cites that there are about 6,000 tongues spoken today throughout the earth, some used by hundreds of millions and some by less than a thousand. *The Cambridge Encyclopedia of Language* states:

> Every culture which has been investigated, no matter how "primitive" it may be in cultural terms, turns out to have a fully developed language, with a complexity comparable to those of the so-called "civilized" nations.

Evidence is against speech evolving, as Harvard Professor Steven Pinker wrote in *The Language Instinct* (1994):

> There is no such thing as a Stone Age language.

Linguist Dr. Mason wrote in *Science News Letter* (Sept. 3, 1955, p. 148):

> The idea that "savages" speak in a series of grunts, and are unable to express many "civilized" concepts, is very wrong ... Many of the languages of non-literate peoples are far more complex than modern European ones.

A *Science Illustrated* article stated (July 1948, p. 63):

> Older forms of the languages known today were far more difficult than their modern descendants ... man appears not to have begun with a simple speech, and gradually made it more complex, but rather to have gotten hold of a tremendously knotty speech somewhere in the unrecorded past, and gradually

simplified it to the modern forms.

Oriental language scholar Sir Henry Rawlinson wrote in *The Journal of the Royal Asiatic Society of Great Britain and Ireland* (London, 1855, Vol. 15, p. 232):

> If we were to be thus guided by the mere intersection of linguistic paths, and independently of all reference to the scriptural record, we should still be led to fix on the plains of Shinar, as the focus from which the various lines had radiated.

Sir William Jones addressed the Asiatic Society in Calcutta, Feb. 2, 1786:

> The Sanskrit language, whatever be its antiquity, is of a wonderful structure; more perfect than the Greek, more copious than the Latin, and more exquisitely refined than either, yet bearing to both of them a stronger affinity, both in the roots of verbs and in the forms of grammar, than could possibly have been produced by accident; so strong, indeed, that no philoger could examine them all three, without believing them to have sprung from some common source which, perhaps, no longer exists.

The *New Encyclopedia Britannica* explains:

> The earliest records of written language, the only linguistic fossils man can hope to have, go back no more than about 4,000 or 5,000 years.

The appearance of fully developed languages is reflected in the story of the Tower of Babylon, where speech was confused and people scattered.

Historical references to a Great Ziggurat of Babylon, called Etemenanki (House of the platform of Heaven and Earth) are cited in Andrew R. George's article, "The Tower of Babel: Archaeology, History & Cuneiform Texts" (2007; Archiv fuer Orientforschung, 51, 2005/06, pp. 75–95):

> The reference to a ziggurat at Babylon in the Creation Epic (Enûma Eliš· VI 63: George 1992: 301–2) is more solid evidence, however, for a Middle Assyrian piece of this poem survives to prove the long-held theory that it existed already in the SECOND

MILLENNIUM BC. There is no reason to doubt that this ziggurat, described as ziggurat apsî elite, "the upper ziggurat of the Apsû," was E-temenanki.

In 689 BC, the King of Assyria, Sennacherib, invaded Babylon and claims to have destroyed Etemenanki – the Great Ziggurat of Babylon. Assyria was then conquered by the Babylonian King Nabopolassar (658–605 BC), who, together with his son Nebuchadnezzar II (634–562 BC), spent 88 years rebuilding the Great Ziggurat. This is the same Nebuchadnezzar II who infamously destroyed the Temple in Jerusalem in 587 BC and took Judah captive to Babylon. Nebuchadnezzar II described the Great Ziggurat:

> This edifice…the most ancient monument of Borsippa (Birs Nimrud). A former king built it, (they reckon 42 ages) but he did not complete its head. Since a remote time, people had abandoned it, without order expressing their words. Since that time the earthquake and the thunder had dispersed the sun-dried clay. The bricks of the casing had been split, and the earth of the interior had been scattered in heaps.
>
> Merodach, the great god, excited my mind to repair this building. I did not change the site nor did I take away the foundation. In a fortunate month, in an auspicious day, I undertook to build porticoes around the crude brick masses, and the casing of burnt bricks. I adapted the circuits, I put the inscription of my name in the Kitir of the portico. I set my hand to finish it. And to exalt its head. As it had been done in ancient days, so I exalted its summit.

A tablet gave the ziggurat's dimensions:

1st level 300ft by 300ft – 110ft high;

2nd level 260ft by 260ft – 60ft high;

3rd level 200ft by 200ft – 20ft high;

4th level 170ft by 170ft – 20ft high;

5th level 140ft by 140ft – 20ft high;

6th level possibly – 20ft high;

7th level 70ft by 80ft – 50ft high.

Greek historian Herodotus confirmed the existence

of the Great Ziggurat in 440 BC, but what remained was demolished by Alexander the Great in 331 BC, who intended to rebuild it till he suddenly died. The 2nd millenium BC is the assumed time period of the original Great Ziggurat of Babylon and the appearance of different languages.

ISRAEL–FIRST NATION WHERE ALL READ

At the time when the children of Israel left Egypt, sometimes dated around 1,400 BC:

- –the Hittite language had 375 cuneiform characters;
- –the Indus Valley Harappan language had 417 symbols;
- –the Luwian language of Anatolian had over 500 logographic hieroglyphs;
- –the Akkadian language prevalent in Mesopotamia had over 1,500 Sumerian cuneiform characters;
- –the Egyptian language had over 3,000 hieroglyphic characters;
- –the Chinese language had nearly 10,000 pictogram and ideogram characters, invented by scribes of China's Yellow Emperor.

When Moses came down from Mount Sinai, he not only had the Ten Commandments, but he had them in a 22 CHARACTER ALPHABET. With so few characters, everyone in the nation learned to read, even children.

In most countries, reading and writing was only practiced by kings, pharaohs, emperors, their scribes, together with the ruling class and merchants. In Ancient Egypt, the literacy rate was less than one percent. The National Archaeological Museum in Athens, Greece, has a section on "Scribes" in its section on Egyptian Artifacts:

Only a small percentage of ancient Egypt's population was literate, namely the pharaoh, members of the royal family, officials, priests and scribes. Particularly popular and lucrative, the scribe's profession was mostly hereditary.

Scribes had careers in the government, priesthood,

and army. They began their rigorous training in their early childhood. Most of their training took place inside a building called the "House of Life," attached to the temple. Scribes wrote one stone or clay sherds, wooden boards, linen, papyrus, and parchment.

In many cases, writing was kept intentionally complicated to maintain control over uneducated masses. George Orwell wrote in *Nineteen Eighty-Four*:

> In the long run, a hierarchical society was only possible on a basis of poverty and ignorance.

It is theorized that scribes wanted to keep writing complicated as job security. Writing was their secret knowledge. They were needed to decipher the hieroglyphs.

Writing was initially invented by scribes to keep track of everything the king possessed, a tally accounting method of markings to keep track of inventories. Writing then evolved to keep track of a king's genealogy, decrees, astrological observations, myths, and royal propaganda.

There was no need for common people and slaves to read as they had no possessions to keep track of, and obviously made no decrees. Slaves not only had no need to read, they were actually forbidden to learn to read.

In the Middle Ages, clergy and upper classes could read but most common Europeans could not, contributing to the people being controlled more easily by a monarch.

A stronger viewpoint was taken by Anthropologist Claude Levi Strauss (1908–2009), who wrote:

> Ancient writing's main function was to facilitate the enslavement of other human beings.

This view was similar to the United States prior to the Civil War, where some slave-holding States, such as Virginia and Maryland, had laws making it illegal to teach slaves to read, as it was understood that illiterate, uneducated people were easier to control.

Frederick Douglass, who had been born a slave in Baltimore, Maryland, told the story of a time when he was about 12 years old. His master's sister-in-law, Sophia

Auld, was teaching Frederick the alphabet. When her husband found out, he forbade it, saying that if slaves could read, they would grow discontent, desire freedom, and run away. Frederick Douglass considered this the "first decidedly anti-slavery lecture" he had ever heard, causing him to be determined to read all-the-more.

Frederick Douglas wrote in his autobiography of learning to read from neighborhood white children. He would carefully observe the writings of men he worked with. He remembered reading a newspaper and it being snatched away from him with a scolding. (*The Life and Times of Frederick Douglass: His Early Life as a Slave, His Escape from Bondage, and His Complete History*, Dover Value Editions, Courier Dover Pub., 2003, p. 50).

In Israel, not only could everyone learn to read, they were required to, as the law was addressed to each person. Everyone was held personally accountable to obey the law.

ISRAELITE–EDUCATED & MORAL CITIZEN

A "subject" is a person who is under the rule of another. A "citizen" is a person possessing rights and responsible as a freeman to participate in ruling." An "Israelite" was originally similar to an Athenian "citizen," as W.D. Ross wrote in *Aristotle* (London, Methuen, 1937, p. 247):

> Aristotle's conception of a citizen is widely different from the modern conception ... His citizen is not content to have a say in the choosing of his rulers; every citizen is actually to rule in turn, and not merely in the sense of being a member of the executive, but in the sense, a more important one for Aristotle, of helping to make the laws of his state ... It is owing to this lofty conception of a citizen's duties that he so closely narrows the citizen body.

Supreme Court Justice James Wilson wrote in *Chisholm v. State of Georgia* (1793):

> Let a State be considered as subordinate to the People ... By a State I mean, a complete body of free

persons united together for their common benefit, to enjoy peaceably what is their own, and to do justice to others ... Under that Constitution there are citizens, but no subjects ...

As a citizen, I know the Government of that State to be republican; and my short definition of such a Government is, one constructed on this principle, that the Supreme Power resides in the body of the people.

Israel is quite possibly the first instance in history of an entirely literate population. Reading and writing allowed for the accumulation of thought and laid the foundation for science, inventions, manufacturing, and medicine.

E.C. Wines wrote in *Commentaries on the Laws of the Ancient Hebrews, with an Introductory Essay on Civil Society & Government* (NY: Geo. P. Putnam & Co., 1853):

A fundamental principle of the Hebrew government was education; the education of the whole body of the people; especially, in the knowledge of the constitution, laws and history of their own country.

An ignorant people cannot be a free people. Intelligence is essential to liberty. No nation is capable of self-government, which is not educated to understand and appreciate its responsibilities ...

Upon this principle Moses proceeded in the framing of his commonwealth ... The Mosaic law required, that the greatest pains should be taken to mold the minds, the principles, the habits, and manners of the young.

Parents were, again and again, commanded to teach their children, from infancy, all the words of the law, and all the glorious facts of their national history. They were enjoined to talk of them, when they sat in the house, and when they walked by the way, when they lay down, and when they rose up ...

Hebrew parents were required, not only to teach their children orally, but also to impart to them the arts of reading and writing. Since they were commanded to write them, they must themselves have learned the art of writing; and since they were to write them for the use of their children, these must have been taught the art of reading.

There is reason to believe, that the ability to read and write was an accomplishment, more generally possessed by the Hebrews, than by any other people of antiquity.

E.C. Wines continued:

Our Savior ... in his addresses to the common people ... constantly appealed to them in such words as these: "Have ye not read what Moses saith? Have ye not read in the scriptures?"

Such language implies an ability, on the part of the people, to examine the scriptures for themselves ...

The writings of Josephus are crowded with testimonies as to the great care of the Hebrews in the education of their children ...

Maimonides, in his treatise on the study of the law, says: "Every Israelite, whether poor or rich, healthy or sick, old or young, is obliged to study the law ... " He asks, "How long ought a man to pursue the study of the law?" and replies, "Till death."

An important function of the Levites was to superintend the education of the people ... In the reformation undertaken by Jehoshaphat, that excellent prince, in the true spirit of the Mosaic institution, commanded the priests to go through the land, and teach the people, city by city, the laws of Moses ...

The schools of the prophets were seminaries... instructed in the divine law, being best fitted to convey God's commands to the people ... Bishop Warburton argues ... that they were seminaries designed chiefly for the study of the Jewish law.

It is probable, however, that they were not devoted exclusively to that department of study, but embraced within their scope other branches of knowledge, which were reckoned among the pursuits of learning in that day.

They corresponded to the colleges and universities of modern times. They must have exercised a powerful influence on the mind and manners of the Jewish people ...

There was a peculiarity in the Mosaic system of education, which deserves our notice. It did not overlook the fact, that every man has what Dr. Arnold calls two businesses; his particular business, as of a farmer, merchant, lawyer, or the like, and his general business, that which he shares in common with all his fellow-citizens, his business as a man and a citizen ...

Moses ... intended, that all his people should share in the management of the public affairs. He meant each to be a depositary of political power ... as a solemn trust ... On the subject of education, he appears chiefly anxious to have his people instructed in the knowledge of ... their duties as men and citizens.

He belonged neither to that class of political philosophers, who desire to see the mass of the people shut out from all political power ... nor to that class, who wish to see the power of the masses increased, irrespective of their ability to discharge so important a trust beneficially to the community.

In his educational scheme, power and knowledge went hand in hand. The possession of the latter was regarded as essential to the right use of the former.

E.C. Wines continued:

The education, enjoined by Moses, was not ... merely of the children of the highborn and the rich, but of all ranks and conditions. It was a fundamental maxim of his policy, that no citizen, not even the lowest and the poorest, should grow up in ignorance...

In proportion as this idea enters into the constitution of a state, tyranny will hide its head, practical equality will be established, party strife will abate its ferocity, error, rashness, and folly will disappear, and an enlightened, dignified, and venerable public opinion will bear sway.

Upon the whole, it may be affirmed, that in no part of the Hebrew constitution does the wisdom, of the lawgiver shine with a more genial lustre, than in what relates to the education of the young ... that every citizen should be acquainted with the laws and constitution of his country.

Patriotism itself is but a blind impulse, if it is not founded on a knowledge of the blessings we are called upon to secure, and the privileges which we propose to defend.

It is political ignorance alone, that can reconcile men to the tame surrender of their rights; it is political knowledge alone, that can rear an effectual barrier against the encroachments of arbitrary power and lawless violence.

In full accordance with the spirit of the Mosaic legislation is the beautiful prayer of David, "that our sons may be as plants grown up in their youth; that our daughters may be as cornerstones, polished after the similitude of a palace."

Such was the political philosophy of the founder of the Hebrew state ... The education of the Hebrew people, conducted mainly ... under the domestic roof, was, nevertheless, a national education, and worthy of the imitation of other nations ...

The Hebrew law required an early, constant, vigorous, and efficient training of the disposition, judgment, manners, and habits both of thought and feeling. The sentiments, held to be appropriate to man in society, were imbibed with the milk of infancy. The manners, considered becoming in adults, were sedulously imparted in childhood.

The habits, regarded as conducive to individual advancement, social happiness, and national repose and prosperity, were cultivated with the utmost diligence. The greatest pains were taken to acquaint the Hebrew youth with their duties, as well as their rights, both personal and political.

In a word, the main channel of thought and feeling for each generation was marked out by the generation which preceded it, and the stream for the most part flowed with a steady current. Such a system of mental and moral culture as that for which the Hebrew constitution made provision, could not be without rich fruits.

The result was, that the nation reached a high point of literary attainment.

Vice-President Richard Nixon stated in an address "The Meaning of Communism to Americans," Aug. 21, 1960:

> Throughout the ages, among men of all nations and creeds, LAW has generally been thought of as a curb on arbitrary power. It has been conceived as a way of substituting reason for force in the decision of disputes, thus liberating human energies for the pursuit of aims more worthy of man's destiny than brute survival or the domination of one's fellows ...
>
> During most of the world's history, men have thought that the questions worthy of discussion were how the institutions of LAW could be shaped so that they might not be perverted into instruments of power or lose the sense of their high mission through sloth or ignorance.

E.C. Wines explained the Levites' role as educators:

> There was, indeed, one cardinal feature in the Hebrew polity (form of government), which was preeminently favorable, at all times, to the cultivation of knowledge. By divine appointment the whole tribe of Levi was set apart for the service of religion and letters; and while many were employed before the altar and in the temple, others were devoted to study ...
>
> Among the Hebrews there was no monopoly of knowledge by a favored few. Intelligence was general ... available for the advantage of all; of the shepherd and vine-dresser, as well as of the sons of the prophets.

The first letter in the Hebrew alphabet is "Alef" and the second letter is "Bet" – thus the word "Alphabet." This easy-to-learn alphabet allowed the entire nation to read and be a "nation of scribes" – the People of the Book.

Not only were they freed from the control of the Pharaoh, they were freed from being illiterate. They could maintain their freedom by being a literate people able to read the Law. British Prime Minister Benjamin Disraeli (1868; and 1874–1880), commented:

> Upon the education of the people of this country, the fate of this country depends.

Some scholars even speculate that the order of the

Hebrew Alphabet ('A', 'B', 'C', 'D', etc.) might have been an acrostic mnemonic to remember the lines of Ten Commandments, where each letter began a new line across Moses' stone tablets. (See Miles R. Jones, Ph.D., *The Writing of God–Secret of the Real Mount Sinai*, Johnson Publishers, Dallas, TX, 2010)

The use of an acrostic as a memory aid is found repeatedly in Hebrew Scriptures: Lamentations 3, Psalms 25, 31, 34, 37, 111, 112, 145, and Psalm 119, which is arranged with each line in a paragraph begining with the consecutive Hebrew letter:

aleph, beth, gimel, daleth, he, vav, zayin, heth, teth, yodh, kaph, lamed, mem, nun, samekh, ayin, pe, tsadhe, ooph, resh, shin, tav.

A famous early Christian acrostic was the Greek word "fish" — ICHTHYS, where each letter stood for a word in the Greek acclamation "**I**esous **CH**ristos, **TH**eou **Y**ios, Soter" (Jesus Christ Son of God Savior).

In Sumeria, Egypt, China and other ancient civilizations meanings were conveyed through the use of hieroglyphic symbols, pictograph images and ideograms which resembled physical objects.

In contrast, the Hebrew alphabet has each letter be a sound which could be combined with other letters to form words. The Hebrew alphabet was better suited to convey concepts and ideas. To the Hebrews, the "WORD" is sacred.

South of Mt. Sinai was the nation of Sabea or Sheba (modern day Yemen and Ethiopia). Distantly related, Sheba and Midian were sons of Abraham by Keturah, whom Abraham married after Sarah died, and they migrated south into the Arabian Peninsula. Shortly after the time of Moses, Sabeans began using an alphabet similar both in characters and order to the Hebrew alphabet.

After the Hebrews wandered for forty years, they arrived in the land of Canaan. (Canaan was the son of Ham, who was a son of Noah.) The land of Canaan was near the Ugarites and Phoenicians, with their cities of

Tyre, Sidon and Byblos (present-day Lebanon). Though scholarly debate exists in the dating, it appears that around this time the Ugarites and Phoenicians began using an alphabet surprisingly similar to the Hebrews.

Where the Children of Israel stayed in their Promised Land were prohibited from making hewn stone altars and monuments, the Phoenicians were a sea-faring merchant people who carried their alphabet around the Mediterranean to Carthage, Greece, and the Etruscans of Rome, leaving their writing on stone monuments.

ISRAEL–EVERYONE EQUAL

Most kings viewed themselves as divinely-apponted and superior to the people, with the "law" being the expression of their will. The Hebrews had a different concept of the Law, that it was given by God directly to the people, and therefore superior to both people and king.

Deuteronomy 4:8:

> And what nation is there so great, that hath statutes and judgments so righteous as all this law, which I set before you this day?

Lyman Beecher, D.D., (1775-1863) was a New England clergyman and father of Harriett Beecher Stowe, author of the abolitionist novel *Uncle Tom's Cabin* (1852). Beecher wrote "Republicanism of the Bible," published in Select Miscellany, *The Hesperian; or Western Monthly Magazine* (May 1838, p. 47-48, Discourses to the Mechanics of Cincinnati, 1837), in which he stated:

> Evidence of the inspiration of the Bible (is) ... the Old Testament in the production of such a state of liberty and equality as never before or since blessed the earth, save perhaps, in our own country. Instead of being unfriendly to civil liberty, we possess in the Old Testament, the first pattern that ever existed of national liberty and equality.

Instead of laws being a collection of a king's decrees,

the Hebrew Law limited the king as well as the people.

In opposition to King George III's Stamp Act, Jonathan Mayhew stated in 1765:

> As soon as the prince sets himself above the law, he loses the king in the tyrant. He does, to all intents and purposes, un-king himself.

Ancient Israel was the first nation where everyone was equal before the law, as compared to other nations where "equality" depended on how close of a relationship they had with the king. Instead of a hierarchical system with the king and royalty at the top getting special treatment, the Hebrew Law saw everyone, both male and female, made in the image of God. There was to be no respect of persons in judgment. E.C. Wines wrote:

> Under the Hebrew constitution, the poor and the weak were not to be the victims of the rich and the strong. The small as well as the great were to be heard, and equal justice awarded to all, without fear or favor.

Franklin D. Roosevelt stated Jan. 6, 1942:

> We are fighting to cleanse the world of ancient evils, ancient ills. Our enemies are guided by brutal cynicism, by unholy contempt for the human race.

> We are inspired by a faith that goes back through all the years to the first chapter of the Book of Genesis: "God created man in His own image"...

> We are fighting, as our fathers have fought, to uphold the doctrine that all men are equal in the sight of God. Those on the other side are striving to destroy this deep belief and to create a world in their own image–a world of tyranny and cruelty and serfdom.

This inspired America's founders, as Lord Acton wrote:

> In England Parliament is above the law. In America the law is above Congress.

Massachusetts Governor Samuel Adams stated in a Proclamation of a Day of Fasting, March 20, 1797:

> We cannot better express ourselves than by humbly supplicating the Supreme Ruler of the World that

the rod of tyrants may be broken to pieces, and the oppressed made free again.

In Israel, judges must not show partiality to the poor because they feel sorry for them, nor show favoritism to the rich because of they are powerful.

Leviticus 19:15:

> Ye shall do no unrighteousness in judgment: thou shalt not respect the person of the poor, nor honor the person of the mighty: but in righteousness shalt thou judge thy neighbor.

Lord Acton wrote:

> The object of civil society is *justice* — not truth, virtue, wealth, knowledge, glory or power. *Justice* is followed by equality and liberty.

Even the stranger living among them was under the same law they were under.

Numbers 15:14-16; 29:

> And if a stranger sojourn with you ... and will offer an offering ... as ye do, so he shall do. One ordinance shall be both for you of the congregation, and also for the stranger that sojourneth with you ... as ye are, so shall the stranger be before the LORD. One law and one manner shall be for you, and for the stranger that sojourneth with you.
>
> Ye shall have one law ... both for him that is born among the children of Israel, and for the stranger that sojourneth among them.

Leviticus 24:22:

> Ye shall have one manner of law, as well for the stranger, as for one of your own country: for I am the LORD your God.

A law instructing that strangers be treated under the same law as citizens was extremely rare, as most nations normally xenophobic, treating those outside their people group as inferior: Egyptians looked down on "shepherd peoples"; Romans looked down on Germanic peoples; Chinese looked down upon foreigners; Japanese looked down upon non-Japanese; Vikings looked down on non-Vikings; and Greeks looked down upon non-Greeks.

The Greek philosopher Aristotle counseled young Alexander the Great that he should be:

> a leader to the Greeks and a despot to the barbarians, to look after the former as after friends and relatives, and to deal with the latter as with beasts or plants.

In Islamic sharia law, non-Muslims are called dhimmi, who are treated as second-class citizens with virtually no rights as compared to Muslim males.

Hebrew Law instructed leaders to make a copy of the Law and read it every day so they would not think of themselves more highly than their brethren.

Deuteronomy 17:18–20:

> He shall write him a copy of this law in a book out of that which is before the priests the Levites ... and he shall read therein all the days of his life: that he may learn to fear the LORD his God, to keep all the words of this law and these statutes, to do them: That his heart be not lifted up above his brethren.

The New International Version words it: "not consider himself better than his fellow."

Centuries later, New Testament Christianity enlarged on the idea that everyone was equal before God. As the Old Testament High Priest approached God carrying the blood of the lamb sacrificed to pay for the sins of each person in the nation, New Testament believers approach God through the blood of the lamb – Christ Jesus – sacrificed to pay for the sins of each individual in the world.

The enthusiastic preaching of this by New England pastors undermined the idea that the king was the divinely appointed intermediary, thus effectively pulling the rug out from under the concept of "the divine right of kings."

On June 24, 1826, just ten days before his death, Thomas Jefferson wrote to Roger C. Weightman, condemning "the divine right of kings":

> All eyes are opened, or opening, to the rights of

man ... that the mass of mankind has not been born with saddles on their backs, nor a favored few booted and spurred, ready to ride them legitimately, by the grace of God.

THE TEN COMMANDMENTS

Hebrew Law gave birth to the idea of "the individual." This made a profound impact on the development of western civilization and ultimately the United States.

Prime Minister Margaret Thatcher stated Feb. 5, 1996:

> The Decalogue (TEN COMMANDMENTS) are addressed to each and every person. This is the origin... of the sanctity of the individual."

Soviet Communist leader Nikita S. Khrushchev stated:

> Comrades! We must abolish the cult of the individual decisively, once and for all.

Kelly O'Connell wrote in "Pagan Government Theory Insures Tyranny Returns to the West" (*Canada Free Press*):

> A lack of the Rule of Law is easily detected in Marxism ... Clarence B. Carson's *Basic Communism* details how the Soviets went to great lengths to create the masquerade of a functional democratic government... (though) the USSR was only ever a tyranny ...
>
> While the Soviet constitution set out the powers of government and "rights of the people," this work was not in the least a foundational law from which the rest of government powers and laws were drawn.
>
> In fact, one internal Soviet apologist wrote: "In the Soviet Union, the Constitution is regarded far more as a symbol ... than as an immutable blueprint; it is descriptive rather than prescriptive."
>
> This explanation defies the very definition of a Constitution which is everywhere else understood as the law above the law ... The entire Soviet theory of constitutionalism was set in a "class" context, whereas rights were premised upon what 'class' any individual

was considered to represent ...

Rights and duties were likewise described in "class" terms. So for example, one writer states, "Members of the exploiting classes—businessmen, monks and priests, etc were disenfranchised and denied the right to hold office."

The Bill of Rights was restated in "class" terms. Freedom of speech, of press, association, of assembly and of access to education was reserved to the "working class." This model of fake democratic organs obscuring tyranny is the essential aspect of all Liberal, Marxist and socialist movements ...

Yet, anyone with even a cursory knowledge of Soviet history realizes that no average citizen, whether in the working class, or not—had any of these powers.

Behind the typical constitutional language adopted by the Russians, the fact remained that no independent freedom of decision was given ... Instead, the Soviet Union was controlled by a very small cadre of party elites, numbering perhaps no more than seventy, who made all decisions.

The one-party system was a functional tyranny, and any who stepped outside this model brought down inevitable banishment to the gulag (forced labor camp) or death ... Tyrannies ... led to horrific human rights disasters ...

The chief problem in leftism is a lack of a Rule of Law—inherent in a system denying a divine law-giving function. Why this is true can be summed up in the juxtaposition between the "TEN COMMANDMENTS" versus any random boiler plate humanistic philosophy.

Harry S Truman addressed the Attorney General's Conference, Feb. 1950:

The fundamental basis of this nation's laws was GIVEN TO MOSES ON THE MOUNT ... I don't think we emphasize that enough these days ... . If we don't have a proper fundamental moral background, we will finally end up with a totalitarian government which does not believe in rights for anybody except for the State.

Rev. Martin Luther King, Jr., stated:

A just law is a man-made code that squares with the moral law or the law of God.

John Adams wrote to Jefferson, Nov. 4, 1816:

THE TEN COMMANDMENTS and the Sermon on the Mount contain my religion.

Alfred Smith, four-term Governor of New York, and 1928 Democratic Presidential candidate, stated in May of 1927:

The essence of my faith is built upon THE COMMANDMENTS OF GOD. The law of the land is built on THE COMMANDMENTS OF GOD. There can be no conflict between them.

In 1954, President Dwight David Eisenhower, said:

The purpose of a devout and united people was set forth in the pages of The Bible ... (1) to live in freedom, (2) to work in a prosperous land ... and (3) to obey THE COMMANDMENTS OF GOD ... This Biblical story of the Promised Land inspired the founders of America. It continues to inspire us.

The U.S. District Court stated in *Crockett v. Sorenson*, (W.D. Va. 1983):

THE TEN COMMANDMENTS have had immeasurable effect on Anglo-American legal development ... A basic background in the Bible is essential to fully appreciate and understand both Western culture and current events.

Senator Robert Byrd told Congress, June 27, 1962:

Above the head of the Chief Justice of the Supreme Court are THE TEN COMMANDMENTS, with the great American eagle protecting them. Moses is included among the great lawgivers in Herman A. MacNeil's marble sculpture group on the east front.

Chief Justice Rehnquist wrote in dissenting the Supreme Court's refusal to hear an Elkhart, Indiana, "Ten Commandment" case, (2001):

The text of THE TEN COMMANDMENTS no

doubt has played a role in the secular development of our society and can no doubt be presented by the government as playing such a role in our civic order...

A carving of Moses holding THE TEN COMMANDMENTS, surrounded by representations of other historical legal figures, adorns the frieze on the south wall of our courtroom, and we have said that the carving signals respect not for great proselytizers but for great lawgivers.

President William McKinley stated in his Inaugural Address, March 4, 1897:

Our faith teaches that there is no safer reliance than upon the God of our fathers ... who will not forsake us so long as we obey HIS COMMANDMENTS.

Herbert Hoover stated in San Diego, Sept. 17, 1935:

Our Constitution ... is based upon certain inalienable freedoms and protections which in no event the government may infringe ... It does not require a lawyer to interpret those provisions. They are as clear as THE TEN COMMANDMENTS ...

The freedom of worship, freedom of speech and of the press, the right of peaceable assembly, equality before the law ... behind them is the conception which is the highest development of the Christian faith ... individual freedom with brotherhood.

Ronald Reagan stated at a National Rifle Association banquet in Phoenix, May 6, 1983:

If we could just keep remembering that Moses brought down from the mountain THE TEN COMMANDMENTS, not ten suggestions – and if those of us who live for the Lord could remember that He wants us to love our Lord and our neighbor, then there's no limit to the problems we could solve.

Franklin D. Roosevelt stated on Dec. 24, 1942:

There is no better way of fostering good will toward man than by first fostering good will toward God. If we love Him we will keep HIS COMMANDMENTS.

G.K. Chesterton wrote:

> If man will not subject himself to the TEN
> COMMANDMENTS of God, he will be made subject
> to the ten thousand commandments of men.

In 1956, Cecil B. DeMille directed the epic Paramount Pictures movie, *THE TEN COMMANDMENTS*, starring Charlton Heston as Moses and Yul Brynner as Pharaoh Rameses II. While filming on-location in Egypt, Cecil B. DeMille, then 75 years old, climbed a 107-foot ladder to shoot the famous Exodus scene from atop of the massive Per Rameses set. The intense heat gave DeMille a near-fatal heart attack. Doctors ordered him to rest, but DeMille insisted on finishing the movie. He never fully recovered and died of a heart condition on Jan. 21, 1959. He had planned on doing a film on the Biblical Book of Revelation.

At the 1956 New York opening of the movie, *THE TEN COMMANDMENTS*, Cecil B. DeMille stated:

> THE TEN COMMANDMENTS are not the laws. They are THE LAW. Man has made 32 million laws since THE COMMANDMENTS were handed down to Moses on Mount Sinai more than three thousand years ago, but he has never improved on God's law.
>
> THE TEN COMMANDMENTS are the principles by which man may live with God and man may live with man. They are the expressions of the mind of God for His creatures. They are the charter and guide of human liberty, for there can be no liberty without the law ...
>
> What I hope for our production of THE TEN COMMANDMENTS is that those who see it shall come from the theater not only entertained and filled with the sight of a big spectacle, but filled with the spirit of truth. That it will bring to its audience a better understanding of the real meaning of this pattern of life that God has set down for us to follow.

Franklin D. Roosevelt stated in a radio address on Washington's Birthday, Feb. 22, 1943:

> Skeptics and the cynics of Washington... are like the people who carp at THE TEN COMMANDMENTS because some people are in the habit of breaking one

or more of them.

Roosevelt stated in a Press Conference, Dec. 22, 1944:

We don't all live up to THE TEN COMMANDMENTS, which is perfectly true, but on the whole they are pretty good. It's something pretty good to shoot for. The Christian religion most of us in the room happen to belong to, we think it is pretty good. We certainly haven't attained it.

Well, the Atlantic Charter ... not comparing it with the Christian religion or THE TEN COMMANDMENTS ... was a step towards a better life for the population of the world.

On March 8, 1983, at the National Association of Evangelicals in Orlando, Florida, President Reagan stated:

There's a great spiritual awakening in America ... One recent survey by a Washington–based research council concluded ... 95 percent of those surveyed expressed a belief in God. A huge majority believed THE TEN COMMANDMENTS had real meaning in their lives.

Dr. Billy Graham stated in accepting with the Congressional Gold Medal, May 2, 1996:

We have lost sight of the moral and spiritual principles on which this nation was established – principles drawn largely from the Judeo-Christian tradition as found in the Bible ... There is hope! Our lives can be changed ... The Scripture says, "You must be born again" ...

Think how different our nation would be if we sought to follow the simple and yet profound injunctions of THE TEN COMMANDMENTS and the Sermon on the Mount.

On Aug. 11, 1992, U.S. Rep. Nick Joe Rahall introduced a bill to declare Nov. 22–28, "America's Christian Heritage Week," stating:

While ... emerging democracies ... turn from the long held atheism of communism to true religious freedoms, we find ourselves, with heavy hearts, watching our own Government succumb to pressures to distant itself from God and religion.

Our own Government ... has ... evolved into bans against the simple freedom as ... representation of THE TEN COMMANDMENTS on government buildings ... Such a standard of religious exclusion is absolutely and unequivocally counter to the intention of those who designed our Government.

In 1973, as Governor of California, Ronald Reagan stated:

With freedom goes responsibility. Sir Winston Churchill once said you can have 10,000 regulations and still not have respect for the law. We might start with THE TEN COMMANDMENTS. If we lived by the Golden Rule, there would be no need for other laws.

On Feb. 5, 1997, Governor Fob James threatened to call out the National Guard to prevent removal of a Ten Commandments display in a Gadsden, Alabama, courtroom:

The only way those TEN COMMANDMENTS and prayer would be stripped from that courtroom is with the force of arms.

Mark Twain humorously wrote:

If the TEN COMMANDMENTS were not written by Moses, then they were written by another fellow of the same name.

ISRAEL–NO POLICE

Ancient Israel had no police. Everyone was taught the law and everyone was expected to enforce the law. The remnant of this was seen in English common law, where sheriffs encouraged ordinary citizens to help apprehend law breakers, and in American law, known as a "citizen's arrest."

ISRAEL–NO STANDING ARMY

Ancient Israel had no standing army, as every man was in the militia, armed, and ready at a moments notice to defend his community. E.C. Wines wrote in *Commentaries on the Laws of the Ancient Hebrews, with an Introductory Essay on Civil Society & Government* (NY: Geo. P. Putnam & Co., 1853):

> Moses' constitution made no provision for a standing army; and a soldiery under pay was an innovation long posterior to the time of Moses. The whole body of citizens, holding their lands on condition of military service, when required, formed a national guard of defense. Thus the landholders (and every Israelite was a landholder) formed the only soldiery, known to the Mosaic constitution.

Lyman Beecher wrote in "Republicanism of the Bible":

> Their land belonged to them, and they did not ask the nation whether they might drive off trespassers and invaders. While at the same time, they were Federal for ... their common defense against enemies.

On Oct. 26, 1774, the Provincial Congress of Massachusetts reorganized their defenses with one-third of their regiments being "Minutemen," ready to fight at a minute's notice. This followed the example of the earliest known militia in history – Ancient Israel, where every man was armed and always ready to defend his community.

Denver University Law Review, Jul. 15, 2013 published David B. Kopel's article "Ancient Hebrew Militia Law":

> New Englanders intensely self-identified with ancient Israel–from the first days of settlement in early 17th century (Israel in the wilderness) to the days of the American Revolution, when New England's "black regiment" of clergymen incited the Revolution as a religious duty, and described the thirteen American colonies as the modern version of the twelve confederate tribes of Israel.
>
> Thus, ancient Hebrew militia law is part of the intellectual background of the American militia system, and of the Second Amendment ...
>
> Every male "from the age of twenty years up, all those in Israel who are able to bear arms" ... were obliged to fight, to go forth "armed to battle." Men

who failed this duty "sinned against the Lord."

Although God may work miracles ... the righteous ... may never force God's hand by demanding a miracle–putting good people in danger and expecting God to protecting them.

David B. Kopel continued:

Israel's military system was "based on the duty of every able-bodied male to bear arms and serve."

Israel relied on a militia, in which citizen soldiers would spend most of their time cultivating their farms, or engaged in other economic production, and would fight only for limited periods (ideally, after the harvest), and only when necessary.

Similarly, during the American Revolution, most men served in their state militias, rather than the Continental Army. Thus, they were most able to keep their farms in production, and other economic activity in progress.

This was an important reason why the United States was able to economically sustain a war that lasted eight years.

Kopel added:

Another purpose of the Hebrew militia system was the decentralization of power, for the preservation of liberty. *The Etz Hayim*, (a modern Conservative Jewish version of the Pentateuch with commentary), explains:

"Deuteronomy does not intend that the Israelites maintain a standing army ... Instead, they are to have a civilian army, or militia, mobilized at times of need ... Reliance on a militia rather than a standing army for military needs is another example of Deuteronomy's dispersal of power among different officials."

David B. Kopel concluded:

In Battles of the Bible, Chaim Herzog (a former President of Israel) and Mordechai Gichon (a professor of military history at Tel Aviv University) summarized how the militia system preserved popular participation in the government:

"The people in arms formed the national assembly of initially sovereign peoples ... Ancient Jewish society ... never gave way to absolutism. The 'people' always remained ... a body with influence on the affairs of state. This fact was instrumental not only in the preservation of the people in arms as the mainstay of the Israelite armed forces until the destruction of the First Temple (586 BC) ... but also in the apparent readiness of the Israelites to bear the constant burden of military preparedness" ...

If Western Civilization can be said to be founded on two pillars of "Athens and Jerusalem," the Jewish pillar matches the Greek pillar in recognizing the importance of an armed people in preserving liberty through service in a militia of all free and able-bodied men.

Dutch politician Geert Wilders was born the year John F. Kennedy was shot. He gave a speech titled "America the Last Man Standing" in New York, Sept. 25, 2008:

Europe ... is changing ... by Muslim mass-migration ... with mosques on many street corners... controlled by religious fanatics ... Muslim neighborhoods ... are mushrooming in every city across Europe ...

Islam is not compatible with freedom and democracy, because what it strives for is sharia. If you want to compare Islam to anything, compare it to communism or national-socialism, these are all totalitarian ideologies ...

With an Islamic Europe, it would be UP TO AMERICA ALONE to preserve the heritage of ROME, ATHENS and JERUSALEM.

Justice William J. Brennan Jr., explained in *U.S. v. Verdugo-Urquidez* (494 U.S. 247, 288, 1990), that "the people" means "the people":

The term "the people" is better understood as a rhetorical counterpoint "to the government" ... that rights that were reserved to "the people" were to protect all those subject to "the government" ...

The Bill of Rights did not purport to "create" rights. Rather, they designed the Bill of Rights to prohibit our government from infringing rights and liberties presumed to be pre-existing.

The Supreme Court wrote in *U.S. v. Verdugo-Urquidez*:

> "The people" protected by the Fourth Amendment, and by the First and Second Amendments, and to whom rights and powers are reserved in the Ninth and Tenth Amendments, refers to a class of persons who are part of a national community ... The Fourth Amendment's drafting history shows that its purpose was to protect the people of the United States against arbitrary action by their own government.

The U.S. Constitution mentions "militias" in Article 1, Section 8. Samuel Adams explained at the Massachusetts Convention to ratify the U.S. Constitution, 1788:

> And that the said Constitution be never construed to authorize Congress to infringe the just liberty of the press, or the rights of conscience; or to prevent the people of the United States, who are peaceable citizens, from keeping their own arms.

James Madison wrote in *Federalist No. 46,* published in the *New York Packet*, Jan. 29, 1788:

> The ultimate authority ... resides in the people alone ... The advantage of being armed, which the Americans possess over the people of almost every other nation ... forms a barrier against the enterprises of ambition ...

> In the several kingdoms of Europe ... the governments are afraid to trust the people with arms.

Attempts of activist judges to redefine words was warned against by Thomas Jefferson in a letter to Supreme Court Justice William Johnson, June 12, 1823:

> On every question of construction, carry ourselves back to the time when the Constitution was adopted, recollect the spirit manifested in the debates, and instead of trying what meaning may be squeezed out of the text, or invented against it, conform to the probable one in which it was passed.

The individual citizen's right to be armed was acknowledged in the Supreme Court cases of *McDonald v. Chicago,* 561 U.S. 742 (2010), and *District of Columbia v. Heller,* 554 U.S. 570 (2008), in which the Court stated:

> The Second Amendment protects an individual right to possess a firearm unconnected with service in a militia, and to use that arm for traditionally lawful purposes, such as self-defense within the home. (p. 2–53); The operative clause's text and history demonstrate that it connotes an individual right to keep and bear arms. (p. 2–22);

> The Anti-Federalists feared that the Federal Government would disarm the people in order to disable this citizens' militia, enabling a politicized standing army or a select militia to rule. The response was to deny Congress power to abridge the ancient right of individuals to keep and bear arms, so that the ideal of a citizens' militia would be preserved. (p. 22–28).

ISRAEL–NO PRISONS

Ancient Israel had no prisons. If someone committed a crime they were taken to the gates of the city where the elders pronounced swift punishment and the payment of restitution. If someone were falsely accused, they could run to a city of refuge and wait for a more formal trial.

E.C. Wines wrote in *Commentaries on the Laws of the Ancient Hebrews, with an Introductory Essay on Civil Society & Government* (NY: Geo. P. Putnam & Co., 1853):

> A cheap, speedy, and impartial administration of justice was another of those great ideas, on which Moses founded his civil polity (form of government)... That terrible and ruinous evil, "the law's delay," was unknown to the Hebrew jurisprudence ...

> Justice could be administered promptly, while provision was made against the evils of hasty decisions, in the right of appeal to higher courts; in important cases, even to the venerable council of seventy, composed of the wisest, the gravest, the ablest, the most upright, and trustworthy men in the nation ...

> Care was thus taken, that in suits and proceedings

at law, every man should have what was just and equal, without going far to seek it, without waiting long to obtain it, and without paying an exorbitant price for it ...

Justice could be administered promptly, while provision was made against the evils of hasty decisions, in the right of appeal to higher courts.

ISRAEL–BUREAUCRACY–FREE WELFARE

Ancient Israel had a bureaucracy free welfare system, where farmers would charitably leave the gleanings in their fields and vineyards for the poor to gather.

Leviticus 19:9-10:

> And when ye reap the harvest of your land, thou shalt not wholly reap the corners of thy field, neither shalt thou gather the gleanings of thy harvest. And thou shalt not glean thy vineyard, neither shalt thou gather every grape ... thou shalt leave them for the poor and the stranger.

Today, churches and non-profit organizations generously fulfill this charitable role in our society, for the most part with no government oversight and little waste. Charity, in a sense, is the opposite of selfishness. Thinking of the others first is the glue that holds society together, keeping it from falling into the abyss of tyranny and chaos.

ISRAEL–NO CONQUEST BEYOND BORDERS

Ancient Israel was unique from other nations, which continually desired to expand their borders. Israel was to be content within the borders given them by the Lord, and not transition into a nation of conquest outside its borders.

This is seen by the Law's prohibition on multiplying horses – the primary military assets of conquering armies.

Deuteronomy 17:16:

But he shall not multiply horses to himself, nor cause the people to return to Egypt, to the end that he should multiply horses: forasmuch as the LORD hath said unto you, Ye shall henceforth return no more that way.

E.C. Wines wrote in *Commentaries on the Laws of the Ancient Hebrews, with an Introductory Essay on Civil Society & Government* (NY: Geo. P. Putnam & Co., 1853):

A thirst of conquest ... had no place ... The intensely agricultural character of the Hebrew government served to impress upon it an almost equally pacific character ... Permanent landed possessions, improved habitations, and a too curious attention to domestic conveniences and comforts, would beget in the tillers of the soil an affection for the spots they cultivated which would produce sentiments and manners, quite repugnant to their own schemes of conquest and military aggrandizement ...

The use of cavalry, at once the effect and the cause of a passion for war, was prohibited by the constitution. On the occasion of a certain victory, when a large number of the enemy's horses had fallen into his hands, Joshua was directed by the oracle to "trough," or hamstring them, that is, to cut their thigh sinews.

This was practiced on similar occasions, even as late as the reign of David. The law against multiplying horses appears to have been faithfully observed, till the proud ambition of Solomon swept away this, in common with many other wholesome provisions of the national constitution.

In governments, which have made conquest a leading object of pursuit, the principal military force has consisted in cavalry ... In ... military art, the superiority of cavalry over infantry is very conspicuous. The fate of battle depended on that part of the army, which fought on horseback, or in chariots.

It is obvious, that no founder of an empire, in those early ages, who intended his people for a career of conquest and military grandeur, would or could have dispensed with cavalry in his armies. The fact that

Moses forbade the use of this species of force, is a proof that he designed his people for peaceful pursuits, and not for military glory.

E.C. Wines wrote in *Commentaries on the Laws of the Ancient Hebrews, with an Introductory Essay on Civil Society & Government* (NY: Geo. P. Putnam & Co., 1853):

Moses had another motive for his prohibition of cavalry. The political equality of all the citizens, as we have seen under a former head, was a darling object with him. But in all ancient nations, where cavalry was employed, the horsemen, being necessarily the wealthier members of the community, became also the more powerful. The system threw the chief political power into the hands of a few rich citizens, who could afford to mount and bring into the field themselves and their dependents.

This naturally tended to the establishment of monarchical and aristocratical governments. Moses could not but perceive this tendency, and on this account, as well as on account of his repugnance to an aggressive military policy, he excluded a mounted soldiery from the forces of the republic.

It is remarkable, how speedily the substitution of the monarchical for the republican form of polity (form of government), led to the introduction and use of cavalry in the Israelitish armies.

ISRAEL–NO GOVERNMENT TRACKING

Ancient Israel restricted the centralized government from numbering and tracking citizens. In the ancient world, a person counted what belonged to them. If a king counted the people he was implying that the people belonged to him.

Exodus 30:12 cited how the people belonged to the Lord:

When you take the census of the children of Israel for their number, then every man shall give a ransom for himself to the Lord, when you number them, that there may be no plague among them when you number them.

Kings would also count the number of fighting men at their command as a preliminary step to going to war. Jesus stated in Luke 14:31:

> Or what king, going to make war against another king, sitteth not down first, and consulteth whether he be able with ten thousand to meet him that cometh against him with twenty thousand?

The Lord wanted to make it clear that his nation of Israel was to be content with the land He had given them. Israel was different from other nations and was not to have a king tempted to turn the nation into a conquering force like the Egyptians, Hittites, Assyrians, Babylonians, Persians, Alexander the Great, or the Romans.

E.C. Wines wrote in *Commentaries on the Laws of the Ancient Hebrews, with an Introductory Essay on Civil Society & Government* (NY: Geo. P. Putnam & Co., 1853):

> The sin of David in numbering the people ... consisted ... in openly aspiring at the establishment of a military government, and in attempting, with that view, to subject the whole nation to martial regulations, to form a standing army, and so to break down and ride over one of the fundamental provisions of the constitution,—the many successful wars which he had carried on having, in all likelihood, filled his mind with the spirit of conquest ...
>
> We ... admire the wisdom of a lawgiver (Moses), who, in an age of barbarism and war, established a government upon the broad principles of equity and peace.

ISRAEL–PEOPLE CHOOSE LEADERS

Ancient Israel had the people in each tribe choose their leaders from amongst themselves.

Deuteronomy 1:3–13:

> Moses spake unto the children of Israel ... How can I myself alone bear ... your burden? ... TAKE YOU wise men, and understanding, and KNOWN

AMONG YOUR TRIBES, and I will make them
rulers over you.

Deuteronomy 16:18–19:

Judges and officers SHALT THOU MAKE THEE
IN ALL THY GATES which the Lord thy God giveth
thee throughout thy tribes; and they shall judge the
people with just judgment: thou shalt not wrest
judgment; thou shalt not respect persons, neither take
a gift; for a gift doth blind the eyes of the wise, and
pervert the words of the righteous.

The Law gave specification on who should be chosen
to serve in leadership.

Exodus 18:21:

Thou shalt provide out of all the people able men,
such as fear God, men of truth, hating covetousness; to
be rulers of thousands, and rulers of hundreds, rulers
of fifties, and rulers of tens.

A footnote to the 1828 edition of Josephus's *Antiquities
of the Jews – Book 3*, regarding "The Exodus Out of Egypt,
to the Rejection of That Generation," stated:

This manner of electing the judges and officers
of the Israelites by the testimonies and suffrages of
the people, before they were ordained by God, or
by Moses, deserves to be carefully noted, because it
was the pattern of the like manner of the choice and
ordination of bishops, presbyters, and deacons, in the
Christian church.

E.C. Wines wrote in *Commentaries on the Laws of
the Ancient Hebrews, with an Introductory Essay on Civil
Society & Government* (NY: Geo. P. Putnam & Co., 1853):

A magistracy elected by the people, the public
officer chosen by the public voice, was another of
those great principles, on which Moses founded his
civil polity (form of government).

The magistrates are not properly the ministers of
the people unless the people elect them. It is, therefore,
a fundamental maxim in every *popular* government,
that their people should choose their ministers, that
is to say, their magistrates.

The people need councillors of state and executive officers, as much as monarchs, perhaps even more than they. But they cannot have a just confidence in these officers, unless they have the choosing of them. And the people, in every nation capable of freedom, are well qualified to discharge this trust. Facts, obvious to sense, and to which they cannot be strangers, are to determine them in their choice.

The merits of their neighbors are things well known to them. "Should we doubt of the people's natural ability in respect to the discernment of merit, we need only cast an eye on the continual series of surprising elections made by the Athenians and Romans, which no one surely will attribute to hazard."

The people, therefore, though in the mass incapable of the administration of government, are, nevertheless, capable of calling others to this office. They are qualified to choose, though, as a general thing not qualified to be chosen. "In their sentiments," said the great Edmund Burke, "the people are rarely mistaken."

Lyman Beecher wrote in "Republicanism of the Bible":

The administration of these laws was committed to men of their own choosing. The direction of Moses is "take ye wise men and understanding, and known among your tribes, and I will make them rulers over you" ... You elect and I will commission them for there several offices.

E.C. Wines stated similarly:

The election by the Hebrew people of Jehovah himself to be the civil head of their state, is a point, which has been already established, in the introductory essay. The proofs need not be repeated here. No fact can be plainer, or more certain, than that the judges, instituted at the suggestion of Jethro, were chosen by the suffrages (vote) of all Israel.

The direction of Moses to the people, upon that occasion, is very explicit. His words are, "Take you wise men, and understanding, and known among your tribes, and I will make them rulers over you." The meaning is ... "You elect the proposed officers, and I will commission and induct them into office."

It is very observable, that these magistrates were to be taken "out of all the people," and not from any privileged class. The only qualifications for office required were, that they should be "able men, such as fear God, men of truth, hating covetousness," "wise men, and understanding, and known among their tribes."

The possession of these high attributes was enough; no other patent of nobility was required. Mr. Jefferson's test of official competency is expressed in the three interrogatories, "Is he honest? Is he capable? Is he faithful?"

If he had added a fourth, "Does he fear God?" he would have had the Mosaic test to a tittle. Moses demanded four qualifications in a civil ruler, namely, ability, integrity, fidelity, and piety.

E.C. Wines wrote further:

When the land of Canaan was to be divided among the tribes, Joshua addressed all Israel thus: "Give out from among you three men from each tribe, and I will send them" ... "Give out from among you;" that is, "Select, choose for yourselves." When Jephthah was made judge, it is expressly said, "The PEOPLE made him head and captain over them."

These instances, and others which might be cited, prove, that the great principle, that rulers should be elected by the ruled, that authority should emanate from those over whom it is to be exercised, was fully embodied in the Hebrew constitution.

AUTHORITY: GOD TO PEOPLE TO LEADERS

Lord Acton wrote

Authority that does not exist for Liberty is not authority but force.

Samuel Rutherford (c.1600–1661) was Rector of St. Andrew's Church in Scotland and one of the commissioners at Westminster Assembly in London, 1643–47. In 1644, he wrote his controversial book, *Lex, Rex*, which is Latin for, *The Law is King.*

Lex, Rex challenged the "divine right of kings" by advocating placing limitations on government with a constitution. Rutherford wrote *Lex, Rex* to counter John Maxwell's book *Sacro-Sanctum Regus Majestas* which is Latin for "The Sacredness of Royal Majesty."

Rutherford reasoned that even though kings derived their authority from God, Romans 13:1-4, they received it **through the people.** Because Rutherford advocated kings being under the law rather than above it, his book was banned in Scotland and publicly burned in England. He was placed under house arrest and summoned to stand trial for treason before the Parliament in Edinburgh, but he died before the orders could be carried out. Samuel Rutherford cited the following biblical passages in support of **kings deriving their authority through the people:**

II Samuel 16:18, "Hushai said to Absalom, Nay, but whom the Lord and the people, and all the men of Israel choose, his will I be, and with him will I abide";

Judges 8:22, "The men of Israel said to Gideon, Rule thou over us";

Judges 9:6, "The men of Shechem made Abimelech king";

II Kings 14:21, "The people made Azariah king";

I Samuel 12:1, II Chronicles 23:3.

Kelly O'Connell wrote in "Pagan Government Theory Insures Tyranny Returns to the West" (*Canada Free Press*, 2012):

Consider the opposite vision, as described by John Coffey in *Politics, Religion and the British Revolutions, the Mind of Samuel Rutherford ...*

Scottish divine (theologian) and professor of theology, Samuel Rutherford is the author of *Lex, Rex*, the most famous study of the Rule of Law in history... Rutherford recognized the divine origin of government. He appeals to Scripture to make an opening argument of authority in such texts as Romans 13 and 1 Peter 2. He then affirms government as rooted in *popular* consent, as established by people.

Rutherford concentrated on describing how humans and God together create a proper government... Rutherford understands government as properly based upon the covenant theory between man and God, such as seen in 1 Samuel 10. What is remarkable about Rutherford's theory of covenant... was it not only established the government's lawful role, but also set standards for lawful resistance ...

This follows from the belief that the king's power comes from the people from whom he borrows their authority. And this addressed both the secular and religious aspects of proper kingship. This subject presupposed a dialectic relationship between God, king and the people as described in the famed Huguenot tract *Vindiciae Contra Tyrannos.*

While the religious aspect was important, Rutherford concentrated on the civil relationship between king and subjects in *Lex, Rex* ... Rutherford stressed the federal nature of proper human authority. Federalism is a theory of power located not nationally, or regionally, or locally—but shared between all three. Federalism presumes a covenanted theory of government. Such ideas were gleaned from governmental theory colossus Johann Althusis, especially *Politica Methodice Digesta*, whom Rutherford quoted freely.

Lord Acton wrote:

> The true natural check on absolute democracy is the federal system, which limits the central government by the powers reserved, and the state governments by the powers they have ceded.

Kelly O'Connell continued:

> Rutherford rejected the notion of passive obedience sometimes associated with the Bible. Instead, Rutherford used Natural Law theory as a foundation for defensive wars, which he claimed were a kind of innocent violence. He also grounds his defense of the right of violent resistance to a tyrant in Roman law ...

Rutherford grounded proper civil authority

in *popular* consent. He derived this from radical scholastic theory which claimed that authority was originally vested in the community.

He used language later employed by such writers as Rousseau, claiming that all men were born free from the authority of government officials. The community held all political power in abstract which it then used to set up a concrete government to rule justly.

ISRAEL–PEOPLE RATIFIED CONSTITUTION

Ancient Israel ratified their constitution and confirmed their leaders. E.C. Wines noted:

> A principle, closely allied to this, namely, that the people should have an authoritative voice in the enactment of the laws, is another of those great ideas, which underlie the Hebrew government; and this principle, like the preceding one, is fundamental in every *popular* government.
>
> When Moses, on descending from the mount, rehearsed to the people the laws which he had received from the Lord, with one voice, they answered and said, "All the words that the Lord has said, we will we do."
>
> What is this, but an acceptance by the nation of the constitution proposed to them? The Hebrew constitution was adopted by the Hebrew people, as truly as the American constitution was adopted by the American people.

Lyman Beecher wrote "Republicanism of the Bible" (Select Miscellany, *The Hesperian; or Western Monthly Magazine*, May 1838, p. 47-48, Discourses to the Mechanics of Cincinnati, 1837), stating:

> We observe ... that this new combination of patriarchates and tribes was adopted by the suffrages (vote) of the people.
>
> When Moses had written them on the mount, he came down and repeated to the people all the words of the Lord. And the people answered with one voice

and said "All the words which the Lord hath said will we do." Thus they accepted and adopted their constitution. They were chosen and adopted by the Jewish nation as truly as the Constitution of this country was adopted by the people.

This adoption, by the Jewish nation, of the laws, which Moses brought from God, was repeated at the death of Moses, and by a statute, once in seven years was to be repeated ever after by the assembled nation. So that, from generation to generation, once in seven years, the tribes met in a great national convention, and solemnly ratified the constitution. They took what might be called the freeman's oath to observe that constitution ...

These republican institutions introduced by Moses, contain strong internal evidence of the Divine original of the Old Testament ... This evidence is, that no existing knowledge in or around the nation — no examples and no powers of the human mind, were sufficient to account for the existence of an institution to whose excellence the world has scarcely reached, down to the present day.

E.C. Wines wrote:

The government, then, was, in a solid and just sense, a government of the people; for the magistrates were chosen by their suffrages, and the laws were enacted by their voice. The responsibility of public officers to the people was the seventh fundamental maxim of the Hebrew polity (form of government). In proof of this the reader is referred to the closing scene of Samuel's public administration.

The aged statesman resigns his authority to the convention of the people, by whom it had been conferred. History records no sublimer or more touching scene. He calls upon his constituents, if any had been injured by his public acts, or knew of any abuse of the trusts confided to him, to step forward and accuse him. With one voice they reply, "Thou hast injured, oppressed, defrauded none."

Several incidents, related in the history of the kings, confirm this view. When Saul was chosen king, a writing, limiting the royal prerogative, was prepared by Samuel, and deposited in the sanctuary, where reference might afterwards be made to it, in case of royal usurpation.

A similar writing was exacted of his successors. Solomon, during the latter period of his life, had reigned as a despot. When his son mounted the throne, Judah and Benjamin were the only tribes, which acknowledged him. The other tribes offered to submit to his authority, on conditions which were not accepted. But when the young king rejected their terms, they rejected him, chose a sovereign for themselves, and established a separate kingdom.

These instances show, that the people held their rulers to a stern responsibility for the manner in which they discharged their public trusts.

All this was the action of the republican spirit of the nation; a spirit, inspired, cherished, and sanctioned by the constitution. Who can doubt whether it was a constitution, intended for a free and self-governing community? A cheap, speedy, and impartial administration of justice was another of those great ideas, on which Moses founded his civil polity (form of government).

A HEBREW SENATE

In Hebrew, the senate is referred to as the sanhedrin, which means "sitting together," "assembly" or "council," consisting usually of 23 chosen from the cities in the Land of Israel. The **Great Sanhedrin** was made up of 71 prominent national leaders: 70 members, of which one was the chief of the court, called the "Av Beit Din"; and the person overseeing The Great Sanhedrin as the president was called the "Nasi." E.C. Wines wrote:

> Courts of various grades were established, from high courts of appeal down to those ordained for every town. "Judges and officers shalt thou make thee in all thy gates," was the constitutional provision on this subject ...

To what a ... subdivision the judiciary system was carried, appears from the ordinance, which required that there should be "rulers over thousands, rulers over hundreds, rulers over fifties, and rulers over tens, who should judge the people at all seasons" ....

Certainly, with a judiciary constituted in this manner, justice could be administered promptly, while provision was made against the evils of hasty decisions, in the right of appeal to higher courts; in important cases, **even to the venerable council of seventy, composed of the wisest, the gravest, the ablest, the most upright, and trustworthy men in the nation.**

Lyman Beecher wrote in "Republicanism of the Bible":

The doctrine of appeals from the lower to the higher courts, is distinct and remarkable. It was similar to what takes place in our own country. — The appeal might travel up from the lowest to the highest courts in each tribe, and thence up to the seventy elders, elected as assistants to Moses - the federal court - similar to the United States superior court.

Hebrew leaders were referred to as "the senate" in *Josephus: The Complete Works*, Chapter 11: *What befell the sons of Eli, the Ark, and how Eli died miserably*:

About this time it was that the Philistines made war against the Israelites, and pitched their camp at the city Aphek. Now when the Israelites had expected them a little while, the very next day they joined battle, and the Philistines were conquerors, and slew above four thousand of the Hebrews, and pursued the rest of their multitude to their camp. So the Hebrews being afraid of the worst, **sent to the senate**, and to the high priest, and desired that they would bring the ark of God.

ISRAEL–HIGHEST VALUE OF HUMAN LIFE

Ancient Israel had a decentralized system that looked disorganized from the outside, but inside had maximum individual freedom, liberty and opportunity. It established the highest possible value of human life by requiring the taker of innocent life to pay with their own.

Genesis 9:6:

> Whoso sheddeth man's blood, by man shall his blood be shed: for in the image of God made he man.

ISRAEL–PRIVATE LAND OWNERSHIP

Ancient Israel was the first nation with private land ownership – the promised "LAND."

Richard Pipes was director of Harvard's Russian Research Center, 1968–1973, then Harvard University's Baird Professor Emeritus of History. In *Communism–A History* (Random House, 2001), Richard Pipes wrote:

> In the oldest civilizations, dating back 5,000 years – pharaonic Egypt and Mesopotamia – agricultural land belonged to palaces and temples ... Ancient Israel is the first country where we possess firm evidence of private land ownership.

Numbers 26:52–56:

> And the LORD spake unto Moses, saying, Unto these the land shall be divided for an inheritance according to the number of names.
>
> To many thou shalt give the more inheritance, and to few thou shalt give the less inheritance: to every one shall his inheritance be given according to those that were numbered of him.
>
> Notwithstanding the land shall be divided by lot: according to the names of the tribes of their fathers they shall inherit. According to the lot shall the possession thereof be divided between many and few.

Deuteronomy 27:17:

> Cursed be he that removeth his neighbor's landmark.

Lyman Beecher wrote in "Republicanism of the Bible":

> The most admirable trait in this republican system,

is the distribution of land which made every adult male a landholder.— not a mere tenant, but the owner himself of the soil on which he lived. —

This is the great spring of civil liberty, industry and virtue. By this simple arrangement, the great body of the nation were elevated from the pastoral to the agricultural state, and were at once exempted from the two extremes most dangerous to liberty — an aristocracy of wealth , and a sordid , vicious poverty...

This single principle of universal ownership in fee simple of the soil, secured at once intense patriotism, indomitable courage, untiring industry and purity of morals — neither an hereditary nobility, nor a dependent peasantry, nor abject poverty could exist ...

If by any means ... the family was compelled to alienate a portion of its land, it could not be done for a longer period than fifty years ...

Thus the whole land was kept in the line of the family descent – no poverty, nor vice on the part of a man, could deprive his family of the privilege of inheriting their portion of the soil – and attaching them to the community as independent members, with all the inducements to freedom, and intelligence and virtue, appertaining to owners and cultivators of the soil.

E.C. Wines wrote in *Commentaries on the Laws of the Ancient Hebrews, with an Introductory Essay on Civil Society & Government* (NY: Geo. P. Putnam & Co., 1853):

Property in the soil is the natural foundation of power, and consequently of authority ... Hence, the natural foundation of every government may be said to be laid in the distribution of its territories.

And here three cases are supposable, namely, the ownership of the soil by ONE, the FEW, or the MANY.

First, if the prince own the lands, he will be absolute; for all who cultivate the soil, holding of him, and at his pleasure, must be so subject to his will, that they will be in the condition of slaves, rather than of freemen.

Secondly, if the landed property of a country be shared among a few men, the rest holding as vassals under them, the real power of government will be in the hands of an aristocracy, or nobility, whatever authority may be lodged in one or more persons, for the sake of greater unity in counsel and action.

But, thirdly, if the lands be divided among all those who compose the society, the true power and authority of government will reside in all the members of that society; and the society itself will constitute a real democracy, whatever form of union may be adopted for the better direction of the whole, as a political body.

Under such a constitution, the citizens themselves will have control of the state.

If someone owns land, they can accumulate possessions. The Bible called this being blessed. Karl Marx called this capitalism. Lord Acton wrote:

Property, not conscience, is the basis of liberty.

Noah Webster wrote in the preface of his *Webster's Dictionary*, republished 1841:

Let the people have property and they will have power.

E.C. Wines added:

"The profit of the earth is for all" was a Hebrew maxim, which grew into a proverb. The monopoly of the soil is a sore evil. It makes the many the slaves of the few. It produces ignorance, improvidence, destitution, turbulence, and crime. It is essential to the progress of man, that he be unshackled, that his faculties have free play.

But this can never be, unless the earth be owned by those who till it. Ownership of the soil will give tone to the mind, vigor to the body, and earnestness to industry ... As the attraction of gravity is the great principle of motion in the material world, so the possession of the earth in fee simple by the cultivator, is the great principle of action in the moral world.

Nearly all the political evils, which have afflicted mankind, have resulted from the unrighteous monopoly of the earth; and the predicted renovation can never be accomplished, until, to some extent, this monopoly has passed away, and the earth is extensively tilled by the independent owners of the soil.

Great proprietorships are the scourge of any country. All history attests this truth. The multiplication of farms, and their cultivation by the actual owners, is the dictate of true political wisdom. It is this, which peoples the country, and even the cities. It is this, which elevates the masses. It is this, which confers dignity upon the common people. It is this, which stimulates industry, quickens genius, and develops the resources of a state.

It is this, which gives true freedom and independence to a nation. And this, to the broadest extent ever known in practical legislation, was the policy of Moses. These observations will, perhaps, be sufficient to establish the wisdom of the Hebrew constitution in its partition of the territories of the republic.

E.C. Wines wrote in *Commentaries on the Laws of the Ancient Hebrews, with an Introductory Essay on Civil Society & Government* (NY: Geo. P. Putnam & Co., 1853):

There is no truth in political science more easy to comprehend, more open to the view of all, or more certainly known in universal experience, than that the men who own the territories of a state will exercise a predominating influence over the public affairs of such state.

This is agreeable to the constitution of human nature, and is confirmed by the concurrent testimony of all history. The provision of the Hebrew constitution in reference to the ownership of the soil, is that of my third supposition.

Moses ordered, that the national domain should be so divided, that the whole six hundred thousand free citizens should have a full property in an equal part of it. And to render this equality solid and lasting, the tenure was made inalienable, and the estates, thus originally settled upon each family, were to descend by an indefeasible entail (irrevocable inheritance), in perpetual succession.

The principle which lies at the bottom of this argument for the political equality of the Hebrew citizens, is strongly developed, in its application to our own country, by one of our ablest political writers.

"The agrarian in America," says the elder Adams, "is divided into the hands of the common people in every state, in such a manner, that nineteen twentieths of the property would be in the hands of the commons, let them appoint whom they might for chief magistrate and senators.

The sovereignty, then, in fact as well as theory, reside in the whole body of the people; and even an hereditary king and nobility, who should not govern according to the public opinion, would infallibly be tumbled instantly from their places."

E.C. Wines continued:

Mr. Adams ... held, that the sovereignty of a state is an inseparable attribute of property in the soil. Lord Bacon and Harrington were of the same opinion. The former uses property and dominion as convertible terms; and the latter says expressly, that empire follows the balance of property, whether lodged in one, few, or many bands.

The details of the agrarian law of Moses ... made extreme poverty and overgrown riches alike impossible, thus annihilating one of the most prolific sources as well as powerful engines of ambition ... a titled and wealthy aristocracy.

It gave to every member of the body politic an interest in the soil, and consequently in the maintenance of public order and the supremacy of law ... It made the virtues of industry and frugality necessary elements in every man's character. Its tendency was to secure to all the citizens a moderate independence, and to prevent those extremes of opulence and destitution, which are the opprobrium of modern civilization.

Great inequality of wealth in a nation is a great evil, to be avoided by the use of all just and prudent means. It was a leading object with Moses to give to his constitution such a form, as would tend to equalize the distribution of property.

Under his polity (form of government), the few could not revel in the enjoyment of immense fortunes while the million were suffering from want. Misery was not the hereditary lot of one class, nor boundless wealth of another ...

The agrarian of Moses elevated labor to its just dignity, and removed the odium, which adhered to it in all other ancient states ... It was as honorable among the ancient Hebrews, as it is even in New England ... A common Hebrew sentiment ... was ... intelligent labor, manly labor, independent labor, labor thinking, and acting, and accumulating for itself, was the great substantial interest, on which the whole fabric of Hebrew society rested ...

Not content with establishing originally a full equality among the citizens, the constitution of Moses made provision for its permanent continuance. With such jealous care ... that the people might never... be lost to the state in the condition of slaves, that it provided for a general periodical release of debts and servitudes;— partially by the institution of the sabbatical year, but more completely by that of the jubilee. No matter how often the property had changed hands, at the return of the jubilee year, it was restored, free of encumbrance, to the original owners or their heirs.

The Israelite, whom calamity or improvidence had driven abroad, needed no longer to wander for want of a home of his own to welcome him. This was a wise, as well as benevolent provision of the constitution. It was admirably suited to preserve a wholesome equality among the citizens. The rich could not accumulate all the lands.

In other nations, even if one owned land, they really did not, as it was always conditional of them staying in the king's favor. If one crossed the king, his land could be taken away, as well as his life.

In Ancient Israel land was permanently titled to each

family. If a family got in financial difficulty and sold their land, every 50 years, the year of Jubilee, the land reverted back to the original family. This prevented a dictator from accumulating all the land and making the people into serfs and slaves. E.C. Wines wrote:

> The fiftieth year, beyond which no lease could run, was always approaching, with silent, but sure tread, to relax their tenacious grasp.

> However alienated, however unworthily sold, however strongly conveyed to the purchaser an estate might be, this long- expected day annulled the whole transaction, and placed the debtor in the condition, which either himself or his ancestor had enjoyed.

> At the return of this day, the trumpet peal was heard, in street and field, from mountain top and valley, throughout the length and breadth of the land. The chains fell from the exulting slave. The burden of debt, like that of Bunyan's Pilgrim, rolled off from shoulders, long galled by its pressure.

> The family mansion and the paternal estate again greeted eyes, from which misfortune, through many a weary year, had divorced them. The inequalities of condition, which the lapse of half a century had produced, once more disappeared. Garlands of flowers crowned all brows; and the universal gladness found vent in music, feasting, and merriment.

∽

PRIESTS COULD NOT OWN LAND.

The priestly class in other nations, such as Egypt, held a superior social position since they validated the king as the supposed divinely-appointed political intermediary between the people and heaven. The pagan priests' superstitious rituals supported the hierarchical structure.

Kelly O'Connell wrote in "Pagan Government Theory Insures Tyranny Returns to the West":

> (In) both Greece and Rome ... there was **the priestly college**, a number of unrelated religious castes who received their marching orders from the

state. For example, during a war the Roman Senate might call for augury, that is a study of bird behavior, to predict the future. Yet it was up to the Senate whether the findings of the augurs were accepted, or how their findings might be applied.

Harvard Professor Richard Pipes stated: "In the oldest civilizations ... agricultural land belonged to *palaces and temples*." "**Palaces**" referred to kings owning land, and "**temples**" referred to the pagan priestly class owning land.

In ancient Israel, there was no king and the priestly class - the Levites, were prohibited from owning land.

Deuteronomy18:1:

> The priests the Levites, and all the tribe of Levi, shall have no part nor inheritance with Israel.

Ancient Israel's Levite priests taught the Law in which there was no respect of persons; that each individual was directly accountable to God; and that the people would choose their own leaders "known among your tribes" who "fear God, men of truth, hating covetousness."

Since the priests role included teaching all the people to read the Law, the priests were prohibited from owning an allotment of land as other tribes and instead were scattered all around the nation.

∽

ISRAEL–LOCAL RULE

Ancient Israel's political structure was originally the exact opposite of every monarchy that existed on the globe – a complete inversion of the flow of power.

Lyman Beecher wrote "Republicanism of the Bible" (Select Miscellany, *The Hesperian; or Western Monthly Magazine*, May 1838, p. 47-48, Discourses to the Mechanics of Cincinnati, 1837), stating:

> It is not generally known, and would scarcely be believed without inspection, that the Mosaic institute comprehends in a high degree, all the elements of a federal republican government, more resembling

our own than any government on earth ... It was the object of God, in the Mosaic institute, to ... stop the march of despotism ... which darkened and cursed... the whole earth ...

After the bondage of the descendants of Abraham, for four hundred years in Egypt, Moses was raised up to be their lawgiver ... to establish institutions for the preservation of the true religion, till Christ the Messiah should visit the world and die for its redemption.

The laws of Moses, revealed to him by God ... include ... 1. The moral laws ... 2. Rites and forms of Jewish worship ... 3. The constitution and laws of their civil government ...

It is of the political laws of the Old Testament that I shall now particularly speak ... because it is in this view of the Mosaic institute that we shall perceive the republican tendencies ...

The laws which God condescended to bestow... preserve in the hands of the people as much personal liberty as ever was or can be combined with a permanent and efficient national government ...

The patriarchal system of families and heads of families was the first, and simplest, and purest government. But all its features were preserved by heaven and united with the national government.

These families, united, constituted tribes, and the tribes, united for national purposes, constituted the Federal Republic ... The purity of the family was guarded also, with peculiar care, and the rights and relative duties of parents and children.

Lord Acton wrote:

Towns were the nursery of freedom.

Lyman Beecher continued:

We have called the civil constitution of the Old Testament, a Federal Republic, — It was so in the highest sense. Each tribe, as to all purposes of government within itself, was perfectly independent, as each State is in our Union. They regulated their own peculiar matters, and the national government did not inter-meddle with them. — So the tribes were each governed by their own laws, and those laws were in full liberty as it is possible for laws to be ...

I do not believe it possible for a people to be more free, and be subject to a good conservative government, than the Israelites were in their respective tribes.

ISRAEL–ROLE OF PRIESTS & PROPHETS

The secret to Ancient Israel's system was the Levites and priests teaching the people the system – the Law.

Imagine if every computer sold is pre-loaded with a virus. The customer has to immediately take it to a computer tech to have the virus cleaned off. In the human experience, every child is born with a pre-loaded virus of selfishness. In ancient Israel, the children were immediately be taken to Levite priests – "computer techs" – to have each line of code rewritten so as to prevent them from surrendering to their selfish nature.

Since the natural pull of human nature is towards selfish sin, what Israel was attempting to do was "counter-fallen human nature." For example: human nature wants to lie – the Law says do not lie; human nature wants to steal – the Law says do not steal; human nature wants to commit adultery – the Law says do not commit adultery; etc. The Law instructed them to "love thy neighbor as thyself."

Lyman Beecher wrote in "Republicanism of the Bible":

For the religious instruction and reproof of the people, a succession of prophets were raised up, and continued through an extended portion of their history... These persons ... were able to warn and rebuke and exhort ... The sanctity of their lives and their fearless patriotism ... carried reproof and admonition alike to the cottage and the palace ...

The perpetuity of liberty among a people ... so free as the Israelites ... demanded universal and immediate intellectual and moral culture. But how shall this be secured? They had come from ... Egypt, and from a condition of bitter oppression, and had remained in forty years in the wilderness, untaught, and were as unprepared for liberty, as a people could be ... Some system of education must go into operation ... How then was this to be secured? The power of the press was unknown, and the transcription of books impossible.

The exigency demanded an immediate supply of oral instruction, both to minister at the altar, and for the schools: — and Divine Wisdom met the exigency, by setting apart the whole of one tribe out of twelve, to superintend the comprehensive interests of literature and religion. It was God's potent arm that did it. No other nation in the world, at that day, was educated as fully as the children of Israel ...

The priesthood ... were released from the care of the soil ... The Jewish priesthood was sustained ... for the support for teaching ... This priesthood was not sequestered in cells and cloisters ... The heart of the Levite and the heart of the nation beat in unison.

INTEGRAL COMPONENT – THE GOD OF THE BIBLE

Why would individuals voluntarily deny their selfish impulses? Israel had the integral component, the key motivgation, namely, the belief in:

1) a God who is watching everyone;

2) who wants everyone to be fair; and

3) will hold each person accountable in the future.

This belief motivated everyone to modify their behavior to be fair to each other. The awareness of being accountable to God creates inside each person's head something called "a conscience." Order was maintained while individual liberty was preserved. Each person governed their own actions according to the Law, rather than being governed by the surveillance of a police state.

Imagine if someone was presented with an opportunity

to steal and never get caught. If that person did not believe there was a God watching who wanted him to be fair and would hold him accountable in a future life, this person would be more incline to carry out his act of stealing. In fact, it would be irrational for him not to steal.

But at the moment this person is about to carry out his deed he remembers that there: 1) is a God watching; 2) who wanted him to be fair; and 3) who will hold him accountable in the future, this person would have a propensity to hesitate and reconsider his actions. He would have a "conscience."

Israel was basing the maintenance of order in society upon each individual's awareness of PERSONAL ACCOUNTABILITY to an ever-present, all-seeing God who wants each person to treat his fellowman fairly as he would want to be treated.

Secretary of State William Jennings Bryan was three times the Democrat Party's candidate for U.S. President. His statue is in the U.S. Capitol's Statuary Hall. Bryan gave over 600 public speeches in his Presidential campaigns, the most famous being "The Prince of Peace" (*New York Times*, Sept. 7, 1913), in which he stated:

> A religion which teaches *personal responsibility* to God gives strength to morality. There is a powerful restraining influence in the belief that an all-seeing eye scrutinizes every thought and word and act of the individual.

Prime Minister Margaret Thatcher stated Feb. 5, 1996:

> The Decalogue (TEN COMMANDMENTS) are addressed to each and every person. This is the origin ... of the sanctity of the individual ... You don't get that in any other political creed ... It is personal liberty *with personal responsibility*. Responsibility to your parents, to your children, to your God ... Your Founding Fathers came over with that.

Some might deny their selfish desires because they want to preserve societal order, but they are the exception, not the norm. Some might deny their selfish desires out of fear of punishment or to avoid public embarrassment.

Some might deny their selfish desires because of peer pressure, or to fit in, or be socially acceptable, or even be honored. Some might deny their selfish desires because they are subconsciously adhering to a remnant of faith held by a parent, grandparent or people group. Some might even be virtuous for the sake of virtue.

But for the large percentage of people, these reasons would not be enough for them to consistently resist the temptation to fulfill their selfish desires. It is likely many people would act selfishly if they felt like they could get away with it, or if they had a desperate need, or if they felt they were wronged or were being unjustly deprived, or were working hard and felt they were not being fairly compensated.

Motivation for virtue works best with a Judeo-Christian belief that each individual is made equal in the image of God. It is like a mathematical concept of inverse proportion: LESS external law requires MORE internal law to maintain order in society.

Both EXTERNAL law and INTERNAL law are powerless without consequences.

EXTERNAL law requires temporal, physical consequences, of both a positive & negative nature.

These consequences are the government having a police force and legal system which holds each individual accountable. Government dispenses temporal rewards and incentives for compliance, and physical restraints and punishment, including death, for non-compliance.

INTERNAL law requires eternal, spiritual consequences, of both a positive & negative nature.

These consequences are a God who holds each individual accountable, dispensing eternal rewards in heaven for compliance, and eternal punishments in hell for non-compliance.

So the long version of the equation is:

(External Law x Temporal Consequences) + (Internal Law x Eternal Consequences) = Order in Society.

What Israel was attempting to do was to replace the prideful EXTERNAL desire for a king's recognition and rewards, together with fear of the king's dishonor and punishment, with an individual's INTERNAL desire for God's eternal recognition and rewards, together with fear of God's eternal wrath and punishment.

Martin Luther King, Jr., wrote in *Strength to Love*, 1963:

> The Church must be reminded that it is ... the conscience of the state. It must be the guide and the critic of the state ...
>
> If the church does not recapture its prophetic zeal, it will become an irrelevant social club without moral or spiritual authority.

For virtue to truly be effective, it must be more than just a list of *dos and don'ts*, as the selfishness inherent in human nature is continually pulling people to find ways to get around the *dos and don'ts*. Police would need to follow everyone around, making sure they obeyed.

In Western Judeo-Christian civilization, the original and most commonly accepted idea of "virtue" is striving to live up to a moral standard where people treat each other equally. (This is a different definition from that used by French Revolution philosophers, who attempted to twist the meaning of virtue to be the raw exercise of power.)

Using the traditional understanding of virtue, the question has to be asked, why would someone voluntarily deny their selfish human nature and live up to a moral standard to treat others fairly? Other than the external fear of being caught, the most effective motivation is an internal spiritual motivation.

Other beliefs are not as effective. For example, Buddhism has a spiritual belief in a fate or "karma," a sort of cosmic circle of what goes around comes around – that how one treats others will be how others treat them in the future. This is an impersonal force which lacks the expectations from a personal relationship.

In Islam, the religion actually gives instructions as to when it is "halal" (permissible) to steal, lie, rape or kill apostates or infidels. There is no concept of equality, and women are consider property.

The most consistently powerful motivation in Western Civilization for people to treat others fairly is the belief in a just God to whom each individual is accountable. Though secularists hate to admit it, the anticipation of a heavenly reward, or the dread of an eternal punishment, are strong motivations. Benjamin Franklin wrote to Yale President Ezra Stiles, March 9, 1790:

> The soul of Man is immortal, and will be treated with justice in another life respecting its conduct in this.

Benjamin Franklin recorded his beliefs:

> That there is one God, Father of the Universe ... That He loves such of His creatures as love and do good to others: and will reward them either in this world or hereafter, That men's minds do not die with their bodies, but are made more happy or miserable after this life according to their actions.

Secretary of State Daniel Webster was asked what the most profound thought was that ever passed through his mind. He responded: "My accountability to God."

John Adams wrote to Judge Van der Kemp, Jan. 13, 1815:

> My religion is founded on the love of God and my neighbor; in the hope of pardon for my offenses; upon contrition ... in the duty of doing no wrong, but all the good I can, to the creation, of which I am but an infinitesimal part. I believe, too, in a future state of rewards and punishments.

John Adams, in discussing the alternative, wrote to Judge F.A. Van de Kemp, Dec. 27, 1816:

> Let it once be revealed or demonstrated that there is no future state, and my advice to every man, woman, and child, would be, as our existence would be in our own power, to take opium. For, I am certain there is

nothing in this world worth living for but hope, and every hope will fail us, if the last hope, that of a future state, is extinguished.

John Adams further wrote in a Proclamation of Humiliation, Fasting, and Prayer, March 6, 1799:

No truth is more clearly taught in the Volume of Inspiration ... than ... acknowledgment of ... a Supreme Being and of the accountableness of men to Him as the searcher of hearts and righteous distributor of rewards and punishments are conducive equally to the happiness and rectitude of individuals and to the well-being of communities.

Abraham Lincoln told Rev. Byron Sunderland of the First Presbyterian Church, Washington, DC, Nov. 25, 1862:

I believe in the supremacy of the human conscience, and that men are responsible beings, that God has a right to hold them, and will hold them, to a strict account for the deeds done in the body. But, sirs, I do not mean to give you a lecture upon the doctrines of the Christian religion. These are simply with me the convictions and realities of great and vital truths.

Pennsylvania's Constitution, 1776, ch. 2, sec. 10, stated:

Each member, before he takes his seat, shall make and subscribe the following declaration, namely:

I do believe in one God, the Creator and Governor of the Universe, the Rewarder of the good and Punisher of the wicked, and I do acknowledge the Scriptures of the Old and New Testament to be given by Divine Inspiration.

Pennsylvania's Supreme Court stated in *Commonwealth v. Wolf* (3 Serg. & R. 48, 50, 1817:

Laws cannot be administered in any civilized government unless the people are taught to revere the sanctity of an oath, and look to a future state of rewards and punishments for the deeds of this life.

South Carolina's Constitution, 1778, Article 7, stated:

Every ... person, who acknowledges the being of a God, and believes in the future state of rewards and punishments ... [is eligible to vote].

South Carolina's Constitution, 1790, Article 38, stated:

> That all persons and religious societies, who acknowledge that there is one God, and a future state of rewards and punishments, and that God is publicly to be worshiped, shall be freely tolerated.

Mississippi's Constitution, 1817, stated:

> No person who denies the being of God or a future state of rewards and punishments shall hold any office in the civil department of the State.

Maryland's Constitution, 1851, required to hold office:

> A declaration of belief in the Christian religion; and if the party shall profess to be a Jew the declaration shall be of his belief in a future state of rewards and punishments.

Maryland's Constitution, 1864, required to hold office:

> A declaration of belief in the Christian religion, or of the existence of God, and in a future state of rewards and punishments.

Tennessee's Constitution, 1870, art. 9, sec. 2, stated:

> No person who denies the being of God, or a future state of rewards and punishments, shall hold any office in the civil department of this State.

An oath is to call a higher power to hold you accountable to perform what you said you would do. This accountability is expressed in all three branches of government:

–President's oath of office ends with "So Help Me God";

–Congressmen & Senators' oath of office ends with "So Help Me God";

–Federal Judges' oath of office ends with "So Help Me God." The traditional courtroom oath for witnesses ended "to tell the truth, the whole truth and nothing but the truth, So Help Me God."

–The military's oath of enlistment and oath for commissioned officers ends with "So Help Me God."

Sir William Blackstone, one of the most quoted authors

by America's founders, wrote in *Commentaries on the Laws of England*, 1765–1770:

> The belief of a future state of rewards and punishments, the entertaining just ideas of the main attributes of the Supreme Being, and a firm persuasion that He superintends and will finally compensate every action in human life (all which are revealed in the doctrines of our Savior, Christ), these are the grand foundations of all judicial oaths, which call God to witness the truth of those facts which perhaps may be only known to Him and the party attesting.

It was known that a witness or politician would have opportunities to twist the truth and do back room deals for their own benefit and never get caught.

But it was reasoned that if that witness or politician believed God existed and was looking over their shoulder, they would hesitate when presented with the temptation. They would have a conscience. They would think twice before giving in, considering "even if I get away with this unscrupulous action in this life, I will still be accountable to God in the next."

If a person did not believe in God and in a future state of rewards and punishments, when presented with the same temptation to do wrong and not get caught, they would give in. In fact, if there is no God and this life is all there is, they would be a fool not to.

President Reagan referred to this while speaking on the Equal Access Bill in Dallas, Texas, Aug. 23, 1984:

> Without God there is no virtue because there is no prompting of the conscience.

John Jay wrote to John Bristed, April 23, 1811:

> If there was no God there could be no moral obligations, and I did not see how society could subsist without them.

William Linn, who was unanimously elected the first Chaplain of the U.S. House, May 1, 1789, stated:

> Let my neighbor once persuade himself that there

is no God, and he will soon pick my pocket, and break not only my leg but my neck. If there be no God, there is no law, no future account; government then is the ordinance of man only, and we cannot be subject for conscience sake.

The less internal moral code a nation has will result in government enacting more external legal codes to keep order – and each new law takes away individual freedom.

Clay Christensen, Professor of Business Administration at the Harvard Business School, wrote Feb. 8, 2011:

Sometime ago I had a conversation with a Marxist economist from China. He was coming to the end of a Fulbright Fellowship here in Boston, and I asked him if he had learned anything that was surprising or unexpected.

And without any hesitation he said "Yes, I had no idea how critical religion is to the functioning of democracy."

"The reason why democracy works," he said, "is not because the government was designed to oversee what everybody does. But rather democracy works because most people, most of the time, voluntarily choose to obey the law. And in your past, most Americans attended a church or synagogue every week. And they were taught there by people who they respected."

My friend went on to say that "Americans followed these rules because they had come to believe that they weren't just accountable to society, they were accountable to God."

My Chinese friend heightened a vague but nagging concern I harbored inside that as religion loses its influence over the lives of Americans what will happen to our democracy? Where are the institutions that are going to teach the next generation of Americans that they too need to voluntarily choose to obey the laws? Because if you take away religion, you cannot hire enough police.

McGuffey's Fifth Eclectic Reader (Cincinnati & NY: Van

Antwerp, Bragg & Co., 1879), included lesson 93, "Religion The Only Basis of Society" by William Ellery Channing:

> How powerless conscience would become without the belief of a God ... Erase all thought and fear of God from a community, and selfishness and sensuality would absorb the whole man.
>
> Appetite, knowing no restraint, and suffering, having no solace or hope, would trample in scorn on the restraints of human laws.
>
> Virtue, duty, principle, would be mocked and spurned as unmeaning sounds. A sordid self-interest would supplant every feeling; and man would become, in fact, what the theory in atheism declares him to be, – a companion for brutes.

Patrick Henry noted:

> A corrupted public conscience is incompatible with freedom.

John Adams wrote to Jefferson, April 19, 1817:

> Without religion, this world would be something not fit to be mentioned in polite company ... The most abandoned scoundrel that ever existed, never yet wholly extinguished his conscience and while conscience remains, there is some religion.

General Omar Bradley stated in his address on Armistice Day, Nov. 11, 1948:

> We have grasped the mystery of the atom and rejected the Sermon on the Mount ... The world has achieved brilliance without conscience. Ours is a world of nuclear giants and ethical infants.

U.S. Supreme Court Justice James Wilson, who was appointed by George Washington, wrote:

> The eminent distinction between right and wrong... [is revealed] by our conscience, by our reason, and by the Holy Scriptures.

In 1745, copying the *110 Rules of Civility*, George Washington wrote:

> Labor to keep alive in your breast that little spark of Celestial fire called Conscience.

Apart from a belief in a future accountability, situation ethics renders virtue ineffective and to a certain extent, irrational. The philosopher Plato argued that pagan Greeks with their vague concept of an afterlife could only pretend to be virtuous. If they were given the choice of giving up their virtue or giving up their lives, they would always give up their virtue to save their lives.

HONESTY BASIS FOR COMMERCE

Ancient Israel had a code of honesty in business dealings which provided a strong foundation for commerce.

Leviticus 19:11-13, 35–36:

Ye shall not steal, neither deal falsely, neither lie one to another ... Thou shalt not defraud thy neighbor ... You shall do no injustice in judgment in measurement of length, weight, or volume. You shall have honest scales and honest weights, an honest ephah, and an honest hin: I am the Lord your God, who brought you out of the land of Egypt.

Deuteronomy 25:13 –16:

You shall not have in your bag differing weights, a heavy and a light. You shall not have in your house differing measures, a large and a small, You shall have a perfect and just weight, a perfect and just measure, that your days may be lengthened in the land which the Lord your God is giving you. For all who do such things, all who behave unrighteously, are an abomination to the Lord your God.

Proverbs 11:1:

Dishonest scales are an abomination to the Lord, but a just weight is His delight.

Proverbs 16:11:

Honest weights and scales are the Lord's. All the weights in the bag are His work.

Proverbs 20:10, 23:

Diverse weights and diverse measures; they are

both alike, an abomination to the Lord ... Diverse weights are an abomination to the Lord, and dishonest scales are not good.

Israel's law condemned unjust weights and measures, as well as the taking of bribes. It laid the foundation for public trust in commerce.

Mark Twain wrote in an article "Concerning The Jews," published in *Harper's New Monthly Magazine* (Sept. 1899, p. 527–535):

Of the Jews from Germany ... the great and lucrative businesses of all sorts in Germany were in the hands of the Jewish race. Isn't it an amazing confession? It was but another way of saying that in a population of 48,000,000, of whom only 500,000 were registered as Jews, eight-five percent of the brains and honesty of the whole was lodged in the Jews. I must insist upon the honesty – it is an essential of successful business, taken by and large. Of course it does not rule out rascals entirely, even among Christians, but it is a good working rule, nevertheless.

David P. Goldman is author of *How Civilizations Die* (Regnery Press, 2011), and is Senior Fellow at the London Center for Policy Research and Associate Fellow at the Middle East Forum. He wrote "Why Jews are good at money," *Asia Times*, Feb. 12, 2015 (http://www.atimes. com/atimes/World/WOR-02-120215.html):

Free capital markets require governments to win the faith of the people. Capital markets require belief in the viability of investments, trust among counterparties, and faith in the future. It is fitting that Jews created capital markets, because the Jews invented faith. The secret of Jewish success in public finance is to be found in the Jewish encounter with the divine.

The gods of the pagan world did not require faith. The gods simply were there, as much as the natural world which they personified. The "god-infested world" (Gilson) of the pagans was simply the natural world as it presented itself to man, with all its arbitrariness and cruelty.

To the extent that gods demanded loyalty, it was in their capacity as the patrons of a particular policy protected by that god, for example, Athena in the case of Athens. Nowhere in the pagan world, though, do we encounter a God who could instruct Abraham to leave his homeland and his father's house, and betake himself to a place which God would later show him.

Never do we meet a God who offers his laws (the Torah) to a people, as YHWH did at Mount Sinai, and ask that people's free assent to accept these laws. In no other instance do we hear of a single, universal creator God who enters into a covenant of mutual obligations with humans.

That is the origin of faith, emunah in Hebrew, meaning loyalty as well as belief. The Jewish concept of emunah implies not only that we conceive something to be true, but that we also must be steadfast in acting according to that truth.

That is the Jewish genius: to be able to inspire faith (or what is usually called "confidence" in markets) to make possible long-term investments in capital markets involving millions of participants. The investors in a bond or stock issue are not linked by ties of family or personal loyalty, but rather by contract, law and custom.

Their obligations extend beyond the ancient loyalties of family and clan. That may seem obvious on first reflection. But most countries in the world lack functioning capital markets, because faith is absent.

The public does not trust the government to enforce contracts, or the management of a company not to steal money. That is emphatically true in China, which is struggling to create modern capital markets rather than depend on state banks and shadow financing. In backward countries, trust is inconceivable outside the narrow circle of blood relations. Firms remain small because trust is restricted to family members. That is what Chinese can learn from Jews about business.

The Jews have no special aptitude for trading. But we have a special gift for promoting the rule of law and public and private institutions which promote credit, that is, faith in future outcomes and the fair treatment of market participants. In the absence of faith, there never will be enough lawyers to enforce contracts, or policemen to arrest embezzlers, or watchdogs to extirpate government corruption.

Something more fundamental is required: a sense that the law is sacred, and if any of us breaks the public trust, all of us are damaged. Our rabbis of antiquity said, "All of Israel stands surety for each other."

Adam Smith's invisible hand isn't enough. Capital markets require more than the interaction of self-interested individuals: they require a common sense of the sanctity of covenant, of mutual obligations between government and people, and between one individual and the next.

That is why the United States of America is the most successful nation in economic history. It was founded by devout Christians who hoped to construct a new nation in emulation of ancient Israel.

Jamie Glazov's book, *United in Hate: The Left's Romance With Tyranny and Terror* (Los Angeles: WND Books, 2009), was reviewed by George Jochnowitz in Midstream (winter, 2011; reprinted FrontPage Mag (3/11/11):

Ulrike Meinhof, one of the founders of the terrorist Baader-Meinhof Gang, said, " ... Anti-Semitism is really a hatred of capitalism." Meinhof was proud of her anti-Semitism. Meinhof, to be sure, was a terrorist. Unfortunately, many leftists ... take positions approaching hers ...

Glazov feels that there are two basic reasons that the left has joined Muslim terrorists to oppose Jews and Israel. "First...leftism, like Islamism, detests modernity, individual freedom, and any value placed on individual human life... In addition, Jews are seen as being synonymous with the oppressive structures of corporate capitalism ... "

Marxism is not a religion, but it does demand belief—blind belief—in the doctrines it teaches. Leftists today may ignore Marx's writings about economics, but they support and have always supported regimes that suppress free thought ...

Glazov writes of many leftists ... are ... supporters of totalitarianism ... But there is a more profound factor in the hostility that totalitarians feel toward Jews: Jews argue.

They think dangerous thoughts. Marxist regimes reject thinkers and intellectuals. Chairman Mao exiled teachers and writers to the countryside to learn from the peasants. Pol Pot simply killed them ...

Hitler, to be sure, never explained why he had to kill people who were Jews or descended from Jews. Perhaps he felt that the genetic flaw he had to eradicate was the argument gene. Since Jews argue, a variety of beliefs may be found among them.

There have certainly been Jews who were Communists; there are even Jews today who are sympathetic to Islamism.

All the same, it is logical that argument and free thought are a problem for totalitarians. Totalitarians hate Jews ... Hitler knew he needed scientists because he wanted Germany to be able to produce atomic weapons, but anti-Semitism took priority over this need. Einstein fled Germany; Edward Teller and Szilard fled Germany's ally, Hungary. Enrico Fermi, who was not Jewish but was married to a Jew, fled Europe when Mussolini extended Hitler's racial laws to Italy.

Hitler ... felt that killing Jews ... took precedence over his country's military needs ... Today, Mahmoud Ahmadinejad is echoing the irrationality that Hitler put into effect 70 years ago ... He is amassing atomic bombs as part of a policy ... announced ... in the annual Al-Quds (Jerusalem) sermon given on Dec. 14, 2001 ... that if one day the world of Islam comes to possess nuclear weapons, Israel could be destroyed ...

Glazov writes, "Palestinian children blew themselves into smithereens while their parents celebrated, proud that their offspring had become shahid (martyrs)." Totalitarians love death, unlike Jews, which may be another factor in explaining why totalitarians are so anti-Semitic.

"Two of the most outstanding Jewish characteristics are the love of life and the enduring struggle to survive. For Islamists, as for Nazis and communists, this is an egregious transgression against their faith."

Genocide was Hitler's primary goal. Stalin engineered a famine in his war against the kulaks that killed millions. Mao caused the greatest famine in all human history. Pol Pot killed about a third of his own people. The Kim Dynasty has caused years and years of starvation in North Korea. Ahmadinejad is looking forward to fighting a nuclear war against Israel.

Totalitarianism is about death. Life is about learning more every day. Those who fear learning also hate life. As Glazov shows us, that is why totalitarians are united in hate.

The Iona Institute for Religion & Society published the article, "Christianity the reason for West's success, say the Chinese," March 3, 2011, in which Tom O'Gorman wrote:

In the West we are doing our best to destroy our Christian heritage but in China, Chinese intellectuals are coming around to the view that it is precisely this heritage that has made the West so successful.

Former editor of the *Sunday Telegraph*, Dominic Lawson, in a review in the Sunday Times of Niall Ferguson's new book, *Civilization: The West and the Rest*, carries a quote from a member of the Chinese Academy of Social Sciences in which he tries to account for the success of the West, to date. He said:

"One of the things we were asked to look into was what accounted for the success, in fact, the preeminence of the West all over the world. We studied everything we could from the historical, political, economic, and cultural perspective. At first, we thought it was because you had more powerful guns than we had. Then we thought it was because you had the best political system.

"Next we focused on your economic system. But in the past twenty years, we have realized that the heart of your culture is your religion: Christianity. That is why the West is so powerful. The Christian moral foundation of social and cultural life was what made possible the emergence of capitalism and then the successful transition to democratic politics. We don't have any doubt about this."

Note the source. It isn't from a religious leader, or some religious think-tank. The Chinese Academy of Social Sciences is an instrument of the Chinese Communist government which spends a not inconsiderable amount of time and money persecuting Christians and is officially atheistic.

If this is the conclusion it has come to, maybe Europe needs to reconsider whether it mightn't be an idea to encourage rather than eradicate Christianity. Incidentally, just to drive home the point, Lawson also refers to this data point in Ferguson's book: Wenzhou, the Chinese city which is rated as the most entrepreneurial in the country, is also home to 1,400 churches.

Lawson refers to a quote in the book from a prominent Wenzhou business leader, a Mr. Hanping Zhang, who argues that

"an absence of trust had been one of the main factors holding China back; but he feels he can trust his fellow Christians because he knows that they will be honest in their dealings with him."

It has long been accepted that Christianity is one of the core elements of Western civilization; it is too little understood that it is also one of the secrets of the stunning success of that civilization.

THE REPUBLIC OF THE ISRAELITES AN EXAMPLE TO THE AMERICAN STATES

Rev. Samuel Langdon had been a military chaplain in New Hampshire prior to becoming President of Harvard. On a memorial at the North Church in Portsmouth, it states that Rev. Langdon "offered the prayer for the assembled army the night previous to the Battle of Bunker Hill."

Samuel Langdon was a delegate to New Hampshire's ratifying convention in 1788. According the *Portsmouth*

Daily Evening Times, Jan. 1, 1891: "by his voice and example he contributed more perhaps, than any other man to the favorable action of that body" which resulted in New Hampshire becoming the 9th State to ratify the U.S. Constitution, thus putting it into effect.

At New Hampshire's Ratifying Convention in Concord, Rev. Samuel Langdon gave a speech titled **"The Republic of the Israelites An Example to the American States,"** June 5, 1788, which was instrumental in convincing delegates to ratify the U.S. Constitution:

> There is a remarkable paragraph in the sacred writings, which may be very well accommodated to my present purpose, and merits particular attention. You have it in Deuteronomy, 4:5–8.

> "Behold, I have taught you statutes and judgments, even as the Lord my God commanded me, that ye should do so in the land whither ye go to possess it. Keep therefore and do them; for this is your wisdom and your understanding in the sight of the nations, who shall hear all these statutes, and say, surely this great nation is a wise and understanding people: for what nation is there so great, which hath God so nigh unto them as the Lord our God is in all things that we call upon him for? and what nation is there so great, which hath statutes and judgments so righteous as all this law which I set before you this day."

> Here Moses recommends to Israel the strict observance of all the laws which he had delivered to them by God's command, relating both to their CIVIL POLITY and RELIGION, as the sure way to raise their reputation high among all nations as a wise and understanding people; because no other nation was blessed with such excellent national laws, or the advantage of applying to the oracle of the living God, and praying to him in all difficulties, with assurance that all their requests would be answered.

> As to every thing excellent in their CONSTITUTION OF GOVERNMENT, except what was peculiar to them as a nation separated to God from the rest of mankind, THE ISRAELITES MAY BE

CONSIDERED AS A PATTERN TO THE WORLD IN ALL AGES; and from them we may learn what will exalt our character, and what will depress and bring us to ruin.

Let us therefore look over their constitution and laws, inquire into their practice, and observe how their prosperity and fame depended on their strict observance of the divine commands both as to their government and religion.

Samuel Langdon continued:

When first the Israelites came out from the bondage of Egypt, they were a multitude without any other order than what had been kept up, very feebly, under the ancient patriarchal authority. They were suddenly collected into a body under the conduct of Moses, without any proper national or military regulation.

Yet in the short space of about three months after they had passed the Red Sea, they were reduced into such civil and military order, blended together, by the advice of Jethro, as was well adapted to their circumstances in the wilderness while destitute of property. Able men were chosen out of all their tribes, and made captains and rulers of thousands, hundreds, fifties and tens: and these commanded them as military officers, and acted as judges in matters of common controversy.

But the great thing wanting was a permanent constitution, which might keep the people peaceable and obedient while in the desert, and after they had gained possession of the promised land.

Therefore, upon the complaint of Moses that the burden of government was too heavy for him, God commanded him to bring seventy men, chosen from among the elders and officers, and present them at the tabernacle; and there he endued them with the same spirit which was in Moses, that they might bear the burden with him. Thus a Senate was evidently constituted, as necessary for the future government of the nation, under a chief commander.

And as to the choice of this Senate, doubtless the people were consulted, who appear to have had a voice in all public affairs from time to time, the whole congregation being called together on all important occasions: the government therefore was a proper republic.

And beside this general establishment, every tribe had elders and a prince according to the patriarchal order, with which Moses did not interfere; and these had an acknowledged right to meet and consult together, and with the consent of the congregation do whatever was necessary to preserve good order, and promote the common interest of the tribe.

So that the government of each tribe was very similar to the general government. There was a President and Senate at the head of each, and the people assembled and gave their voice in all great matters ...

Moreover, to complete the establishment of civil government, courts were to be appointed in every walled city, after their settlement in Canaan, and elders most distinguished for wisdom and integrity were to be made judges, ready always to sit and decide the common controversies within their respective jurisdictions.

The people had a right likewise to appoint such other officers as they might think necessary for the more effectual execution of justice, according to that order given in Deuteronomy 16:18-19.

– "Judges and officers shalt thou make thee in all thy gates which the Lord thy God giveth thee throughout thy tribes; and they shall judge the people with just judgment: thou shalt not wrest judgment; thou shalt not respect persons, neither take a gift; for a gift doth blind the eyes of the wise, and pervert the words of the righteous."–

But from these courts an appeal was allowed in weighty causes to higher courts appointed over the whole tribe, and in very great and difficult cases to the supreme authority of the general Senate and chief magistrate.

A government, thus settled on republican principles, required laws; without which it must have degenerated immediately into aristocracy, or absolute monarchy.

But God did not leave a people wholly unskilled in legislation, to make laws for themselves: He took this important matter wholly into His own hands, and beside the moral laws of the two tables, which directed their conduct as individuals, gave them by Moses a complete code of judicial laws.

They were not numerous indeed, but concise and plain, and easily applicable to almost every controversy which might arise between man and man, and every criminal case which might require the judgment of the court.

Of these some were peculiarly adapted to their national form, as divided into tribes and families always to be kept distinct; others were especially suited to the peculiar nature of the government as a theocracy, God Himself being eminently their king, and manifesting Himself among them in a visible manner, by the cloud of glory in the tabernacle and temple.

This was the reason why blasphemy, and all obstinate disobedience to his laws, were considered as high treason, and punished with death; especially idolatry, as being a crime against the fundamental principles of the constitution.

But far the greater part of the judicial laws were founded on the plain immutable principles of reason, justice, and social virtue; such as are always necessary for civil society.

Life and property were well guarded, and punishments were equitably adapted to the nature of every crime: in particular, murder stands foremost among capital crimes, and is defined with such precision, and so clearly distinguished from all cases of accidental and undesigned killing, that the innocent were in no danger of punishment, and the guilty could not escape ...

How unexampled was this quick progress of the Israelites, from abject slavery, ignorance, and almost total want of order, to a national establishment perfected in all its parts far beyond all other kingdoms and States!

From a mere mob, to a well regulated nation, under a government and laws far superior to what any other nation could boast! It was a long time after the law of Moses was given before the rest of the world knew any thing of government by law.

Where kings reigned their will was a law. Where *popular* governments were formed, the capricious humor of the multitude ordered every thing just according to present circumstances; or their senators and judges were left to act according to their best discretion.

It was six hundred years after Moses before the Spartans, the most famous of the Grecian republics, received a very imperfect, and in some particulars very absurd code of laws from Lycurgus.

After this feeble attempt of legislation, three hundred years more elapsed before Solon appeared and gave laws to Athens, though a city long famous for arms, arts, eloquence, and philosophy.

And it was about five hundred years from the first founding of the celebrated Roman empire, and nearly three hundred years after Solon, before the first laws of that empire were imported from Greece in twelve tables, by ten ambassadors sent there for that purpose.

But even when that empire had attained the summit of glory, and legislation was carried to great perfection, however well adapted to a government so extensive and complicated their laws might be, they were far from being worthy to be compared with the laws of Israel, as to the security of life, liberty, property, and public morals: and as to their religion, which was from the beginning interwoven with the state, instead of receiving any greater perfection from the increase of knowledge, wealth and power, it only became a more abundant congeries of ridiculous and detestable superstitions.

Moreover; when the Roman empire was overwhelmed and destroyed by an inundation of barbarous nations, and many kingdoms were erected in Europe out of its ruins by the conquerors, laws were extinct under the feudal system; the will of the barons was a law for their vassals; and but a few centuries have passed since kings began to introduce laws into their courts of justice.

Mark Twain wrote "Concerning The Jews" (*Harper's New Monthly Magazine*, Sept. 1899, p. 527–535):

If the statistics are right, the Jews constitute but one per cent of the human race. It suggests a nebulous dim puff of stardust lost in the blaze of the Milky Way. Properly the Jew ought hardly to be heard of; but he is heard of, has always been heard of.

He is as prominent on the planet as any other people, and his commercial importance is extravagantly out of proportion to the smallness of his bulk. His contributions to the world's list of great names in literature, science, art, music, finance, medicine, and abstruse learning are also away out of proportion to the weakness of his numbers. He has made a marvelous fight in this world, in all the ages; and has done it with his hands tied behind him. He could be vain of himself, and be excused for it.

The Egyptian, the Babylonian, and the Persian rose, filled the planet with sound and splendor, then faded to dream-stuff and passed away; the Greek and the Roman followed, and made a vast noise, and they are gone; other peoples have sprung up and held their torch high for a time, but it burned out, and they sit in twilight now, or have vanished.

The Jew saw them all, beat them all, and is now what he always was, exhibiting no decadence, no infirmities of age, no weakening of his parts, no slowing of his energies, no dulling of his alert and aggressive mind. All things are mortal but the Jew; all other forces pass, but he remains. What is the secret of his immortality?

Lyman Beecher wrote "Republicanism of the Bible" (Select Miscellany, *The Hesperian; or Western Monthly Magazine*, May 1838, p. 47-48, Discourses to the Mechanics of Cincinnati, 1837), stating:

> Our own republic, in its constitution and laws, is ... not borrowed from Greece or Rome, but it was borrowed from the Bible.

U.S. Supreme Court Justice David Josiah Brewer wrote in *The United States-A Christian Nation* (published in 1905 by the John C. Winston Company, Philadelphia):

> Our laws and customs are based upon the laws of Moses and the teachings of Christ.

FIRSTS OF ANCIENT ISRAEL'S REPUBLIC

> And what one nation in the earth is like thy people Israel, whom God went to redeem to be his own people.- I Chronicles 17:21.

Ancient Israel was the first well-recorded instance of:

—An entire nation ruled without a king;

—Everyone equal before the Law, no respect of persons in judgment;

—Highest value of human life;

—Private land ownership;

—People could accumulate possessions – "blessed";

—People ratified their constitution;

—People choose their own leaders;

—Local rule, with leaders of tens, fifties, hundreds, thousands;

—A senate comprised of elected leaders of tribes;

—No police, as citizens enforced the law;

—No government tracking;

—No prisons, as swift justice at city gates, and cities of refuge where fugitives could run to await trial;

—No standing army, as every man was in the militia, armed and ready at a moments notice to defend his community;

—No conquest beyond borders;

—Honesty was basis for commerce;

–Bureaucracy-free welfare system;

–Everyone could read;

–Government relied on educated & moral citizens;

–Dependent on priests and Levites teaching Law.

DECLINE OF ISRAELITE REPUBLIC

Ancient Israel's ruling of itself without a king lasted as long as the priests and Levites taught the Law.

The Elementary Textbook Evaluation Guide (San Francico, CA, Textbook Study League, Inc., 1951; John Stormer, *None Dare Call It Education;* cited by Judge Darrell White, American Judicial Alliance, 2015) stated:

> Withhold from the children for one generation the truth of "rights endowed by the Creator" and our Constitution could be altered and our freedom could be voted away without citizens ever knowing the cause of their slavery.

Unfortunately, human nature is fallen and, like a rubber band, wants to snap back toward selfish behavior.

Psalm 10:4:

> The wicked ... will not seek after God: God is not in all his thoughts.

Romans 1:28:

> And even as they did not like to retain God in their knowledge, God gave them over to a reprobate mind, to do those things which are not proper.

Genesis 6:5–6:

> And GOD saw that the wickedness of man was great in the earth, and that every imagination of the thoughts of his heart was only evil continually. And it repented the LORD that He had made man on the earth, and it grieved Him at His heart.

Genesis 8:21:

> And the LORD smelled a sweet savor; and the LORD said in His heart, I will not again curse the

ground any more for man's sake; for the imagination of man's heart is evil from his youth; neither will I again smite any more everything living, as I have done.

Jeremiah 16:12:

And ye have done worse than your fathers; for, behold, ye walk every one after the imagination of his evil heart, that they may not hearken unto me.

Jeremiah 7:24:

But they hearkened not, nor inclined their ear, but walked in the counsels and in the imagination of their evil heart, and went backward, and not forward.

While the priests and Levites taught the Law, the people of Israel had virtue and self-control. They enjoyed unprecedented individual freedom, opportunity, equality and prosperity.

Deuteronomy 24:8:

Take heed ... that thou observe diligently, and do according to all the priests (and) the Levites shall teach you.

When priests and Levites neglected teaching the Law and ceased being the conscience of the nation, the people devolved into embracing a moral relativism. They reverted to their selfish fallen nature where **"every man did that which was right in his own eyes."**

Prophets called for the people to repent, but the people did not heed. Chaos weakened the nation internally and Israel was overrun by immigrant strangers who rose up and ruled over them.

Deuteronomy 28:15, 43-44:

But it shall come to pass, if thou wilt not hearken unto the voice of the Lord thy God ... that all these curses shall come upon thee ... The stranger that is within thee shall get up above thee very high; and thou shalt come down very low. He shall lend to thee, and thou shalt not lend to him: he shall be the head, and thou shalt be the tail.

When Israel repented, the Lord raised up deliverers.

Israel renewed its covenant, recommitted to following the Law, and experienced blessings, beginning the cycle again:

Covenant > Blessed > Backslide >

Prophets sent > Nation unrepentant >

Judgment > Nation repentant > Deliverer sent >

Renewed Covenant > Blessed

Lyman Beecher wrote in "Republicanism of the Bible":

Besides the regular officers of the constitution, there were judges who were military leaders, raised up for special emergencies, and inspired with courage and skill for temporary purposes.

After a crisis with the Moabites, the people of Israel tried to make Gideon a king.

Judges 8:22–23:

Then the men of Israel said unto Gideon, Rule thou over us, both thou, and thy son, and thy son's son also: for thou hast delivered us from the hand of Midian.

And Gideon said unto them, I will not rule over you, neither shall my son rule over you: the LORD shall rule over you.

Thomas Paine wrote in his third edition of *Common Sense*, Philadelphia, Feb. 14, 1776:

Monarchy is ranked in scripture as one of the sins of the Jews, for which a curse in reserve is denounced against them.

The history of that transaction is worth attending to. The children of Israel being oppressed by the Midianites, Gideon marched against them with a small army, and victory through the divine interposition decided in his favor. The Jews, elated with success, and attributing it to the generalship of Gideon, proposed making him a king, saying, "Rule thou over us, thou and thy son, and thy son's son."

Here was temptation in its fullest extent; not a kingdom only, but an hereditary one; but Gideon in the piety of his soul replied, "I will not rule over you, neither shall my son rule over you. THE LORD

SHALL RULE OVER YOU."

Words need not be more explicit: Gideon doth not decline the honor, but denieth their right to give it; neither doth he compliment them with invented declarations of his thanks, but in the positive style of a prophet charges them with disaffection to their proper Sovereign, the King of Heaven.

LEVITES NEGLECTED TEACHING LAW

The morals of Israel declined as the Levites neglected teaching the Law. The Law commanded "Thou shalt not make unto thee any graven image ... Thou shalt not bow down thyself to them, nor serve them: for I the Lord thy God am a jealous God" (Ex. 20:4-5), yet the Book of Judges (ch. 17–18), told of a Levite with a graven image:

> And there was a man of mount Ephraim, whose name was Micah ... and his mother took two hundred shekels of silver, and gave them to the founder, who made thereof a graven image ...
>
> In those days there was no king in Israel, but **every man did that which was right in his own eyes** ...
>
> And there was a young man ... who was a Levite, and he sojourned ... to the house of Micah ... And Micah said unto him, Whence comest thou?
>
> And he said unto him, I am a Levite of Bethlehemjudah ... And Micah said unto him, Dwell with me, and be unto me a father and a priest, and I will give thee ten shekels of silver by the year, and a suit of apparel, and thy victuals.
>
> So the Levite went in ... And there went from thence of the family of the Danites, out of Zorah and out of Eshtaol, six hundred men appointed with weapons of war ...
>
> And they ... came to the house of the young man the Levite, even unto the house of Micah, and saluted him ... and came in thither, and took the graven image... Then said the priest unto them, What do ye?
>
> And they said unto him ... go with us, and be to us

> a father and a priest: is it better for thee to be a priest unto the house of one man, or that thou be a priest unto a tribe and a family in Israel?
>
> And the priest's heart was glad, and he took the ephod, and the teraphim, and the graven image, and went in the midst of the people ... Micah ... said, Ye have taken away my gods which I made, and the priest ...
>
> And the children of Dan set up the graven image: and Jonathan, the son of Gershom, the son of Manasseh, he and his sons were priests to the tribe of Dan until the day of the captivity of the land. And they set them up Micah's graven image, which he made.

Another account illustrating that the Levites had neglected to teach the law is the disturbing story in Judges 19:

> And it came to pass in those days, when there was no king in Israel, that there was a certain Levite sojourning on the side of mount Ephraim, who took to him a concubine ... And his concubine played the whore against him.

The observation is that the Levite priest had a concubine – a woman he was not legitimately married to, and that she "played the whore." This was against the Law, which instructed a Levite to marry a virgin of his own tribe and specifically forbabe him from having a whore.

Leviticus 21:1, 7, 13–15:

> And the LORD said unto Moses, Speak unto the priests the sons of Aaron ... They shall not take a wife that is a whore, or profane; neither shall they take a woman put away from her husband: for he is holy unto his God ...
>
> And he shall take a wife in her virginity. A widow, or a divorced woman, or profane, or an harlot, these shall he not take: but he shall take a virgin of his own people to wife. Neither shall he profane his seed among his people: for I the LORD do sanctify him.

The Levites who were supposed to be teaching the Law were not keeping it themselves. The tragic story continues with an event similar to Lot in Sodom and Gomorrah.

Judges 19:10–22:

> But the Levite ... came over against Jebus, which is Jerusalem; and there were with him two asses saddled, his concubine also was with him ... And, behold, there came an old man ... and the old man said, Whither goest thou? ... And he said unto him... I am now going to the house of the LORD ... So he brought him into his house ...
>
> Behold, the men of the city, certain sons of Belial, beset the house round about, and beat at the door ... saying, Bring forth the man that came into thine house, that we may know him.

The nation had departed so far away from following the Law that there existed "sons of Belial" who wanted to "know him," a term for aggressive homosexual behavior. The account continued in shocking detail.

Judges 19:23:

> And the man, the master of the house, went out unto them, Nay, my brethren, nay, I pray you, do not so wickedly; seeing that this man is come into mine house, do not this folly. Behold, here is my daughter a maiden, and his concubine; them I will bring out now, and humble ye them, and do with them what seemeth good unto you: but unto this man do not so vile a thing.
>
> But the men would not hearken to him: so the man took his concubine, and brought her forth unto them; and they knew her, and abused her all the night until the morning: and when the day began to spring, they let her go. Then came the woman in the dawning of the day, and fell down at the door of the man's house where her lord was, till it was light.

This most disturbing passage revealed the moral depravity which resulted from the Levites failing to teach the Law. In addition, the Levite was so callous and indifferent that instead of defending his concubine, he shoved her out the door to be abused to death.

Judges 19:28:

> And her lord (the Levite) rose up in the morning, and opened the doors of the house, and went out to go

his way: and, behold, the woman his concubine was fallen down at the door of the house, and her hands were upon the threshold.

And he said unto her, Up, and let us be going. But none answered. Then the man took her up upon an ass, and the man rose up, and gat him unto his place.

And when he was come into his house, he took a knife, and laid hold on his concubine, and divided her, together with her bones, into twelve pieces, and sent her into all the coasts of Israel. And it was so, that all that saw it said, There was no such deed done nor seen from the day that the children of Israel came up out of the land of Egypt unto this day: consider of it, take advice, and speak your minds.

Judges 20:1, 35; 21:25:

Then all the children of Israel went out, and the congregation was gathered together as one man, from Dan even to Beer-sheba, with the land of Gilead, unto the LORD in Mizpeh ... and the children of Israel destroyed of the Benjamites that day twenty and five thousand and an hundred men ...

In those days there was no king in Israel: **every man did that which was right in his own eyes.**

Deuteronomy 12:1–8:

These are the statutes and judgments, which ye shall observe to do in the land, which the LORD God of thy fathers giveth thee to possess it, all the days that ye live upon the earth ... Ye shall not do after all the things that we do here this day, **every man whatsoever is right in his own eyes.**

Jeremiah 18:12–17:

And they said ... **we will walk after our own devices, and we will every one do the imagination of his evil heart.** Therefore thus saith the LORD ... Because my people hath forgotten me ... I will scatter them as with an east wind before the enemy; I will show them the back, and not the face, in the day of their calamity.

Why did **every man do what was right "in his own**

eyes," walk after their "own devices" and "every one do the imagination of his evil heart"? **Because the priests and Levites neglected their responsibility to teach the people what was right IN THE LORD'S EYES.** The Levites and priests failed to teach the people virtue and to obey the Law of God.

Alexis de Tocqueville wrote in *Democracy in America*, Chapter XVII: Principal Causes Maintaining The Democratic Republic – Part II:

> Despotism may govern without faith, but liberty cannot. Religion is much more necessary in the republic which they set forth in glowing colors than in the monarchy which they attack; and it is more needed in democratic republics than in any others.

> How is it possible that society should escape destruction if the moral tie be not strengthened in proportion as the political tie is relaxed? and what can be done with a people which is its own master, if it be not submissive to the Divinity?

On the eve of the French Revolution, the first U.S. Minister to France, Gouverneur Morris, wrote April 29, 1789:

> The materials for a revolution in France are very indifferent ... There is an utter prostration of morals... depravity ... extreme rottenness of every member... The great masses of the common people have no religion ... no law but their superiors, no morals but their interest ... In the high road a la liberte ... the first use they make of it is to form insurrections everywhere.

Gouverneur Morris wrote *Observation on Government, Applicable to the Political State of France*, 1792:

> Religion is the only solid basis of good morals; therefore education should teach the precepts of religion, and the duties of man toward God ... Provision should be made for maintaining divine worship as well as education ... Religion is the relation between God and man; therefore it is not within the reach of human authority.

Gouverneur Morris, who died Nov. 6, 1816, had

spoken 173 times during the Constitutional Convention, more than any other delegate. As head of the Committee on Style, it was Gouverneur Morris who penned the final draft of the Constitution and originated the phrase: "We the people of the United States ... "

Gouverneur Morris helped write New York's Constitution, was elected U.S. Senator and pioneered the Erie Canal. In 1785, he addressed the Pennsylvania Assembly regarding the Bank of North America:

> How can we hope for public peace and national prosperity, if the faith of governments so solemnly pledged can be so lightly infringed? ... This hour of distress will come. It comes to all, and the moment of affliction is known to Him alone, whose Divine Providence exalts or depresses States and Kingdoms... in proportion to their obedience or disobedience of His just and holy laws.

John Jay, Chief Justice of New York, charged the Grand Jury of Ulster County, Sept. 8, 1777:

> The convention by whom that constitution was formed were of opinion that the gospel of Christ, like the ark of God, would not fall, though unsupported by the arm of flesh ...
>
> But let it be remembered that whatever marks of wisdom ... may be in your constitution, yet like the ... forms of our first parents before their Maker breathed into them the breath of life, it is yet to be animated ... from the people it must receive its spirit ...
>
> Vice, ignorance, and want of vigilance will be the only enemies able to destroy it ... Hence it becomes the common duty ... **to unite in repressing the licentious.**

Numbers 15:37:

> And the LORD spake unto Moses, saying, Speak unto the children of Israel ... that they make them fringes in the borders of their garments ... that ye may look upon it, and remember all the commandments of the LORD, and do them ... and THAT YE SEEK NOT AFTER YOUR OWN HEART AND YOUR OWN EYES, after which ye use to go a whoring.

HE WHO CONTROLS THE PURSE STRINGS HAS THE POWER

Someone who attempted to end Israel's self-rule earlier was Abimelech, the illegitimate son of Gideon. He usurped power and became a tyrant by taking money out of the city treasury and paying political agitators.

The Book of Judges tells of how Abimelech went to the city of Shechem and persuaded them to let him take public money kept in the pagan temple of Baal-Berith, and used it to hire thugs to murder his brothers.

Judges 9:4–5:

> So they gave him seventy shekels of silver from the Temple of Baal-Berith, with which Abimelech hired worthless and reckless men; and they followed him. Then he went to his father's (Gideon's) house at Ophrah and killed his brothers, the seventy sons of Jerubbaal (Gideon), on one stone. But Jotham the youngest son of Jerubbaal (Gideon) was left, because he hid himself.
>
> And all the men of Shechem gathered together, all of Beth Millo, and they went and made Abimelech king beside the terebinth tree at the pillar that was in Shechem. After several years, Abimelech was killed while assaulting a city and a woman dropped a stone from the tower on his head. Abimelech's tactic was used over and over again though history by aspiring tyrants who took money, often from the very people they desired to dominate, and using that money to hire "vain and worthless persons" to be thugs to defeat political opponents.

Later we will read how Philip of Macedon used money to bride citizens to betray the Athenian Democracy; and Julius Caesar raided the treasury to buy supporters against his political opponent, ending the Roman Republic.

"I GAVE YOU A KING IN MY ANGER"

Hosea 13:11: "I gave thee a king in mine anger." Israel descended into lawlessness. The First Book of Samuel 2:12-17, related how the High Priest Eli did not respect the Law to the same extent Moses did:

Now the sons of Eli were sons of Belial; they knew not the LORD. And the priests' custom with the people was, that, when any man offered sacrifice, the priest's servant came, while the flesh was in seething, with a fleshhook of three teeth in his hand; And he struck it into the pan, or kettle, or cauldron, or pot; all that the fleshhook brought up the priest took for himself ...

The priest's servant came, and said to the man that sacrificed, Give flesh to roast for the priest; for he will not have sodden flesh of thee, but raw.

And if any man said unto him, Let them not fail to burn the fat presently, and then take as much as thy soul desireth; then he would answer him,

Nay; but thou shalt give it to me now: and if not, I will take it by force. Wherefore the sin of the young men was very great before the LORD: for men abhorred the offering of the LORD.

I Samuel 2:27–36 recorded a prophet's rebuke of Eli:

And there came a man of God unto Eli, and said unto him ... Wherefore kick ye at my sacrifice and at mine offering, which I have commanded in my habitation; and honorest thy sons above me, to make yourselves fat with the chiefest of all the offerings of Israel my people?

Wherefore the LORD God of Israel saith, I said indeed that thy house, and the house of thy father, should walk before me forever: but now the LORD saith, Be it far from me; for them that honor me I will honor, and they that despise me shall be lightly esteemed.

Behold, the days come, that I will cut off thine arm, and the arm of thy father's house, that there shall not be an old man in thine house. And thou shalt see an enemy in my habitation, in all the wealth which God shall give Israel: and there shall not be an old man in thine house forever.

And the man of thine, whom I shall not cut off from mine altar, shall be to consume thine eyes, and to grieve thine heart: and all the increase of thine house shall die in the flower of their age.

And this shall be a sign unto thee, that shall come upon thy two sons, on Hophni and Phinehas; in one day they shall die both of them ... Every one that is left in thine house shall come and crouch to him for a piece of silver and a morsel of bread.

The High Priest Eli refused to change his ways, so another warning was delivered.

I Samuel 3:11–18:

And the LORD said to Samuel, Behold, I will do a thing in Israel, at which both the ears of every one that heareth it shall tingle. In that day I will perform against Eli all things which I have spoken concerning his house: when I begin, I will also make an end.

For I have told him that I will judge his house for ever for the iniquity which he knoweth; because his sons made themselves vile, and he restrained them not. And therefore I have sworn unto the house of Eli, that the iniquity of Eli's house shall not be purged with sacrifice nor offering forever.

And Samuel lay until the morning, and opened the doors of the house of the LORD. And Samuel feared to show Eli the vision. Then Eli called Samuel, and said, Samuel, my son. And he answered, Here am I. And he said, What is the thing that the LORD hath said unto thee? I pray thee hide it not from me: God do so to thee, and more also, if thou hide anything from me of all the things that he said unto thee.

And Samuel told him every whit, and hid nothing from him. And he said, It is the LORD: let him do what seemeth him good.

Samuel righteously led Israel, but unfortunately his owns sons grew up to act as bad as Eli's sons, resulting in the people clamoring for a king.

Moses had instructed in Exodus 18:21 "Thou shalt

provide out of all the people able men, such as fear God, men of truth, HATING COVETOUSNESS," but Samuel's sons "turned aside after lucre, and took bribes."

In the New Testament, Paul wrote to Titus "A bishop must be blameless, as the steward of God ... not given to filthy lucre (greedy for money)."

I Samuel 8:1–22:

> And it came to pass, when Samuel was old, that he made his sons judges over Israel ... And his sons walked not in his ways, but turned aside after lucre, and took bribes, and perverted judgment.
>
> Then all the elders of Israel gathered themselves together, and came to Samuel unto Ramah, And said unto him, Behold, thou art old, and thy sons walk not in thy ways: now make us a king to judge us like all the nations. But the thing displeased Samuel, when they said, Give us a king to judge us.

The response of the people was to reject altogether the system of self-rule. After repeated cycles of backsliding and repentance, this time, instead of repenting, the people demanded a king. Thomas Paine reflected on this in his third edition of *Common Sense*, Philadelphia, Feb. 14, 1776:

> About one hundred and thirty years after this, they fell again into the same error. The hankering which the Jews had for the idolatrous customs of the Heathens, is something exceedingly unaccountable; but so it was, that laying hold of the misconduct of Samuel's two sons, who were entrusted with some secular concerns, they came in an abrupt and clamorous manner to Samuel, saying,
>
> "Behold thou art old, and they sons walk not in thy ways, now make us a king to judge us like all the other nations."
>
> And here we cannot observe but that their motives were bad, namely, that they might be LIKE unto other nations, i.e. the Heathens, whereas their true glory lay in being as much UNLIKE them as possible.
>
> "But the thing displeased Samuel when they said, give us a King to judge us; and Samuel prayed unto

the Lord, and the Lord said unto Samuel, hearken unto the voice of the people in all that they say unto thee, for they have not rejected thee, but they have rejected Me, THAT I SHOULD NOT REIGN OVER THEM.

"According to all the works which they have done since the day that I brought them up out of Egypt even unto this day, wherewith they have forsaken me, and served other Gods: so do they also unto thee."

Then comes the warning of how a king with centralized power will take away their freedom, their children, and their property. Samuel described how they would regret it, detailing how the king would take complete control of their lives. Paine continued, quoting I Samuel 8:

"Now therefore hearken unto their voice, howbeit, protest solemnly unto them and show them the manner of the King that shall reign over them," (i.e. not of any particular King, but the general manner of the Kings of the earth whom Israel was so eagerly copying after. And notwithstanding the great distance of time and difference of manners, the character is still in fashion.)

"And Samuel told all the words of the Lord unto the people, that asked of him a King. And he said, This shall be the manner of the King that shall reign over you. He will take your sons and appoint them for himself for his chariots and to be his horsemen, and some shall run before his chariots" (this description agrees with the present mode of impressing men).

Instead of the people of Israel choosing their own leaders "to be rulers of thousands, and rulers of hundreds, rulers of fifties, and rulers of tens," the king "will appoint him captains over thousands, and captains over fifties." The king will take the land and redistribute it to those who support him. Paine continued from the Book of I Samuel:

"And he will appoint him captains over thousands and captains over fifties, will set them to clear his ground and to reap his harvest, and to make his instruments of war, and instruments of his chariots, And he will take your daughters to be confectionaries, and to be cooks, and to be bakers" (this describes the expense and luxury as well as the oppression of Kings)

"And he will take your fields and your vineyards, and your olive yards, even the best of them, and give them to his servants. And he will take the tenth of your seed, and of your vineyards, and give them to his officers and to his servants" (by which we see that bribery, corruption, and favoritism, are the standing vices of Kings)

"and he will take the tenth of your men servants, and your maid servants, and your goodliest young men, and your asses, and put them to his work: and he will take the tenth of your sheep, and ye shall be his servants, and ye shall cry out in that day because of your king which ye shell have chosen, AND THE LORD WILL NOT HEAR YOU IN THAT DAY."

This accounts for the continuation of Monarchy; neither do the characters of the few good kings which have lived since, either sanctify the title, or blot out the sinfulness of the origin; the high encomium of David takes no notice of him OFFICIALLY AS A KING, but only as a MAN after God's own heart.

Paine further quoted the Book of Samuel:

"Nevertheless the people refused to obey the voice of Samuel, and they said, Nay, but we will have a king over us, that we may be like all the nations, and that our king may judge us, and go out before us and fight our battles."

Samuel continued to reason with them but to no purpose; he set before them their ingratitude, but all would not avail; and seeing them fully bent on their folly, he cried out, "I will call unto the Lord, and he shall send thunder and rain" (which was then a punishment, being in the time of wheat harvest)

"that ye may perceive and see that your wickedness is great which ye have done in the sight of the Lord, IN ASKING YOU A KING. So Samuel called unto the Lord, and the Lord sent thunder and rain that day, and all the people greatly feared the Lord and Samuel. And all the people said unto Samuel, Pray for thy servants unto the Lord thy God that we die not, for WE HAVE ADDED UNTO OUR SINS THIS EVIL, TO ASK A KING."

These portions of scripture are direct and positive. They admit of no equivocal construction. That the Almighty hath here entered his protest against monarchical government is true, or the scripture is false.

I Samuel 8:21-22:

And Samuel heard all the words of the people, and he rehearsed them in the ears of the LORD. And the LORD said to Samuel, Hearken unto their voice, and make them a king. And Samuel said unto the men of Israel, Go ye every man unto his city.

Jonathan Mayhew, pastor of West Church in Boston, stated in a 1766 sermon on repealing the Stamp Tax:

Having been initiated in youth in the doctrines of civil liberty as they were taught by such men as Plato, Demosthenes, Cicero, and other renowned persons, among the ancients; and such as Sydney and Milton, Locke and Hoadley, among the moderns, I liked them; they seemed rational.

And having learned from the holy Scriptures that wise, brave, and virtuous men were always friends to liberty, – that God gave the Israelites a king in his anger, because they had not sense and virtue enough to like a free commonwealth, – and that where "the Spirit of the Lord is, there is liberty," – this made me conclude that freedom was a great blessing.

Israel was given a king as a judgment and punishment on them. On the spectrum of power, one side is "total government" and the other side is "no government." The "no government" side is anarchy if the people do not follow the law and **"every man did that which was right in his own eyes."** The Lord told Samuel: "They have not rejected thee, but they have rejected Me, that I should not reign over them."

The inference is that the Lord was ruling over them "from the bottom up," when each person knew and followed the Law taught to them by the priests and rabbis. Israel was punished by being given a king like all the other nations who ruled "from the top down." Out of Israel's chaos and anarchy, they got a despotic tyrant,

Saul changed citizens' highest character quality from **virtue** — the following of the Law taught to them by the priests — to **loyalty to the king,** where being **honored** by the king soon became prized above anything else, and disloyalty to the king was punishable by death.

I Samuel 22:6-10:

> When Saul heard that David was discovered... Saul said unto his servants ... All of you have conspired against me, and there is none that showeth me that my son hath made a league with the son of Jesse, and there is none of you that is sorry for me ... Then answered Doeg the Edomite ... said, I saw the son of Jesse coming to Nob, to Ahimelech ... and he inquired of the Lord for him, and gave him victuals, and gave him the sword of Goliath the Philistine.

Ahimelech and the priests were focused solely on their spiritual responsibilities, as this was the old system since the founding of the nation. They were not involved in politics and were completely unaware of the political rivalry that had arisen in between Saul and David. Their being uninvolved in politics cost them their lives.

I Samuel 22:11-16;

> Then the king sent to call Ahimelech the priest, the son of Ahitub, and all his father's house, the priests that were in Nob: and they came all of them to the king. And Saul said, Hear now, thou son of Ahitub. And he answered, Here I am, my lord.
>
> And Saul said unto him, Why have ye conspired against me, thou and the son of Jesse, in that thou hast given him bread, and a sword, and hast inquired of God for him, that he should rise against me, to lie in wait, as at this day?
>
> Then Ahimelech answered the king, and said, And who is so faithful among all thy servants as David, which is the king's son in law, and goeth at thy bidding, and is honorable in thine house?
>
> Did I then begin to inquire of God for him? be it far from me: let not the king impute any thing unto his servant, nor to all the house of my father: for thy

servant knew nothing of all this, less or more.

And the king said, Thou shalt surely die, Ahimelech, thou, and all thy father's house.

The soldiers of Saul hesitated carrying out his order, as they were still operating under the old system which respected the religious leaders.

I Samuel 22: 17:

And the king said unto the footmen that stood about him, Turn, and slay the priests of the Lord: because their hand also is with David, and because they knew when he fled, and did not show it to me. But the servants of the king would not put forth their hand to fall upon the priests of the Lord.

Saul turned to a non-Israelite to carry out his order.

I Samuel: 22:18-19:

And the king said to Doeg, Turn thou, and fall upon the priests. And Doeg the Edomite turned, and he fell upon the priests, and slew on that day fourscore and five persons that did wear a linen ephod. And Nob, the city of the priests, smote he with the edge of the sword, both men and women, children and sucklings, and oxen, and asses, and sheep, with the edge of the sword.

In nature, there are animals that are independent and those which can be domesticated. Jared Diamond described in *Guns, Germs, and Steel: The Fates of Human Societies* (W.W. Norton, 1997), that animals which exist in the wild as herds have a pecking order, with one being the leader and the others following. The domestication process involves a human master imprinting himself on the animals as the new herd leader, resulting in the rest following.

What Saul imprinted on Israel was in a sense gene-replacement therapy — he forced citizens with an independent-mentality, where each person is accountable to God; to transition to a herd-mentality with loyalty to the king. Like switching on an electric magnet, the metal filings of human behavior lined up into a conscienceless "yes-man" obedience to a king.

This switch is being implemented in the U.S. Military where soldiers are instructed to deny their impulse to defend the innocent and instead to surrender their consciences to the government and not interfere when witnessing Muslim men beating women or raping boys.

CNN's Jake Tapper reported, Sept. 28, 2015 that Sergeant 1st Class Charles Martland and Captain Daniel Quinn were disciplined by the Army for rescuing a young Afghan boy who had been tied to a post at the home of Afghan Local Police commander Abdul Rahman and raped repeatedly for up to two weeks. Captain Quinn ironically observed:

> The reason we were here is because we heard the terrible things the Taliban were doing to people, how they were taking away human rights ... But we were putting people into power who would do things that were worse than the Taliban did.

Lord Acton wrote:

> Despotic power is always accompanied by corruption of morality.

Lyman Beecher wrote in "Republicanism of the Bible":

> At the expiration of four hundred years, at the request of the nation, the executive authority was placed in the hands of a king, though not without being reproved for their folly, and warned of the encroachment on personal and public liberty, which would be the consequence. Before that, God himself had been the Supreme Executive.

Thomas Paine wrote in his third edition of *Common Sense*, Philadelphia, Feb. 14, 1776:

> In the early ages of the world, according to the scripture chronology there were no kings; the consequence of which was, there were no wars; it is the pride of kings which throws mankind into confusion ...
>
> Antiquity favors the same remark; for the quiet and rural lives of the first Patriarchs have a snappy something in them, which vanishes when we come to

the history of Jewish royalty.

Government by kings was first introduced into the world by the Heathens, from whom the children of Israel copied the custom. It was the most prosperous invention the Devil ever set on foot for the promotion of idolatry.

The Heathens paid divine honors to their deceased kings, and the Christian World hath improved on the plan by doing the same to their living ones. How impious is the title of sacred Majesty applied to a worm, who in the midst of his splendor is crumbling into dust!

As the exalting one man so greatly above the rest cannot be justified on the equal rights of nature, so neither can it be defended on the authority of scripture; for the will of the Almighty as declared by Gideon, and the prophet Samuel, expressly disapproves of government by Kings.

All anti-monarchical parts of scripture have been very smoothly glossed over in monarchical governments, but they undoubtedly merit the attention of countries which have their governments yet to form.

Paine continued:

Near three thousand years passed away, from the Mosaic account of the creation, till the Jews under a national delusion requested a king. Till then their form of government (except in extraordinary cases where the Almighty interposed) was a kind of Republic, administered by a judge and the elders of the tribes.

Kings they had none, and it was held sinful to acknowledge any being under that title but the Lord of Hosts. And when a man seriously reflects on the idolatrous homage which is paid to the persons of kings, he need not wonder that the Almighty, ever jealous of his honor, should disapprove a form of government which so impiously invades the prerogative of Heaven.

Samuel Adams wrote to Elbridge Gerry, Nov. 27, 1780:

Human nature, I am afraid, is too much debased to relish the republican principles... Mankind is prone to political idolatry.

Lyman Beecher continued:

Israel ... stands out conspicuous ... The first and only civil government which God ever instituted and administered ... is undeniably republican — securing religious and intellectual cultural, and liberty, and equality in the highest possible degree ... a republic free as ever existed ... adopted by the people — a nation of landholders - owners of the soil .. We are not more republican than they were.

Harvard President Samuel Langdon wrote in "Government Corrupted by Vice," May 31, 1775, which was distributed to the colonies in the Revolutionary War:

The Jewish government, according to the original constitution which was divinely established, if considered merely in a civil view, was a perfect republic. The heads of their tribes, and elders of their cities, were their counselors and judges.

They called the people together in more general or particular assemblies, took their opinions, gave advice, and managed the public affairs according to the general voice.

Counselors and judges comprehend all the powers of that government, for there was no such thing as legislative authority belonging to it, their complete code of laws being given immediately from God by the hand of Moses.

And let them who cry up the divine right of kings consider, that the only form of government which had a proper claim to a divine establishment, was so far from including the idea of a king, that it was a high crime for Israel to ask to be in this respect like other nations; and when they were thus gratified, it was rather as a just punishment of their folly, that they might feel the burdens of court pageantry, of which they were warned by a very striking description, than as a divine recommendation of kingly authority.

Every nation, when able and agreed, has a right to set up over itself any form of government which to it may appear most conducive to its common welfare.

The civil polity of Israel is doubtless an excellent

general model ... and orders of it may be copied, to great advantage, in more modern establishments.

When a government is in its prime, the public good engages the attention of the whole; the strictest regard is paid to the qualifications of those who hold the offices of the state; virtue prevails–everything is managed with justice, prudence, and frugality; the laws are founded on principles of equity rather than mere policy, and all the people are happy.

But vice will increase with the riches and glory of an empire; and this gradually tends to corrupt the constitution, and in time bring on its dissolution.

This may be considered not only as the natural effect of vice, but a righteous judgment of heaven, especially upon a nation which has been favored with the blessing of religion and liberty, and is guilty of undervaluing them; and eagerly going into the gratification of every lust.

Langdon continued:

> In this chapter the prophet describes the very corrupt state of Judah in his day, both as to religion and common morality; and looks forward to that increase of wickedness which would bring on their desolation and captivity.

They were a sinful nation, a people laden with iniquity, a seed of evil-doers, children that were corrupters, who had forsaken the Lord; and provoked the Holy One of Israel to anger.

The whole body of the nation, from head to foot, was full of moral and political disorders, without any remaining soundness. Their religion was all mere ceremony and hypocrisy; and even the laws of common justice and humanity were disregarded in their public courts.

They had counselors and judges, but very different from those at the beginning of the commonwealth. Their princes were rebellious against God, and the constitution of their country, and companions of thieves, giving countenance to every artifice for seizing the property of the subjects in their own hands, and robbing the public treasury.

Everyone loved gifts, and followed after rewards; they regarded the perquisites more than the duties of their office; the general aim was at profitable places and pensions; they were influenced in everything by bribery; and their avarice and luxury were never satisfied, but hurried them on to all kinds of oppression and violence, so that they even justified and encouraged the murder of innocent persons to support their lawless power, and increase their wealth.

And God, in righteous judgment, left them to run into all this excess of vice to their own destruction, because they had forsaken Him, and were guilty of willful inattention to the most essential parts of that religion which had been given them by a well-attested revelation from heaven.

The Jewish nation could not but see and feel the unhappy consequences of so great a corruption of the state. Doubtless, they complained much of men in power, and very heartily and liberally reproached them for their notorious misconduct. The public greatly suffered, and the people groaned and wished for better rulers and better management.

But in vain they hoped for a change of men and measures and better times, when the spirit of religion was gone, and the infection of vice was become universal. The whole body being so corrupted, there could be no rational prospect of any great reformation in the state, but rather of its ruin; which accordingly came on in Jeremiah's time.

Yet if a general reformation of religion and morals had taken place, and they had turned to God from all their sins—if they had again recovered the true spirit of their religion, God, by the gracious interpositions of His providence, would soon have found out methods to restore the former virtue of the state, and again have given them men of wisdom and integrity, according to their utmost wish, to be counselors and judges.

This was verified in fact, after the nation had been purged by a long captivity, and returned to their own land humbled, and filled with zeal for God and His law.

Yale President Ezra Stiles, May 8, 1783:

> The secular welfare of God's ancient people depended upon their virtue, their religion, their observance of that holy covenant, which Israel entered into with God ...
>
> Our system of ... civil polity would be imperfect without the true religion; or that from the diffusion of virtue among the people of any community would arise their greatest secular happiness.

Colonial Puritan leader Cotton Mather wrote in *Magnalia Christi Americana*, 1702:

> ⟩ Religion begat prosperity, and the daughter devoured the mother.

Benjamin Franklin wrote in *Poor Richard's Almanac*:

> ⟩ When prosperity was well mounted, she let go the bridle, and soon came tumbling out of the saddle.

Alexis de Tocqueville stated:

> Despotism may govern without faith, but liberty cannot. How is it possible that society should escape destruction if the moral tie is not strengthened in proportion as the political tie is relaxed? And what can be done with a people who are their own masters if they are not submissive to the Deity?

M. Stanton Evans wrote in *The Theme Is Freedom*:

> In essence, as the grip of Western faith has weakened, the old gods have come back. Hence not only astrology and Eastern cults, but abortion and euthanasia, the nature-worship of the environmental movement, homosexuality as an "alternative lifestyle," the jihad against expressions of our religion.
>
> Hence also, and most relevant to our central theme, the reemergence of the unlimited state and reduction of the individual. All bespeak a resurgence of the pagan worldview, and behaviors common to the pagan era.

Pope John Paul II wrote in *Centesimus Annus* (46):

> If there is no ultimate truth to guide and direct political activity, then ideas and convictions can

easily be manipulated for reasons of power. As history demonstrates, a democracy without values easily turns into open or thinly disguised totalitarianism.

Jonathan Mayhew preached a sermon, Jan., 1750:

Civil Tyranny is usually small in its beginning like "the drop of a bucket," till at length, like a mighty torrent, or the raging waves of the sea, it bears down all before it, and deluges whole countries and empires.

ISRAEL INFLUENCED AMERICA

Lyman Beecher referred to philosopher David Hume (1711-1776):

It is truly testified by Hume, that the Puritans introduced the elementary principles of republican liberty into the English constitution; and when they came to form colonial constitutions and laws ... they copied the principles of the constitution and laws of Moses. These elementary principles have gone into the Constitution of the Union, and every one of the States, and we have more consistent liberty than ever existed in all the world in all time, out of the Mosaic code ...

Let us ... hold on to our faith in God, that He will not permit the institutions of liberty which he has given to man for freedom, to perish from the earth... The Bible ... is the anchor of republics.

Columnist Don Feder gave an address titled "America And Israel–Two Nations Joined At the Heart," delivered to the Friends of Israel, Grand Rapids, MI, May 15, 2014:

Before there could be an America, there had to be an Israel ... At Sinai, the children of Israel voluntarily bound themselves to Mosaic Law. They agreed to recognize certain rights and assume certain responsibilities. It was the first time in history that rights were universally proclaimed. This was reflected in the commandment not to show partiality to the poor nor favor the powerful in judgment ...

In a world with slavery, exploitation of the weak and human sacrifice, this was a truly revolutionary doctrine. Israel was the first nation in history without a king. The period of the Judges lasted for 365 years – longer than the history of the United States to date. Ancient Israel provided the moral vision of Western Civilization, which eventually led to the founding of America, almost 1,700 years after the destruction of the Second Jewish Commonwealth ...

In the 17th century, a group of English settlers, called dissenters, came to these shores imbued with what can only be described as a Jewish worldview. No Christians have ever identified more closely with the People of the Book (as they called them) than the Pilgrims and Puritans who shaped our political institutions more than any other colonists. Cotton Mather, the great Puritan minister, wanted to make Hebrew the language of the Massachusetts Bay Colony.

They had made their own Exodus – leaving behind them the corruption of the Old World, separating themselves from their brethren in England, and coming here to establish a new Jerusalem. The Atlantic Ocean became their Red Sea, the American wilderness their Canaan and the Geneva Bible their stone tablets. That identification didn't end with the Colonial era.

In his Thanksgiving sermon of 1799, Abiel Tabbot of Andover, Massachusetts told his congregation: "It has often been remarked that the people of the United States come nearer to a parallel with Ancient Israel, than any other nation upon the globe. Hence –Our American Israel– is a term frequently used, and common consent allows it apt and proper."

In his first inaugural address, Thomas Jefferson referred to America as the "chosen country." The original design for the Great Seal of the United States – recommended by Jefferson, Adams and Franklin – showed the Children of Israel crossing the Red Sea, with the motto: "Resistance to tyrants is obedience to God."

The Liberty Bell, which tolled to herald the adoption of the Declaration of Independence, is inscribed with a verse from the Torah (Leviticus

25:10) "Proclaim Liberty throughout the Land unto all the Inhabitants thereof."

From our earliest history, the idea of covenant dominated American political thinking. While they were still aboard the Mayflower, the Pilgrims pledged to found their colony, "For the glory of God, the advancement of the Christian faith and the honor of King and country ... and by these presents solemnly and mutually in the presence of God and one another, covenant and combine ourselves together into a civil body politic ... "

Don Feder continued:

"The Declaration of Independence (America's founding document) was our most important covenant. In this regard, a paper by Daniel J. Elazer of the Jerusalem Center for Public Affairs ("Covenant and America's Founding") is worth quoting at length:

"The Declaration shares many of the characteristics of the classic Biblical covenant at Sinai. Central to this similarity is that the Declaration established the Americans as an organized people bound by a shared moral vision as well as common interests.

"The sense of an American identity, which had been emerging during the previous generation, was formalized and declared to the world much like the Sinai covenant had formally created the people Israel whose sense of shared identity and common destiny had emerged earlier but was concretized during the Exodus.

"Thus the opening paragraph of the Declaration asserts that Americans are no longer transplanted Englishmen, but a separate people entitled, like all peoples, to political independence. There is then a separation from another and a flight from Tyranny. The Americans, moreover, are held to be a single people made up of individuals bound in partnership in a common enterprise."

Like covenants of the Bible, God plays a central role in the Declaration of Independence. The opening paragraph speaks of our infant republic being entitled to assume "the separate and equal station to which the

Laws of Nature and of Nature's God entitle them." It then goes on to proclaim the concept of universal rights and establish their basis, "That all men are created equal, that they are endowed by their Creator with certain unalienable rights ... "

It closes "With a firm reliance on the protection of divine Providence, we mutually pledge our lives, our fortunes and our sacred honor." Just as Israel had to separate itself from Egypt, with the Declaration of Independence, America separated itself from Britain.

Don Feder added:

In the Declaration, God is acknowledged as the source of rights, as He is in Mosaic Law. By establishing a republic (the first in modern times), once again, America followed in Israel's footsteps. Remember, there was no king in Israel for almost four centuries.

Daniel Webster, who was born during the Revolution and was close to the Founding Fathers (intellectually as well as chronically) said of the Jews: "I feel, and have ever felt, respect and sympathy for all that remains of that extraordinary people who preserved through the darkness of so many centuries the knowledge of one supreme spiritual being ... "

Webster continued, and this is crucial, "The Hebrew Scriptures I regard as the fountain from which we draw all we know of the world around us, and of our own character and destiny as intelligent, moral and responsible beings." That knowledge of human nature and the way the world works, gained from the Torah, shaped our political values over the course of almost two centuries.

Often in our national saga, our leaders turned to the Bible to tell us what was in their hearts. On his way to Washington, D.C. for his inauguration in 1861, Abraham Lincoln stopped in Philadelphia to visit Independence Hall, America's Sinai.

Standing at the birthplace of our republic, Lincoln declared, "All my political warfare has been in favor of the teachings coming forth from that sacred hall."

In witness whereof, our 16th president paraphrased Psalm 137, "May my right hand forget its cunning, and may my tongue cleave to the roof of my mouth, if ever I prove false to those teachings."

Three tragic years later, speaking at the dedication of a cemetery at Gettysburg, Lincoln reminded his listeners that the Founding Fathers had brought forth, "A new nation conceived in liberty and dedicated to the proposition that all men are created equal ... " He ended with the prayer "That this nation, under God, shall have a new birth of freedom ... "

Don Feder concluded:

Starting with George Washington, nearly every president has taken his oath of office on a book which includes the story of the patriarchs and prophets, the Exodus, the encounter at Sinai, and the Ten Commandments. The history of Israel is in the marrow of our bones. It flows in our national bloodstream.

More that Athens and Rome – more than Roman Law and English Common Law – Israel shaped America. If Ancient Israel was instrumental in the founding of America, America was crucial to Israel's rebirth in 1948. It's somehow fitting that our support for the fledgling state was due to a president from the Bible Belt ...

There's another consideration worth noting: The enemies of Israel and the Jewish people have invariably been the enemies of America – from Nazism and communism, to Islamism. All of them hate the common ideals on which America and Israel were founded – human rights, equality before the law and tolerance.

On Feb. 5, 1996, Margaret Thatcher stated:

We have to remember that the Jewish people never, ever lost their faith in the face of all the persecution and as a result have come to have their own promised land and to have Jerusalem as a capital city again.

In April 3, 2002, while serving as House Majority Whip, Tom DeLay stated in a speech at Westminster College, titled "The Bonds of Freedom":

The State of Israel has fought five major wars to defend its right to exist since 1948 ... Israel and America are kindred nations. The founders of both countries were profoundly influenced by faith. Both countries drafted governments that practice religious tolerance. Both countries are filled with immigrants summoned by dreams ... Freedom is alive in Israel today. We can't allow the lone light of democracy to be extinguished by a wave of hatred.

Many U.S. Presidents expressed support of Israel, even as far back as John Adams, who wrote to Jefferson:

I will insist that the Hebrews have done more to civilize man than any other nation.

President John Adams stated:

I really wish the Jews again in Judea an independent nation for, as I believe, the most enlightened men of it have participated in the amelioration of the philosophy of the age.

President John Quincy Adams wrote to Major Mordecai Manuel Noah that he believed in: "rebuilding of Judea as an independent nation."

President Abraham Lincoln met a Canadian Christian Zionist, Henry Wentworth Monk, who expressed hope that Jews who were suffering oppression in Russia and Turkey be emancipated "by restoring them to their national home in Palestine." Lincoln said this was "a noble dream and one shared by many Americans."

In 1891, Russian Czar Alexander III incited pogroms against Jews, provoking an outcry by prominent Americans, including the Chief Justice of the Supreme Court and the Speaker of the House. A petition was presented by Cardinal Gibbons and Rev. William E. Blackstone to President Benjamin Harrison and Secretary of State James Blaine calling for the first international conference "to consider the Israelite claim to Palestine as their ancient home, and to promote in any other just and proper way the alleviation of their suffering condition."

In 1917, Lord Balfour sent a letter to Lord Rothschild,

president of the British Zionist Federation, stating that the British Government would facilitate the establishment of a national home for the Jewish people in Palestine.

President Woodrow Wilson stated March 3, 1919:

The allied nations with the fullest concurrence of our government and people are agreed that in Palestine shall be laid the foundations of a Jewish Commonwealth.

President Woodrow Wilson wrote:

Recalling the previous experiences of the colonists in applying the Mosaic Code to the order of their internal life, it is not to be wondered at that the various passages in the Bible that serve to undermine royal authority, stripping the Crown of its cloak of divinity, held up before the pioneer Americans the Hebrew Commonwealth as a model government.

In the spirit and essence of our Constitution, the influence of the Hebrew Commonwealth was paramount in that it was not only the highest authority for the principle, "that rebellion to tyrants is obedience to God," but also because it was in itself a divine precedent for a pure democracy, as distinguished from monarchy, aristocracy or any other form of government.

President Warren G. Harding stated:

It is impossible for one who has studied at all the services of the Hebrew people to avoid the faith that they will one day be restored to their historic national home and there enter on a new and yet greater phase of their contribution to the advance of humanity.

The U.S. House Foreign Affairs Committee reported 1922:

The Jews of America are profoundly interested in establishing a National Home in the ancient land for their race. Indeed, this is the ideal of the Jewish people, everywhere, for, despite their dispersion, Palestine has been the object of their veneration since they were expelled by the Romans. For generations they have prayed for the return to Zion. During the past century this prayer has assumed practical form.

President Calvin Coolidge stated:

The Jews themselves, of whom a considerable number were already scattered throughout the colonies, were true to the teachings of their prophets. The Jewish faith is predominantly the faith of liberty

President Calvin Coolidge expressed:

... sympathy with the deep and intense longing which finds such fine expression in the Jewish National Homeland in Palestine.

President Herbert Hoover stated:

Palestine which, desolate for centuries, is now renewing its youth and vitality through enthusiasm, hard work, and self-sacrifice of the Jewish pioneers who toil there in a spirit of peace and social justice.

President Harry S Truman stated May 26, 1952:

I had faith in Israel before it was established, I have faith in it now ... I believe it has a glorious future before it—not just another sovereign nation, but as an embodiment of the great ideals of our civilization.

President John F. Kennedy stated:

This nation, from the time of President Woodrow Wilson, has established and continued a tradition of friendship with Israel because we are committed to all free societies that seek a path to peace and honor individual right. In the prophetic spirit of Zionism all free men today look to a better world and in the experience of Zionism we know that it takes courage and perseverance and dedication to achieve it.

President Lyndon B. Johnson stated:

The United States and Israel share many common objectives ... chief of which is the building of a better world in which every nation can develop its resources and develop them in freedom and peace.

President Lyndon B. Johnson stated before the B'nai B'rith organization:

Most if not all of you have very deep ties with the land and with the people of Israel, as I do, for my Christian faith sprang from yours ... The Bible stories are woven into my childhood memories as the gallant struggle of modern Jews to be free of persecution is also woven into our souls.

President Richard M. Nixon stated of the United States: "Israel is one of its friends."

President Gerald Ford reaffirmed America's:

Commitment to the security and future of Israel is based upon basic morality as well as enlightened self-interest. Our role in supporting Israel honors our own heritage.

President Jimmy Carter stated:

The United States has a warm and a unique relationship of friendship with Israel that is morally right. It is compatible with our deepest religious convictions, and it is right in terms of America's own strategic interests. We are committed to Israel's security, prosperity, and future as a land that has so much to offer the world.

President Ronald Reagan stated:

Only by full appreciation of the critical role the State of Israel plays in our strategic calculus can we build the foundation for thwarting Moscow's designs on territories and resources vital to our security and our national well-being.

President Reagan stated:

Since the rebirth of the State of Israel, there has been an ironclad bond between that democracy and this one.

President George H.W. Bush stated:

The friendship, the alliance between the United States and Israel is strong and solid, built upon a foundation of shared democratic values, of shared history and heritage, that sustains the life of our two countries. The emotional bond of our people transcends politics. Our strategic cooperation—and I renew today our determination that that go forward—is a source of mutual security.

And the United States' commitment to the security

of Israel remains unshakable. We may differ over some policies from time to time, individual policies, but never over the principle.

President Bill Clinton stated:

Our relationship would never vary from its allegiance to the shared values, the shared religious heritage, the shared democratic politics which have made the relationship between the United States and Israel a special—even on occasion a wonderful—relationship.

President George W. Bush stated:

We will speak up for our principles and we will stand up for our friends in the world ... And one of our most important friends in the world is the State of Israel.

AWARENESS OF A JUST GOD NECESSARY

America's founders drew features from several past attempts of people trying to rule themselves without a king. Features drawn from Israel include the concept of everyone being created equal in the image of the Creator, inalienable rights from the Creator, and an internal law that each person is expected to follow, allowing for a more ordered society without a strong external ruler.

One may suggest rules of ethics without reference to a God. Unfortunately, human nature is selfish, and though a small minority of people may be ethical for ethics sake, a large percentage of people are motivated by positive or negative consequences. There is no greater positive consequence than eternal happiness and no greater negative consequence than eternal damnation.

The continual awareness of God being everywhere, seeing every action, knowing every thought, and holding each person accountable in a future judgment fosters an informed "conscience" which motivates people to follow God's Law even when there are no police around.

This allows for the country to maintain an outward

order because the people have inward self-control, voluntarily modifying their behavior.

Under the oft cited, and vague justification of the "war on terror," governmental control over the general public is amassing at a dramatic rate through massive and comprehensive data collection on all citizens.

This can be seen today with the NSA (National Security Administration) creating a continual awareness that the U.S. Government is saving as "metadata" everyone's emails, Facebook postings, text messages, phone calls and credit card purchases, holding each person potentially accountable in a "future judgment" for their politically incorrect or anti-government sentiments. Information is power, and such power in the wrong hands will most likely be abused.

The more citizens become aware of "big government" surveillance, the more they respond by voluntarily modifying their behavior, self-censoring their emails and postings, in hopes of avoiding future "judgments" of audits, fines or persecution.

The Judeo-Christian concept of an unchanging God means that his Laws are unchanging and gives stability to society that a capricious and unpredictable god cannot give. The God of the Bible has these qualities: being omniscient (all-knowing); omnipresent (everywhere); omnipotent (all-powerful); eternal; and immutable (unchanging).

The Bible concept of God is a Supreme Being who is truthful, keeps His word, hates lying and deceit, and fosters truthfulness in those wanting to please Him.

On the contrary, a non-Bible god is unpredictable, can be deceitful and pretentious, and will foster deception and lying among its devotees. Pagan deities throughout history tend to support hierarchical systems, social castes or classes, even racist systems which pridefully teach adherents that they are superior to unbelievers or infidels.

The concept of a just God who has no favorites, who made every person equal in His image, who wants everyone to love their neighbor as themselves and treat others as they would want to be treated – this concept influences society to be humane and fair to each member.

The concept of a God who gives each person a free will gives rise to the idea that people should be convinced by logical persuasion, not subdued by threat of death or dismemberment, as is common in Islamic sharia countries.

Hinduism has an elaborate system of reincarnation which is generally based on a system of retribution, where one's actions in life affect one's status in the next. Buddhism has a system of karma, where the way one treats others will affect how one ends up being treated.

These impersonal systems are based on a kind of spiritual law where "what goes around comes around" or as the Bible verse observed, "whatever a man soweth, that shall he reapeth." These systems of cause and effect, or action and consequence, provide an internal set of rules, but are impersonal, whereas the Judeo-Christian system is based on a Creator, in whose image everyone is made, who desires an intensely personal loving relationship with each of His children by their own voluntary, free will.

James Madison wrote to Frederick Beasley, Nov. 1825:

> The belief in a God All Powerful, wise and good, is so essential to the moral order of the World and to the happiness of man, that arguments which enforce it cannot be drawn from too many sources nor adapted with too much solicitude to the different characters and capacities to be impressed with it.

Dwight Eisenhower, Feb. 20, 1955, stated for the American Legion Back-To-God Program:

> The Founding Fathers expressed in words for all to read the ideal of Government based upon the dignity of the individual. That ideal previously had existed only in the hearts and minds of men.
>
> They produced the timeless documents upon which the Nation is grounded and has grown great. They, recognizing God as the author of individual rights, declared that the purpose of Government is to secure

those rights.

To you and to me this ideal of Government is a self-evident truth. But in many lands the State claims to be the author of human rights. The tragedy of that claim runs through all history and, indeed, dominates our own times.

If the State gives rights, it can – and inevitably will – take away those rights. Without God, there could be no American form of Government, nor an American way of life. Recognition of the Supreme Being is the first – the most basic – expression of Americanism.

Thus the Founding Fathers saw it, and thus, with God's help, it will continue to be. It is significant, I believe, that the American Legion – an organization of war veterans – has seen fit to conduct a "Back to God" movement as part of its Americanism program.

Veterans realize, perhaps more clearly than others, the prior place that Almighty God holds in our national life. And they can appreciate, through personal experience, that the really decisive battleground of American freedom is in the hearts and minds of our own people ...

Each day we must ask that Almighty God will set and keep His protecting hand over us so that we may pass on to those who come after us the heritage of a free people, secure in their God-given rights and in full control of a Government dedicated to the preservation of those rights.

America's founders drew many ideas from the Bible in formulating their system of self-government. They also drew ideas from other experiments at self-rule, namely, the democracy of Athens, the republic of Rome, and the English common law and Magna Carta.

Ancient Israel often failed in the attempt to rule itself without a king and reverted back to a monarchy similar to the rest of the world. Yale President Ezra Stiles addressed Connecticut's General Assembly, May 8, 1783:

A discourse upon the political welfare of God's American Israel ... Our system of dominion and civil polity would be imperfect without the true religion... From the diffusion of virtue among the people of any community would arise their greatest secular happiness ...

All the forms of civil polity have been tried by mankind, except one, and that seems to have been reserved in Providence to be realized in America.

Most of the states, of all ages ... have been founded in rapacity (aggressive greed), usurpation, and injustice; so that in the contests recorded in history, the public right is a dubious question – it being rather certain that it belongs to neither of the contending parties – the military history of all nations being but a description of the wars and invasions of the mutual robbers and devastators of the human race.

The invasion of the lawless Macedonian (Alexander the Great), who effected the dissolution of the Medo-Persian empire; the widespread Roman conquests; the inundation of the Goths and Vandals; the descents of the Tartars on China; the triumphs of Tamerlane, Ulugh-beg, and Aurengzebe;

and the widespread dominion of the imposter of Mecca, with his successors, the Caliphs and Mamelukes, down to Kouli-Kan, who dethroned his prince, and plundered India of two hundred millions sterling – these, I say ... were all founded in unrighteousness and tyrannical usurpation.

The real interest of mankind, and the public good, has been generally overlooked. It has really been very indifferent to the great cause of right and liberty which of the belligerent powers prevailed – a Tangrolipix or a Mahomet, an Augustus or an Antony, a Scipio or a Hannibal, a Brennus or an Antiochus – tyranny being the sure portion ...

The respective territories to the first nations, was so of God as to give them a divine right defensively to resist the Nimrods and Ninuses (Assyrian conqueror-founder of Nineveh), the first invading tyrants of the ancient ages ...

But after the spirit of conquest had changed the first governments, all the succeeding ones have, in general, proved one continued series of injustice, which has reigned in all countries for almost four thousand years. These have so changed property, laws, rights, and liberties ...

We can only say that there still remains in the body of the people at large ... a power, with which they are invested by the Author of their being, to wrest government out of the hands of reigning tyrants, and originate new policies, adapted to the conservation of liberty ...

But what is the happiest form of civil government... Almost all the polities may be reduced to hereditary dominion, in either a monarchy or aristocracy, and these supported by a standing army ...

Civil dominion, though often wisely administered, is so modeled as to be beyond the control of those for whose end God instituted government.

But a democratical polity for millions, standing upon the broad basis of the people at large, amply charged with property, has not hitherto been exhibited.

"FROM A MERE MOB" TO "LAWS FAR SUPERIOR" TO ANY OTHER NATION

Harvard President Samuel Langdon stated in his address, "The Republic of the Israelites an Example to the American States," June 5, 1788:

Israel had both a civil and military establishment under divine direction, and a complete body of judicial laws drawn up and delivered to them by Moses in God's name.

They had also a form of religious worship ... designed to preserve among them the knowledge of the great Creator of the Universe, and teach them to love and serve him; while idolatry prevailed through the rest of the world ... this religion contained ... a... very concise, system of morals, comprehended in ten commands, which require the perfection of godliness, benevolence, and rectitude of conduct ...

A government, thus settled on republican principles, required laws; without which it must have degenerated immediately into aristocracy, or absolute monarchy ...

How unexampled was this quick progress of the Israelites, from abject slavery, ignorance, and almost total want of order, to a national establishment perfected in all its parts far beyond all other kingdoms and States! from a mere mob, to a well regulated nation, under a government and laws far superior to what any other nation could boast! ...

Upon a review of what has been said, must it not appear quite unaccountable, that the Israelites should so speedily attain to such an height of good policy and legislation, beyond all other nations? Are we not constrained to acknowledge an intermediate interposition and direction of heaven?

Had the unexperienced multitude been left to themselves to draw up a system of civil and military government for themselves, it would have been entirely beyond their abilities to comprehend so complicated a subject; they must have committed innumerable mistakes, in attempting to introduce and establish it; they would have been in danger of jarring opinions, tumults, and insurrections; and probably before the design could be effected, discouragement and confusion would have forced them to surrender into the hands of despotism.

But their God provided everything necessary for their happiness, and nothing more was left to their own wisdom than to submit to his authority, and adhere strictly to his commands: by this, their reputation among the nations would have been equal to the excellency of their laws.

Langdon continued:

Now by the foregoing view of the general state of the nation during the time of the judges, we may plainly see the reason why, instead of rising to fame by the perfection of their polity, religion, and morals, their character sunk into contempt.

But let us see whether they conducted better

afterwards, under their kings. It was their crime to demand such a king as was like the kings of other nations, i.e. a king with the same absolute power, to command all according to his own pleasure.

In this view God only was their king, and the head of the nation was only to be his vice-regent.

Therefore as they had implicitly rejected the divine government, God gave them a king in his anger; the consequence of which was, the total loss of their republican form of government, and sad experience of the effects of despotic power.

Indeed their religious establishment, which had been very much impaired in the days of the judges, was restored, and brought to its greatest glory, by David the most pious, and Solomon the wisest of kings; and during their reigns, the nation gained the height of grandeur; but no national senate was appointed, and the power of the kings continued to be despotic, and so the days of their prosperity were soon over.

As soon as Rehoboam ascended the throne he openly avowed the most despotic principles, so that ten tribes revolted, and made Jeroboam their king ...

Langdon stated further:

Nor is it to be wondered at that false religion so easily gained ground; for the people grew very ignorant: no care was taken to instruct them, in their several cities, in the law of God; but, being without teachers, they were very little acquainted with their own religious institutions.

For this reason when good king Jehoshaphat resolved upon a reformation in church and state, after having taken a circuit thro' his kingdom to "bring the people back to the Lord God of their fathers, he sent out some of his principal officers, with priests and Levites, to teach the people in the cities of Judah; and these carried the book of the law with them, and went about throughout all the cities of Judah, and taught them that religion which God commanded by Moses."

It likewise appears by what immediately follows

this account of his proceedings, that there had been a long omission of the administration of justice in the cities; that no courts had been kept up by the preceding kings, or such as were corrupt, in which the judges paid little regard to law and equity: for the king "set judges in the land, throughout all the fenced cities of Judah, city by city, and said unto the judges, take heed what ye do, for ye judge not for man but for the Lord, who is with you in the judgment: – wherefore now let the fear of Lord be upon you, take heed and do it, for there is no iniquity with the Lord our God, nor respect of persons, nor taking of gifts."

Repeated attempts were made by the few pious kings, to put a stop to the corruption of religion and morals; but all in vain; the people relapsed again and again into ignorance, idolatry, and wickedness: their vices had increased to the utmost degree of enormity in Jeremiah's time; and their complicated crimes at length brought upon them desolation and a long captivity.

Langdon stated further:

And now let us just take a glance at their general state after the captivity in Babylon.

When they returned to their own land they endeavored to conform their religion and government to the mosaic standard; idolatry was entirely purged out; they discovered great zeal for the law of their God and the instituted worship; they appointed a general senate of seventy elders, called by them the Sanhedrin, with a supreme magistrate at the head, for the government of the nation; and while their pious zeal continued they grew and prospered.

But, according to the common course of things in the world ... the affairs of state were badly administered, and the highest honors were gained by favor, bribery, or violence; hypocrisy was substituted in the room of the true fear of God, and the practice of righteousness; all the vices natural to mankind daily increased ...

Therefore upon the whole view we see, that the Israelites never attained to that fame and dignity among the nations which their constitution encouraged them to expect, because they took little care to practice agreeably to the good statutes and judgments given them by Moses.

Their constitution both of government and religion was excellent in writing, but was never exemplified in fact.

WHO LED OUR FOREFATHERS AS ISRAEL OF OLD

Jefferson stated in his Second Inaugural, March 4, 1805:

I shall need, too, the favor of that Being in whose hands we are, who led our forefathers, as Israel of old, from their native land and planted them in a country flowing with all the necessities and comforts of life.

George Washington wrote to the Hebrew Congregations of the city of Savannah, Georgia, 1790:

May the same wonder-working Deity, who long since delivering the Hebrews from their Egyptian Oppressors planted them in the promised land whose Providential Agency has lately been conspicuous in establishing these United States as an independent Nation – still continue to water them with the dews of Heaven and to make the inhabitants of every denomination participate in the temporal and spiritual blessings of that people whose God is Jehovah.

John Jay, as Chief Justice of the State of New York, gave a charge to the Grand Jury of Ulster County, Sept. 8, 1777:

The infatuated sovereign of Britain, forgetful that kings ... ought to be the fathers, not the incendiaries of their people, hath, by destroying our former constitutions, enabled us to erect more eligible systems of government on their ruins ...

This glorious revolution ... is distinguished by so many marks of the Divine favor and interposition, that no doubt can remain of its being ... supported in a manner so singular, and I may say miraculous, that when future ages shall read its history they will be tempted to consider a great part of it as fabulous ...

Will it not appear extraordinary that thirteen colonies ... divided by variety of governments and manners, should immediately become one people, and though without funds, without magazines, without disciplined troops, in the face of their enemies, unanimously determine to be free, and, undaunted by the power of Britain, refer their cause to the justice of the Almighty, and resolve to repel force by force, thereby presenting to the world an illustrious example of magnanimity and virtue scarcely to be paralleled?

However incredible these things may in the future appear, we know them to be true ...

The many remarkable and unexpected means and events by which our wants have been supplied and our enemies repelled or restrained, are such strong and striking proofs of the interposition of Heaven, that our having been hitherto delivered from the threatened bondage of Britain ought, like the emancipation of the Jews from Egyptian servitude, to be forever ascribed to its true cause.

On June 11, 1630, aboard the Arbella, John Winthrop wrote A Model of Christian Charity, which became a guideline for future constitutional covenants of the Colonies:

We shall find that the God of Israel is among us, when ten of us shall be able to resist a thousand of our enemies, when He shall make us a praise and glory, that men of succeeding plantations shall say, "The Lord make it like that of New England."

Yale President Ezra Stiles addressed Connecticut's General Assembly, May 8, 1783:

The American states; their interior as well as exterior civil and jural polities are so nearly perfect, that the rights of individuals, even to numerous millions, are guarded and secured.

The crown and glory of our confederacy is the amphictyonic council (league of ancient Greek city-states) of the General Congress, standing on the annual election of the united respective states, and revocable at pleasure.

This lays the foundation of a permanent union in the American Republic, which may at length convince the world that, of all the policies to be found on earth ... the most perfect one has been invented and realized in America ... So that symbol of union, the American flag, with its increasing stripes and stars, may have an equally combining efficacy for ages.

Ben Franklin stated:

May the God of Wisdom, Strength and Power, the Lord of the Armies of Israel, inspire us with Prudence in this Time of Danger.

On July 13, 1775, Gov. Jonathan Trumbull wrote from Lebanon, Connecticut, to the Gen. George Washington, had recently been placed in command of the Continental Army:

May the God of the armies of Israel shower down the blessings of his Divine Providence on you, give you wisdom and fortitude, cover your head in the day of battle and danger.

In August of 1776, General Washington gave a desperate plea for reinforcements. Governor Jonathan Trumbull sent out an appeal, calling for nine more regiments of volunteers:

To trust altogether to the justice of our cause, without our utmost exertion, would be tempting Providence ... May the Lord of Hosts, the God of the armies of Israel, be your Captain, your Leader, your Conductor, and Saviour.

Don Feder wrote in "Patriot's Prayer–A Statement of Conviction," Dec. 3, 2010:

I believe Israel and America share a unique bond. In the course of human history, they are the only two nations where the vision preceded possession of the land. American values stretch back to Sinai, and come to the West through Jerusalem, Rome and Geneva. Absent Ancient Israel's encounter with God, there would have been no America. To turn our back on Israel would be to betray ourselves.

TIMELINE 1285–594 BC

1285 BC – Khumbannumena, King of the Middle Elamite (Persian) Anzanite Dynasty

1265 BC – Shalmaneser I, King of the Middle Assyrian Empire

1250 BC – King Agamemnon of Mycenea gathers Greeks to sail and conquer Troy on the eastern end of the Hittite Empire, after which 'Sea Peoples', most likely the Greeks, raided and destroyed the Hittite Empire.

1250 BC – Wu Ding, Emperor of China's Shang (Yin) Dynasty LARGEST EMPIRE IN THE WORLD TO THIS DATE, SURPASSING ALL PREVIOUS ONES.

1125 BC – Nebuchadnezzar I, King of the 2nd Isin Dynasty, Babylonian Empire

1122 BC – Shang Zhou, Emperor of China's Shang Dynasty, LARGEST EMPIRE IN THE WORLD TO THIS DATE, SURPASSING ALL PREVIOUS ONES.

1080 BC – Tiglath-Pileser I, Middle Assyrian Empire.

1046 BC – Wu of Zhao, Emperor of China's Western Zhou Dynasty, LARGEST EMPIRE IN THE WORLD TO THIS DATE, SURPASSING ALL PREVIOUS ONES.

970 BC – Solomon of Kingdom of Israel.

900 BC – Po Ngbe, Ruler of the Olmec (Rubber People) of Mesoamerica.

771 BC – Emperor Ping, China's Eastern Zhou Dynasty

764 BC – Sarduri II, King of the Urartu Empire (Kingdom of Van) Caucasus Mountains

745 BC – Tiglath-Pileser III, King of the Neo-Assyrian Empire, LARGEST EMPIRE IN THE WORLD AT THIS DATE, SURPASSING ALL PREVIOUS ONES.

742 BC – Huban-nugash, Ruler of Neo-Elamite Empire

700 BC – Sennacherib – Neo-Assyrian Empire, largest in the world at the time.

690 BC – Taharqa, Nubian Pharaoh of Egypt's 25th

Dynasty, African Kush (Sudan)

622 BC – Draco, King of Athens

611 BC – Nebuchadnezzar II, King of Neo-Babylonian Empire

610 BC – Necho II, Pharaoh of Egypt's 26th Dynasty

594 BC – Solon, chief magistrate of Athens, instituted reforms which led to the Athenian Democracy

∽

GREEK CITY–STATE OF ATHENS

The Greek word for city is "polis" which is the root of "politics." Lord Acton wrote:

> The Laws of Plato, the Politics of Aristotle, are, if I may trust my own experience the books from which we may learn the most about the principles of politics.

Lord Acton wrote:

> Politics = the ethics of public life.

Draco was the King of Athens in 622 BC. He was the first to put their laws down in writing. Unfortunately, these laws were so harsh that they gave birth to the term "draconian."

Athens got a new leader in 594 BC named Solon. As the chief magistrate, called archon, Solon instituted reforms which led to the Athenian Democracy.

John F. Kennedy referred to Solon in his address to the American Newspaper Publishers Association at the Waldorf-Astoria Hotel, New York, April 27, 1961:

> For I have complete confidence in the response and dedication of our citizens whenever they are fully informed ... This Administration intends to be candid about its errors; for, as a wise man once said: "An error doesn't become a mistake until you refuse to correct it."
>
> We intend to accept full responsibility for our errors; and we expect you to point them out when we miss them. Without debate, without criticism, no Administration and no country can succeed—and

no republic can survive. That is why the Athenian law-maker Solon decreed it a crime for any citizen to shrink from controversy.

In order to have the people operate in these democratic reforms, Solon left Athens for ten years, visiting Egypt, Persia and Lydia. Solon's "democracy" worked in Athens for around 6 years, till political confusion allowed Pisistratus to usurp power as a tyrant. Montesquieu wrote in *The Spirit of the Laws*, Book 2, Chapter 2:

> When the body of the people is possessed of the supreme power, this is called a democracy. When the supreme power is lodged in the hands of a part of the people, it is then an aristocracy. In a democracy the people are in some respects the sovereign, and in others the subject. There can be no exercise of sovereignty but by their suffarages (votes), which are their own will. Now, the sovereign's will is the sovereign himself.
>
> The laws, therefore, which establish the right of suffrage, are fundamental to this government. And, indeed, it is as important to regulate, in a republic, in what manner, by whom, to whom, and concerning what, suffrages are to be given, as it is, in a monarchy, to know who is the prince, and after what manner he ought to govern.

Winston Churchill addressed the House of Commons, Nov. 11, 1947:

> Many forms of government have been tried, and will be tried in this world of sin and woe. No one pretends that democracy is perfect or all-wise. Indeed, it has been said that democracy is the worst form of government except all those other forms that have been tried from time to time.

In 525 BC, Cleisthenes became archon and attempted to return to the democratic reforms of Solon. Cleisthenes' brother, Hippocrates, had a famous grandson named Pericles. Pericles led Athens during its Golden Age (461–429 BC), which was the period between the Persian War (478 BC) and the end of the Peloponnesian War

(404 BC). A famous general, Pericles won many battles. He succeeded in having his political enemies ostracized, which means forced out of the city for ten years.

Pericles centralized power, moved the treasury of the Delian League from Delos to Athens, and then raided it for his ambitious building projects, such as the Parthenon.

When the governing body in Athens, called ecclesia, considered prosecuting Pericles for maladministration of funds, he resorted to diverting public attention away from him by allowing relations with Sparta to devolved into the Peloponnesian War. This became the standard practice of usurping leaders who came under public scrutiny as it benefited them in two ways:

> 1) the country falling into a war or a national crisis would divert public attention away from their corruption;
>
> 2) the country always wants a strong leader in times of war or national crisis.

During the period from Solon in 594 BC up to the time Philip of Macedon took control in 338 BC, Athens fluctuated between the rule of a democracy and the rule of tyrants. In the democracy of Athens, everybody, everyday, had to go the agora marketplace and talk politics. Those not keeping up with the politics were called "idiotes."

Plato stated:

> Those who are too smart to engage in politics are punished by being governed by those who are dumber.

John F. Kennedy continued addressing the American Newspaper Publishers Association, April 27, 1961:

> And that is why our press was protected by the First Amendment—the only business in America specifically protected by the Constitution—not primarily to amuse and entertain, not to emphasize the trivial and the sentimental, not to simply "give the public what it wants"—but to inform, to arouse, to reflect, to state our dangers and our opportunities, to indicate our crises and our choices, to lead, mold, educate and sometimes even anger public opinion ...

It means ... that government at all levels, must meet its obligation to provide you with the fullest possible information outside the narrowest limits of national security—and we intend to do it ...

And that is our obligation to inform and alert the American people—to make certain that they possess all the facts that they need, and understand them as well—the perils, the prospects, the purposes of our program and the choices that we face.

The citizens of Athens were meant to work out solutions, Aristotle wrote in *Politics*: "Man is by nature a political animal." A way of promoting political agendas was developed that was different from monarchies.

In a monarchy, if someone had an agenda, they needed to get in to see the king in order to pitch it. This often required bribing the doorkeepers. In China, Mandarin eunuchs kept the Emperor's harem, which sometimes number in the thousands. Mandarins were the doorkeepers for those wanting an audience with the Emperor, and would often demand bribes for their favors.

In democracies, there were no Emperors, as the people made the decisions. The question then arises, how does one pitch an agenda to the entire city? The answer was theater.

∽

GREEK THEATER

Whereas Israel was ruled by laws that were of a divine origin, the Greeks were ruled by laws formed by "general consensus." Those, therefore, who had a political agenda were motivate to develop methods to influence the "general consensus." These methods included: persuasion, propaganda, control of information, manipulation, ridicule, intimidation, and fear-mongering.

One of the ways to influence "general consensus" was theater. Greeks built elaborate outdoor amphitheaters and put on plays, called comedies, satyrs, and tragedies. In these plays, they would praise certain points of view and ridicule others, thus swaying the citizens. In tragedies, particular individuals, groups, or behaviors would be portrayed with honor and respect. In comedies and satyrs, other individuals, groups, or behaviors would be portrayed as foolish, backwards, out-of-step, and simpletons.

The citizens of Athens would leave the amphitheater thinking, "I want to hold the views of the person who was honored," or "I do not want to be like that person who was ridiculed." Saul Alinsky understood this tactic, writing:

> Ridicule is man's most potent weapon ... Pick the target, freeze it, personalize it, and polarize it.

The Athenian leader Pericles paid for the poor to attend the theater, not because he wanted to entertain them, but because he understood it was a way to sway their opinions.

In modern-day application, if one thinks of their favorite movie, sitcom, or television series, there will be a character that they identify with as cute, funny or the hero. As the movie or series progresses, this character begins to make morally compromising decisions, such as lying, cheating, getting revenge, or yielding to lust. The longer one watches, the more they begin to apologize for that character's immoral actions and accept them as normal, thinking to themselves, I know James Bond is with women he is not married to, but he is about to save the world, so can we get on with the story. Thus, highly held moral values are minimized and diminished.

Then the movie, sitcom, or television series portrays actors holding traditional views as being backwards, buffoons, or even hateful. The viewer feels embarrassed for holding the same views and is peer pressured to modify their behavior to refrain from expressing their views publicly, as mentioned earlier in the "spiral of silence" effect. An insider Hollywood comedic tactic has been to "make them laugh at what they hold sacred."

If one watches these movies, sitcoms or television series long enough, one's views will lean in the direction of those who write the scripts, own the studios, or buy the advertising which underwrites the programs.

Edward L. Bernays described in *The Engineering of Consent* (1947) how leaders use media to manipulate voters:

> Any ... organization depends ultimately on public approval, and is therefore faced with the problem of engineering the public's consent ... We expect our elected government officials to try to engineer our consent ... for the measures they propose ...

> The average American adult has only six years of schooling behind him. With pressing crises and decisions to be faced, a leader frequently cannot wait for the people to arrive at even a general understanding...

> Democratic leaders must play their part in leading the public through the engineering of consent ... This role naturally imposes upon them the obligation to use the educational process, as well as other available techniques.

As mentioned earlier, in Athens and in America:

–The COUNTRY is controlled by LAWS

–LAWS are controlled by POLITICIANS

–POLITICIANS are controlled by VOTERS

–VOTERS are controlled by PUBLIC OPINION

–PUBLIC OPINION is controlled by MEDIA
   & EDUCATION.

So whoever controls MEDIA & EDUCATION
   controls the COUNTRY!

George Orwell wrote in *Nineteen Eighty-Four*:

> The invention of print, however, made it easier to manipulate public opinion, and the film and the radio carried the process further.

Edward Bernays wrote in *The Engineering of Consent*:

> We must recognize the significance of modern communication not only as a highly organized mechanical web but as a potent force for social good or possible evil ... By mastering the techniques of communication can leadership be exercised in the vast complex that is modern democracy in the United States.

Theater, media and communications are always political in a nation where the people make the decisions.

RHETORIC: ETHOS – LOGOS – PATHOS

Another Greek tactic of persuading the people was "rhetoric." Greek philosopher Aristotle considered rhetoric "the faculty of observing in any given case the available means of persuasion." Aristotle wrote in *Rhetoric* (translated by W. Rhys Roberts, I:4:1359):

> Rhetoric is a combination of the science of logic and of the ethical branch of politics.

To be a king, all one really has to be good at is intimidation and inspiring fear. Those who are afraid of the king do his bidding, including killing those who do not obey the king. The ripples go out to the entire kingdom. Montesquieu wrote in *The Spirit of the Laws*, 1748:

> As virtue is necessary in a republic ... so fear is necessary in a despotic government ... Fear must therefore depress their spirits, and extinguish even the least sense of ambition ... History informs us that the horrid cruelties of (Roman Emperor) Domitian struck such a terror into the governors ... Such are the principles ... in a particular despotic government by fear.

When a society changes from the people ruling themselves to being ruled by a king, it is like electrons that suddenly become charged and line up from the top to bottom of the empire of individuals vying for positions of patronage handed down from the king.

Muslim Sultans controlled subjects through fear and terror. Ivan the Terrible killed his own son and horribly slaughtered 60,000 in his conquest of the Russian Republic of Novgorod. Robespierre ruled in France with a Reign of Terror. Robespierre controlled France's "Committee of Public Safety," giving a speech to the National Assembly, Feb. 5, 1794, titled "The Terror Justified":

> Lead ... the enemies of the people by terror ...Terror is nothing else than swift, severe, indomitable justice.

Machiavelli wrote:

> Since it is difficult to join them together, it is safer to be feared than to be loved when one of the two must be lacking ...

> It is better to be feared than loved, if you cannot be both ...

> Men shrink less from offending one who inspires love than one who inspires fear.

By contrast, in a democracy, in order to rise in leadership one needs a different set of skills, namely, persuasion. Greeks developed the persuasive techniques of: ethos, logos and pathos.

ETHOS – from where the word "ethics" comes from, is the credibility, trustworthiness and expertise of the person doing the speaking. This has come down to us as the introduction of someone before they give their talk. If the audience knows nothing about the speaker, they may not take what the speaker says very seriously.

The more impressive their reputation, the more persuaded the audience will be. But if the speaker is introduced as someone of great reputation, with a long list of impressive credentials, achievements, awards and distinctions, the audience's estimation of the speaker is elevated and they take what speaker says more seriously.

LOGOS – from where the word "logic" comes from, is the presentation of facts in a convincing way. It appeals to the mind and intellect. Conservatives are said to rely solely on dry, unemotional statistics.

PATHOS – from where the word "passion" comes from, is the appeal to the emotions. It is usually personal stories, where feelings are swayed. Liberals are said to rely largely on this touchy-feely, heartwarming or heart-wrenching appeal. Aristotle stated:

> No appeal to logic is ever successful without an appeal to emotion.

To gain power in a country where the people rule, one has to persuade the people, and it is helpful to be skilled in the techniques of rhetoric.

Athens' famous general Pericles (495–429 BC) was skilled in the use of rhetoric. He had charisma as a persuasive speaker verging on manipulation. Pericles was able to eliminate a political rival, Cimon, by persuading the governing ecclesia to ostracize him. "Ostracizing" was where 6,000 Greek citizens voted to impeach someone for ten years, forcing them to leave the city.

When the Greek historian Thucydides was asked by the Spartan king, Archidamus, who was the better fighter, himself or Pericles? Thucydides replied that Pericles was better because even if he were defeated he could convince the audience that he had won. Historian Thucydides wrote that Athens was a democracy in name only, being governed for all practical purposes by its first citizen – Pericles. Political persuasion is, in a sense, just a slower process of concentrating power.

When accusations spread that Pericles was concentrating too much power, talk spread of 'ostracizing' him. This fall in public opinion polls caused Pericles to employ a tactic of intentionally letting relations with Sparta deteriorate so that a war would start. This would turn the attention of the public away from him, and besides, patriotic citizens always want a strong leader in time of war. The Peloponneisan War started, and unfortunately for him, Pericles and his sons died.

PLATO'S REPUBLIC, CHAPTERS 8 AND 9

Plato lived during the democracy of Athens, 429–347 BC. He was a disciple of Socrates, 470–399 BC, recording many of his teachings. Plato's student was Aristotle (384–322) and Aristotle's student was Alexander the Great (356–323 BC), the son of Philip of Macedon.

In 380 BC, the Plato wrote his work *The Republic*, in which he presented conversations of Socrates. In chapters 8 and 9 of *The Republic*, Plato described five steps in which

State power would concentrate into the hands of a tyrant:

> The constitutions of States are five.

These are:

> 1) Royal or Aristocratical – "aristoi" is Greek for "the best" – rule by capable, virtuous, lovers of truth
>
> 2) Timocratical – rule by lovers of honor and fame
>
> 3) Oligarchical – rule by lovers of money
>
> 4) Democratical – rule by lovers of tolerance
>
> 5) Tyrannical – rule by lovers of power.

Plato wrote:

> States are as the men are; they grow out of human characters ...
>
> Like state – like man.

LOVERS OF TRUTH & PRINCIPLE

Plato called the first stage of city government:

> Royal ... Aristocracy ... whom we rightly call just and good.

This is government by capable, principled and virtuous individuals who love truth, as Plato described:

> Truthfulness. He will never willingly tolerate an untruth, but will hate it as much as he loves truth... And is there anything more closely connected with wisdom than truth?

Being self-less and responsible, these "lovers of truth" know how to successfully run farms and businesses, and they know how to run city government. Their motivation is not what is in their own best interest, but what is genuinely in the best interest of their subjects, as Plato wrote:

> A ruler considers ... always what is for the interest of his subject ... and that alone he considers in everything which he says and does.

E.C. Wines wrote in *Commentaries on the Laws of the Ancient Hebrews, with an Introductory Essay on Civil*

Society & Government (NY: Geo. P. Putnam & Co., 1853):

> Several of the leading political principles of Plato...
> were borrowed from the Hebrew lawgiver; but in
> no other point did his republic so closely resemble
> the Jewish, as in this, that he enjoined it upon all the
> citizens to learn accurately the laws.

LOVERS OF FAME & HONOR

The second stage Plato labeled 'Timocracy' or rule by
lovers of honor and fame. These may include a famous
Greek actor, an Olympic athlete, a battle hero, or just a
busy-body who seeks attention.

Their strong desire to be loved and admired by
peoples leaves them susceptible to manipulation by those
who flatter or threaten ridicule. Machiavelli wrote of
manipulating people's need for love:

> The distinction between children and adults, while
> probably useful for some purposes, is at bottom a
> specious one, I feel. There are only individual egos,
> crazy for love.

Plato wrote:

> Now what man answers to this form of government...
> He is a ... lover of honor; claiming to be a ruler ...

> Busy-bodies are honored and applauded ...

> Is not the passionate element wholly set on ruling...
> and getting fame?

These will enter politics with good intentions, but
having no experience running anything, they yield to
"avarice," as Plato described:

> Not originally of a bad nature, but having kept bad
> company ... becomes arrogant and ambitious ...

> Such an one will despise riches only when he
> is young; but as he gets older he will be more and
> more attracted to them, because he has a piece of the
> avaricious nature in him, and is not single-minded
> towards virtue ...

The love of honor turns to love of money; the conversion is instantaneous ...

Because they have no means of openly acquiring the money which they prize; they will spend that which is another man's.

LOVERS OF MONEY – OLIGARCHY

A covetous "lover of money" is the type of leader Moses warned against in Exodus 18:21:

Thou shalt provide out of all the people able men, such as fear God, men of truth, HATING COVETOUSNESS.

Lord Acton wrote:

Economy cannot be supreme arbiter in politics. Else you might defend slavery where it is economically sound and reject it where the economic argument applies against it.

Benjamin Franklin observed this, stating in his address, "Dangers of a Salaried Bureaucracy," delivered at the Constitutional Convention in Philadelphia, 1787:

Place before the eyes of such men a post of honor, that shall, at the same time, be a place of profit, and they will move heaven and earth to obtain it ...

And of what kind are the men that will strive for this profitable preeminence, through all the bustle of cabal, the heat of contention, the infinite mutual abuse of parties, tearing to pieces the best of characters?

It will not be the wise and moderate, the lovers of peace and good order, the men fittest for the trust. It will be the bold and the violent, the men of strong passions and indefatigable activity in their selfish pursuits. These will thrust themselves into your government and be your rulers.

Plato's third stage, "oligarchy," is when the city is under the control of a ruling class, an insider clique of "lovers of money." They seek money to get elected then funnel money from the city treasury to their family, friends and supporters to help them get re-elected.

They vote themselves favors and raise taxes that everyone else has to pay, but not themselves. They pass laws everyone else has to obey, but they exempt themselves.

This leads to a division of wealthy politicians and their rich friends who receive their favors and entitlements, and the rest of the country which has to pay exorbitant taxes.

Society soon divides into the politically connected rich and the non-politically connected poor. This division of society into "the haves" and "the have-nots" becomes the seedbed for class warfare and domestic unrest.

Aristotle wrote in *Politics*, Book 3, Chapter 7:

Oligarchy has in view the interest of the wealthy.

Frederic Bastiat, in his book, *The Law* (1850) referred to this stage as "legal plunder." Yale President Ezra Stiles addressed Connecticut's General Assembly, May 8, 1783:

A people seized of property, resides the aggregate of original power.

Frederic Bastiat wrote in *The Law* (1850):

Man can live and satisfy his wants only by ceaseless labor; by the ceaseless application of his faculties to natural resources. This process is the origin of property.

But it is also true that a man may live and satisfy his wants by seizing and consuming the products of the labor of others. This process is the origin of plunder.

Now since man is naturally inclined to avoid pain — and since labor is pain in itself — it follows that men will resort to plunder whenever plunder is easier than work. History shows this quite clearly. And under these conditions, neither religion nor morality can stop it. When, then, does plunder stop? It stops when it becomes more painful and more dangerous than labor.

It is evident, then, that the proper purpose of law is to use the power of its collective force to stop this fatal tendency to plunder instead of to work. All the measures of the law should protect property and punish plunder.

But, generally, the law is made by one man or one class of men. And since law cannot operate without the sanction and support of a dominating force, this force must be entrusted to those who make the laws.

This fact, combined with the fatal tendency that exists in the heart of man to satisfy his wants with the least possible effort, explains the almost universal perversion of the law.

Thus it is easy to understand how law, instead of checking injustice, becomes the invincible weapon of injustice. It is easy to understand why the law is used by the legislator to destroy in varying degrees among the rest of the people, their personal independence by slavery, their liberty by oppression, and their property by plunder. This is done for the benefit of the person who makes the law, and in proportion to the power that he holds.

Montesquieu wrote:

There is no crueler tyranny than that which is perpetuated under the shield of law and in the name of justice.

Plato wrote:

Their fondness for money makes them unwilling to pay taxes ...

They invent illegal modes of expenditure; for what do they or their wives care about the law? ...

And so they grow richer and richer ... the less they think of virtue ... and the virtuous are dishonored ...

Insatiable avarice is the ruling passion of an oligarchy.

John Hancock stated at the fourth anniversary of the Boston Massacre, 1774:

Suffer not yourselves to be betrayed, by the soft arts of luxury and effeminacy, into the pit digged for your destruction ... Despise the glare of wealth.

That people who pay greater respect to a wealthy

villain than to an honest, upright man in poverty, almost deserve to be enslaved; they plainly show that wealth, however it may be acquired, is, in their esteem, to be preferred to virtue.

But I thank God that America abounds in men who are superior to all temptation, whom nothing can divert from a steady pursuit of the interest of their country, who are at once its ornament and safeguard.

Aesop, the Greek slave & fable author, stated:

We hang petty thieves and appoint the great thieves to public office.

Oligarchy rulers are not educated in virtue, as Plato wrote:

He has had no education, or he would never have allowed the blind god of riches to lead the dance within him ...

And being uneducated he will have many slavish desires, some beggarly, some knavish, breeding in his soul ...

If he ... has the power to defraud, he will soon prove that he is not without the will, and that his passions are only restrained by fear and not by reason ...

When he is contending for prizes ... he is afraid to incur a loss which is to be repaid only by barren honor.

Benjamin Franklin stated in , "Dangers of a Salaried Bureaucracy," 1787:

There will always be a party for giving more to the rulers, that the rulers may be able, in return, to give more to them.

Plato explained how oligarchs exhibit favoritism by selectively dispensing benefits and enforcing regulations, resulting in:

Inevitable division ... two States, the one of poor, the other of rich men; and they are ... always conspiring against one another ...

The ruling class do not want remedies; they care only for money, and are as careless of virtue as the poorest of the citizens.

Patrick Henry stated at Virginia's Ratifying Convention,

June 5, 1788:

> We have heard that there is a great deal of bribery practiced in the House of Commons in England; and that many of the members raised themselves to preferments, by selling the rights of the people:

Montesquieu described this in *The Spirit of the Laws*, 1748, Book 3:

> They who are to execute the laws against their colleagues will immediately perceive that they are acting against themselves ... Nobles form a body, who by their prerogative, and for their own particular interest, restrain the people; it is sufficient that there are laws in being to see them executed.
>
> But easy as it may be for the body of the nobles to restrain the people, it is difficult to restrain themselves.
>
> Such is the nature of this constitution, that it seems to subject the very same persons to the power of the laws, and at the same time to exempt them.

Plato warned how oligarchs put citizens in debt:

> The rulers, being aware that their power rests upon their wealth, refuse to curtail ... the extravagance of the spendthrift youth because they gain by their ruin ...
>
> They ... gain by the ruin of extravagant youth.

Those not favored by the oligarchs lose their jobs, and as unemployment rises a class-warfare foments between the haves and the have-nots, as Plato wrote:

> Families have often been reduced to beggary ... some of them owe money, some have forfeited their citizenship ...
>
> Thus men of family often lose their property or rights of citizenship; but they remain in the city, full of hatred against the new owners of their estates and ripe for revolution ...
>
> They hate and conspire against those who have got their property, and against everybody else, and are eager for revolution.

When an opportunity arises, the people throw the oligarchs out and set up the 4th stage – "Democracy."

⤚

LOVERS OF TOLERANCE – DEMOCRACY

Plato wrote:

> From the least cause ... the city falls ill and fights a battle ... and democracy comes into power when the poor are the victors, killing some and exiling some, and giving equal shares in the government to all the rest ...

> Next comes democracy and the democratic man, out of ... the oligarchical man.

A democracy is run by lovers of tolerance, as Plato told:

> The great charm is, that you may do as you like; you may govern if you like, let it alone if you like; go to war and make peace if you feel disposed, and all quite irrespective of anybody else ...

> The manner of life in such a State is that of democrats; there is freedom and plainness of speech, and **EVERY MAN DOES WHAT IS RIGHT IN HIS OWN EYES,** and has his own way of life ...

> Is not the city full of freedom ... a man may say and do what he likes?

Tolerance becomes democracy's chief characteristic:

> There will be the greatest variety of human natures... being an embroidered robe which is spangled with every sort of flower ...

> Hence arise the most various developments of character; the State is like a piece of embroidery of which the colors and figures are the manners of men ...

> The State is not one but many, like a bazaar at which you can buy anything ...

> Freedom ... as they tell you in a democracy, is the glory of the State.

Plato's student, Aristotle wrote:

> Tolerance is the last virtue of a dying society.

Plato wrote that ever-expanding tolerance diminishes respect for the law:

When you condemn men to death they remain alive all the same; a gentleman is desired to go into exile, and he stalks about the streets like a hero; and nobody sees him or cares for him ...

Such is democracy; – a pleasing, lawless, various sort of government, distributing equality to equals and unequals alike ...

Democracy ... is a charming form of government, full of variety and disorder, and dispensing a sort of equality to equals and unequals alike.

The city experiences a loss of virtue, giving way to "unnecessary pleasures ... not excepting incest or any other unnatural union," as Plato wrote:

And so the young man passes ... into the freedom and libertinism of useless and unnecessary pleasures...

In all of us, even in good men, there is a lawless wild-beast nature ...

Unnecessary pleasures and appetites I conceive to be unlawful ...

Everyone appears to have them, but in some persons they are controlled ... while in ... others they are stronger ...

and there is no conceivable folly or crime – not excepting incest or any other unnatural union ... which... when he has parted company with all shame and sense, a man may not be ready to commit.

Plato gives a more in depth definition of 'unnecessary pleasures' and 'unnatural union' in *The Laws*:

Whether one makes the observation in earnest or in jest, one certainly should not fail to observe that when male unites with female for procreation the pleasure experienced is held to be due to nature, but contrary to nature when male mates with male or female with female, and that those first guilty of such enormities were impelled by their slavery to pleasure.

Plato continued in *The Laws*:

I had an idea for reinforcing the law about the natural use of the intercourse which procreates children, abstaining from the male, not deliberately killing human progeny or "sowing in rocks and stones," where it will never take root and be endowed with growth, abstaining too from all female soil in which you would not want what you have sown to grow.

This law when it has become permanent and prevails— just as it prevails now regarding intercourse with parents— confers innumerable benefits. In the first place, it has been made according to nature; also, it effects a debarment from erotic fury and insanity, all kinds of adultery and all excesses in drink and food, and it makes man truly affectionate to their own wives: other blessings also would ensue, in infinite number, if one could make sure of this law.

Plato warned that unrestrained liberty leads to licentiousness (unrestrained sexual depravity):

He was supposed from his youth upwards to have been trained under a miserly parent, who encouraged the saving appetites in him ... and then he got into the company of a ... licentious sort of people, and taking to all their wanton ways rushed into the opposite extreme from an abhorrence of his father's meanness ...

Neither does he receive ... advice; if any one says to him that some pleasures are ... of evil desires ... he shakes his head.

Isaiah fortold "the child shall behave himself proudly against the ancient, and the base against the honorable."

Plato described the indulgent youth:

He lives from day to day indulging the appetite of the hour ... His life has neither law nor order ... he is all liberty and equality ... After this manner the democrat was generated out of the oligarch.

Sir Alexander Fraser Tytler wrote in *Universal History from the Creation of the World to the Beginning of the 18th Century* (Boston: Fetridge & Co., 1834; 1850):

The other reflection is, that, from the great variety and opposition of those systems which we have enumerated of the Greek philosophers, we may perceive among that people a liberal spirit of toleration in matters of opinion, which stopped short at absolute irreligion and impiety.

Lord Acton wrote:

Men cannot be made good by the state, but they can easily be made bad.

Lord Acton also wrote:

The common vice of democracy is disregard for morality;

The will of the people cannot make just that which is unjust;

There should be a law to the People besides its own will;

Democracy generally monopolizes and concentrates power;

It is a most striking thing that the views of pure democracy ... were almost entirely unrepresented in (the American) convention;

Americans dreaded democracy and contrived their constitution against it.

Plato warned next:

Can liberty have any limit? ... Certainly not ... By degrees the anarchy finds a way into private houses ...

The son is on a level with his father, he having no respect or reverence for either of his parents; and this is his freedom ...

Citizens ... chafe impatiently at the least touch of authority ... they will have no one over them ...

Liberty overmasters democracy ... The excessive increase of anything often causes a reaction in the opposite direction ...

The excess of liberty, whether in States or individuals, seems only to pass into excess of slavery.

Justice Louis D. Brandeis (1856–1941) stated:

Crime is contagious. If the government becomes a law breaker, it breeds contempt for the law.

Will and Ariel Durant included in *The Lessons of*

History (NY: Simon & Schuster, 1968, p. 74) an excerpt from Plato's *Republic* on how democracy would end:

The democrats contemptuously rejected temperance... Insolence they term breeding, and anarchy liberty and waste magnificence, and impudence courage ...

The father gets accustomed to descend to the level of his son and to fear them, and the son to be on a level with his father, having no shame or fear of his parents ...

The teacher fears and flatters his scholars, and the scholars despise their masters and tutors ... The old do not like to be thought morose and authoritative, and therefore they imitate the young ...

Nor must I forget to tell of the liberty and equality of the two sexes in relation to each other ...

The citizens chafe impatiently at the least touch of authority, and at length ... they cease to care even for the laws, written or unwritten ...

And this is the fair and glorious beginning out of which springs dictatorship (tyrannis) ... The excessive increase of anything causes a reaction in the opposite direction ...

Dictatorship naturally arises out of democracy, and the most aggravated form of tyranny and slavery out of the most extreme form of liberty.

Edmund Burke wrote in *A Letter to a Member of the National Assembly*, 1791:

What is liberty without wisdom and without virtue? It is the greatest of all possible evils; for it is folly, vice, and madness, without restraint.

Men are qualified for civil liberty in exact proportion to their disposition to put moral chains upon their own appetites; in proportion as they are disposed to listen to the counsels of the wise and good in preference to the flattery of knaves.

Society cannot exist, unless a controlling power upon will and appetite be placed somewhere; and the less of it there is within, the more there must be without. It is ordained in the eternal constitution of

things, that men of intemperate minds cannot be free.
Their passions forge their fetters.

Plato warned that citizens, not being educated or trained to be responsible, will yield to avarice. Not cultivating deferred gratification, the people want more now, and so they vote to spread the city's wealth around.

Gary L. Bauer, was Chairman of President Reagan's Special Working Group on the Family, wrote June 5, 2012:

> Yesterday the *Wall Street Journal* summarized the race this way: "Students of democracy from Alexis de Tocqueville to Mancur Olson have pointed out that the greatest threat to self-government comes from the tendency of democracies to become barnacled with special interests that vote themselves more benefits than society can afford."

Dr. Ben Carson stated (*The Hill*, "The heart of the matter is not guns" by Mark Hensch, June 19, 2015):

> You know, we have a war on women, race wars, income wars, age wars, religious wars, anything you could imagine, we have a war on it. And we're giving people a license to hate people who disagree with them ... Well, I hope that we, the American people, can come to the understanding that we are not each other's enemies.
>
> The enemies are those who are stoking the flames of division, trying to divide us into every category and weakening us as a society.

Plato wrote that when the treasury is empty, people will vote to take money from the rich:

> Their leaders deprive the rich of their estates and distribute them among the people; at the same time taking care to reserve the larger part for themselves.

It is a Machiavellian tactic of taking money from political opponents and funneling it to political supporters. This approach is similar to Caesar's "Use money to get men and use men to get money." George Bernard Shaw stated:

> A government policy to rob Peter to pay Paul can be assured of the support of Paul.

Friedrich August Von Hayek stated:

Perhaps the fact that we have seen millions voting themselves into complete dependence on a tyrant has made our generation understand that to choose one's government is not necessarily to secure freedom.

Alexis de Tocqueville stated:

Democracy and socialism have nothing in common but one word, equality. But notice the difference: while democracy seeks equality in liberty, socialism seeks equality in restraint and servitude.

British Prime Minister William Pitt stated:

Necessity is the plea for every infringement of human freedom. It is the argument of tyrants; it is the creed of slaves.

Plato wrote:

And the persons whose property is taken from them are compelled to defend themselves before the people as they best can ...

Observe, too, how grandly democracy sets her foot upon all our fine theories of education,– how little she cares for the training of her statesmen!

John Adams to Thomas Jefferson; July 16, 1814:

Democracy will envy all, contend with all, endeavor to pull down all, and when by chance it happens to get the upper hand for a short time, it will be revengeful, bloody, and cruel.

Plato predicted democracy's undoing:

Such ... is the fair and glorious beginning out of which springs tyranny ...

Does not tyranny spring from democracy ...

Insatiable desire ... and ... neglect ... introduces the change in democracy, which occasions a demand for tyranny ...

Democracy ... of which the insatiable desire brings her to dissolution ...

And so tyranny naturally arises out of democracy, and the most aggravated form of tyranny and slavery out of the most extreme form of liberty.

Lord Acton wrote:

Liberty becomes a question of morals more than of politics.

The people's lack of self-control and deferred gratification finally result in financial irresponsibility. A shortage of money to spread around leads to bickering and fighting, degenerating into chaos and anarchy. Debt and insolvency precedes a government's decline, as seen in:

–Greek City-States following Peloponnesian Wars in the 5th century BC;

–Roman Empire;

–Byzantine Empire;

–Mongolian Yuan Dynasty with its over-printing of paper currency;

–Republic of Venice in 1490;

–Renaissance Genoa of 1555;

–Empire of Spain of 1650;

–Amsterdam in 1770;

–Empire of France, 1797, carrying the debt of fighting in America's Revolution without any recompense;

–Ottoman Empire which owed millions to France and England after World War I;

–Germany's Weimar Republic;

–Italy with its "fiat" currency; and

–U.S.S.R., which went in debt trying to keep up the arms race with the U.S. during Cold War.

–Jefferson advised Indiana Territorial Governor William Henry Harrison, 1803, to acquire land from Indians through debt rather than fighting:

"To promote this ... exchange lands ... we shall push our trading uses, and be glad to see the good and influential individuals among them run in debt, because we observe that when these debts get beyond what the individuals can pay, they become willing to lop them off by a cession of lands."

In Plato's description of an in debt, indulgent, and out-of-control democracy, the more chaotic society gets, the more people begin to look for someone to fix this mess.

LOVER OF POWER – THE TYRANT

The domestic chaos leads to the 5th stage – 'Tyranny'. Samuel Adams wrote to James Warren, Feb. 12, 1779:

> A general dissolution of the principles and manners will more surely overthrow the liberties of America than the whole force of the common enemy. While the people are virtuous they cannot be subdued; but once they lose their virtue, they will be ready to surrender their liberties to the first external or internal invader.

Plato wrote:

> Last of all comes ... the tyrant ...

> In the early days of his power, he is full of smiles, and he salutes every one whom he meets ... making promises in public and also in private, liberating debtors, and distributing land to the people and his followers, and wanting to be so kind and good to every one ...

> This ... is the root from which a tyrant springs; when he first appears above ground he is a protector.

This person, who is a lover of power, begins to blame the rich for all the city's problems, as Plato wrote:

> Hinting at the abolition of debts and partition of lands ... he ... begins to make a party against the rich ...

> That they may be impoverished by payment of taxes, and thus compelled to devote themselves to their daily wants and therefore less likely to conspire against him ...

> And when a man who is wealthy ... is also accused of being an enemy of the people ... he flees... and is not ashamed to be a coward.

George Orwell wrote in *Nineteen Eighty-Four*:

> Do not forget this ... always there will be the

intoxication of power, constantly increasing and constantly growing subtler. Always, at every moment, there will be the thrill of victory, the sensation of trampling on an enemy who is helpless. If you want a picture of the future, imagine a boot stamping on a human face — forever.

The "protector" targets his political opponents, as Plato wrote:

And the protector of the people ... having a mob entirely at his disposal, he is not restrained from shedding the blood of kinsmen; by the favorite method of false accusation he brings them into court and murders them, making the life of man to disappear, and with unholy tongue and lips tasting the blood of his fellow citizen ...

And if any of them are suspected by him of having notions of freedom, and of resistance to his authority, he will have a good pretext for destroying them.

Aristotle wrote in *Politics*, Book 3, Chapter 7:

For tyranny is a kind of monarchy which has in view the interest of the monarch only ...

This is why we do not permit a man to rule ... because a man rules in his own interest, and becomes a tyrant.

Plato continued:

How then does a protector begin to change into a tyrant? ... He begins to grow unpopular.

When the tyrant's life is threatened, Plato stated:

Then comes the famous request for a bodyguard, which is the device of all those who have got thus far in their tyrannical career – "Let not the people's friend," as they say, "be lost to them" ...

The people readily assent; all their fears are for him – they have none for themselves.

William Caxton, the first English printer, published *The Game and Playe of the Chesse*, 1483. It was the second book ever published in England. In it was stated:

For we read that Dionysius of Sicily, a tyrant, was

so suspicious – living in great fear and dread of being hated by everyone – that he expelled his friends from the offices they held, and put in their place strangers to guard his person, choosing those who were cruel and felonious.

And out of fear and distrust of barbers he made his daughters learn how to shave and comb; once they had become good at it he would not let them use any iron in that occupation, except to burn and singe his hairs, and he threatened them and dared not place his trust in them. Likewise, they had no sense of loyalty towards him.

Another thing he did was to surround the palace where he lived with wide, deep ditches like a castle, and he would enter by a drawbridge which could be closed after him. His knights stayed outside with his guards, who kept a strict watch over this fortress.

When Plato saw this Dionysius king of Sicily thus surrounded and with guards and watchmen positioned all around, because of his suspiciousness, he said openly to him, in front of other men:

"King, why have you done so much evil and harm that it is necessary for you to be protected by so many people?"

General Douglas MacArthur addressed Massachusetts State Legislature in Boston, on July 25, 1951:

I find in existence a new and heretofore unknown and dangerous concept that the members of our Armed Forces owe primary allegiance and loyalty to those who temporarily exercise the authority of the executive branch of government, rather than to the country and its Constitution which they are sworn to defend.

No proposition could be more dangerous. None could cast a greater doubt upon the integrity of the armed services. For its application would at once convert them from their traditional and constitutional role as the instrument for the defense of the Republic into something partaking of the nature of a praetorian guard, owing its allegiance to the political master of the hour ...

The armed services ... are accountable as well to the Congress, charged with the policy-making responsibility, and to the people, ultimate repository of all national power. Yet so inordinate has been the application of the Executive power that members of the armed services have been subjected to the most arbitrary and ruthless treatment for daring to speak the truth in accordance with conviction and conscience.

A tyrant is a lover of power, as Plato concluded:

The protector of whom we spoke, is to be seen... the overthrower of many, standing up in the chariot of State with the reins in his hand, no longer protector, but tyrant absolute.

This was put into contemporary language by Grammy Award winning musician Frank Zappa:

The illusion of freedom will continue as long as it's profitable to continue the illusion. At the point where the illusion becomes too expensive to maintain, they will just take down the scenery, they will pull back the curtains, they will move the tables and chairs out of the way and you will see the brick wall at the back of the theater.

This theme of a tyrant usurping power while pretending to be a hero is the story-line of the prequel *Star Wars Episode III: Revenge of the Sith* (2005). The Galactic Republic was persuaded to relinquish power into the hands of Senator Palpatine who promised to end the Clone Wars. They were unaware that the Clone Wars were clandestinely orchestrated by the very same Senator Palpatine so that he could usurp power and become the Supreme Chancellor.

Once in control, Palpatine used his power against the Jedi – the upholders of the Old Republic – accusing them of treason and declaring war on them. As the severity of the manufactured emergency increased, the naive Senate was manipulated to applaud Palpatine as he becomes Emperor.

Palpatine completely purged the noble Jedi, and

replaced them a Jedi–turned–Sith, Darth Vader. The Galaxy was then transformed into a totalitarian dictatorship, tyrannically ruled through constant fear of the evil Emperor Palpatine–the Dark Lord.

George Orwell wrote in *Nineteen Eighty-Four*:

> No one ever seizes power with the intention of relinquishing it. Power is not a means; it is an end. One does not establish a dictatorship in order to safeguard a revolution; one makes the revolution in order to establish the dictatorship. The object of persecution is persecution. The object of torture is torture. The object of power is power.

In recapping, Plato wrote in his work *The Republic*, 380 BC, how government would go through five stages:

> 1) Rule by capable people of virtue, which Plato called royal or aristocracy;

> 2) Rule by those who love fame and being honored, called timocracy;

> 3) Rule by an insider clique that votes themselves favors, called an oligarchy;

> 4) Rule by the people, called democracy, but having no self-control, this ends in chaos and the need for someone to fix the mess;

> 5) Rule by a 'protector' who promises everything to everybody until he consolidates power and is revealed as the tyrant.

Richard Nixon commented, Aug. 21, 1960, on Josef Stalin, responsible for an estimated 40 million deaths:

> Stalin and his followers ... became infected with a mistaken view of Stalin's proper role ... Stalin ruled without the check of constitutional forms ... In the words of Aristotle, written some 23 centuries ago, "This is why we do not permit a man to rule ... because a man rules in his own interest, and becomes a tyrant." It is plain that Stalin ... became a tyrant.

Britain's Lord Thomas MacCauley predicted this for American in a letter to New York's Democrat Secretary of State, Henry S. Randall, May 23, 1857:

Institutions purely democratic must, sooner or later, destroy liberty, or civilization, or both ... France is an example ... a pure Democracy was established there. During a short time there was ...

−a general spoliation,

−a national bankruptcy,

−a new partition of the soil,

−a maximum of prices,

−a ruinous load of taxation laid on the rich for the purpose of supporting the poor in idleness ...

You may think that your country enjoys an exemption from these evils ... I am of a very different opinion. Your fate I believe to be certain, though it is deferred.

Lord MacCauley continued:

The time will come when ... distress everywhere makes the laborer mutinous and discontented, and inclines him to listen with eagerness to agitators who tell him that it is a monstrous iniquity that one man should have a million while another cannot get a full meal.

In bad years there is plenty of grumbling ... and sometimes a little rioting ... Your Government will never be able to restrain a distressed and discontented majority ...

The day will come when, in the State of New York, a multitude of people, none of whom has had more than half a breakfast, or expects to have more than half a dinner, will choose a Legislature ...

On one side is a statesman preaching patience, respect for vested rights, strict observance of public faith. On the other is a demagogue ranting about the tyranny of capitalists and usurers, and asking why anybody should be permitted to drink champagne and to ride in a carriage, while thousands of honest folks are in want of necessaries.

Lord MacCauley concluded:

Which of the two candidates is likely to be preferred by a working man who hears his children cry for more bread?

I seriously apprehend that you will, in some such season of adversity ... devour all the seed-corn, and thus make the next year, a year not of scarcity, but of absolute famine ...

When a society has entered on this downward progress, either civilization or liberty must perish. Either some Caesar or Napoleon will seize the reins of government with a strong hand.

PROPAGANDA AND AGITATORS

President Calvin Coolidge warned in a speech given at the College of William and Mary, May 15, 1926:

But there is another ... recent development ... the greatly disproportionate influence of organized minorities. Artificial propaganda, paid agitators, selfish interests, all impinge upon members of legislative bodies to force them to represent special elements rather than the great body of their constituency. When they are successful, minority rule is established.

Franklin Roosevelt stated in a Campaign Address at Brooklyn, NY, Nov. 1, 1940:

Whoever seeks to set one nationality against another, seeks to degrade all nationalities. Whoever seeks to set one race against another seeks to enslave all races ... So-called racial voting blocs are the creation of designing politicians who profess to be able to deliver them on Election Day.

Booker T. Washington (1856-1915) was a prominent African American educator who founded Tuskegee Institute. He wrote in *My Larger Education–Being Chapters from My Experience* (1911, ch. V: The Intellectuals and the Boston Mob, p. 118):

There is another class of colored people who make a business of keeping the troubles, the wrongs, and the hardships of the Negro race before the public. Having learned that they are able to make a living out of their troubles, they have grown into the settled habit of advertising their wrongs – partly because they want sympathy and partly because it pays.

Community organizer Saul Alinsky wrote in *Rules for Radicals* (1971):

The organizer's first job is to create the issues or problems ...

The organizer must first rub raw the resentments of the people of the community ...

An organizer must stir up dissatisfaction and discontent ...

He must search out controversy and issues, rather than avoid them ...

Fan the latent hostilities of many of the people to the point of overt expression.

Saul Alinsky's tactics were specifically condemned in Scripture, as seen in Proverbs 6:19:

The Lord hates ... a person who stirs up conflict in the community."(NIV)

FDR stated in a radio address for a Birthday Ball for Crippled Children, Jan. 30, 1940:

The answer to class hatred, race hatred, religious hatred ... is the free expression of the love of our fellow men.

FDR prayed on United Flag Day, June 14, 1942:

Grant us victory over the tyrants who would enslave all free men ... We can make ... a planet ... undivided by senseless distinctions of race.

Rep. Fisher Ames, who proposed wording of First Amendment, also predicted:

Democracy could not last ... When the tyranny of the majority leads to chaos, society will submit to rule by the sword.

Noah Webster wrote of the French Revolution ("Political Fanaticism, No. III," *The American Minerva*, Sept. 21, 1796):

The reason why severe laws are necessary in France, is, that the people ... do not know how to govern themselves (and so) must be governed by severe laws and penalties.

Webster wrote in *History of the United States*, 1832:

The brief exposition of the constitution of the United States, will unfold to young persons the principles of republican government; and it is the sincere desire of the writer that our citizens should early understand that the genuine source of correct republican principles is the Bible, particularly the New Testament or the Christian religion.

Unfortunately, this seems to be good advice not well taken with respect to the education. Noah Webster added:

Almost all the civil liberty now enjoyed in the world owes its origin to the principles of the Christian religion ... The religion which has introduced civil liberty is the religion of Christ and His apostles, which enjoins humility, piety, and benevolence; which acknowledges in every person a brother, or a sister, and a citizen with equal rights. This is genuine Christianity, and to this we owe our free Constitutions of Government.

Noah Webster stated:

The moral principles and precepts contained in the Scriptures ought to form the basis of all of our civil constitutions and laws.

Lord Acton wrote:

Moral precepts are constant through the ages and not obedient to circumstances.

Webster wrote in the preface of his *1828 Dictionary*:

The Christian religion is the most important and one of the first things in which all children, under a free government ought to be instructed ... No truth is more evident to my mind than that the Christian religion must be the basis of any government intended to secure the rights and privileges of a free people.

President Harry S Truman, April 3, 1951:

Without a firm moral foundation, freedom degenerates quickly into selfishness and ... anarchy.

Then there will be freedom only for the rapacious and ... more unscrupulous than the rank and file of the people.

Rev. Martin Luther King, Jr., stated April 16, 1963:

I stand in the middle of two opposing forces in the Negro community. One is a force of complacency... The other force is one of bitterness and hatred, and it comes perilously close to advocating violence. It is expressed in the various black nationalist groups that are springing up across the nation, the largest and best-known being Elijah Muhammad's Muslim movement.

Nourished by the Negro's frustration over the continued existence of racial discrimination, this movement is made up of people who have lost faith in America, who have absolutely repudiated Christianity, and who have concluded that the white man is an incorrigible "devil."

Rev. King continued:

I have tried to stand between these two forces, saying that we need emulate neither the 'do-nothingism' of the complacent nor the hatred of the black nationalist. For there is the more excellent way of love and non-violent protest. I am grateful to God that, through the influence of the Negro church, the way of nonviolence became an integral part of our struggle ...

If our white brothers dismiss ... those of us who employ nonviolent direct action ... millions of Negroes will, out of frustration and despair, seek solace and security in black nationalist ideologies – a development that would inevitably lead to a frightening racial nightmare.

James Monroe warned in his Inaugural Address, 1817:

It is only when the people become ignorant and corrupt, when they degenerate into a populace, that they are incapable of exercising the sovereignty. Usurpation is then an easy attainment, and an usurper soon found. The people themselves become the willing instruments of their own debasement and ruin.

Alexis de Tocqueville predicted how Americans would

lose their freedom (*Democracy in America, Vol. 2,* 1840, The Second Part, Bk 4, Ch. VI):

I had noted in my stay in the United States that a democratic state of society similar to the American model could lay itself open to the establishment of despotism with unusual ease ... It would debase men without tormenting them ...

Men, all alike and equal, turned in upon themselves in a restless search for those petty, vulgar pleasures with which they fill their souls ...

Above these men stands an immense and protective power ... It prefers its citizens to enjoy themselves provided they have only enjoyment in mind. It restricts the activity of free will within a narrower range and gradually removes autonomy itself from each citizen.

Alexis de Tocqueville continued:

Thus, the ruling power, having taken each citizen one by one into its powerful grasp ... spreads its arms over the whole of society, covering the surface of social life with a network of petty, complicated, detailed, and uniform rules ... It does not break men's wills but it does soften, bend, and control them ...

It constantly opposes what actions they perform... It inhibits, represses, drains, snuffs out, dulls so much effort that finally it reduces each nation to nothing more than a flock of timid and hardworking animals with the government as shepherd ... a single, protective, and all-powerful government ... Individual intervention ... is ... suppressed.

Alexis de Tocqueville added:

It is ... in the details that we run the risk of enslaving men. For my part, I would be tempted to believe that freedom in the big things of life is less important than in the slightest ... Subjection in the minor things of life is obvious every day ... It constantly irks them until they give up the exercise of their will ... and enfeebles their spirit ...

It will be useless to call upon those very citizens

who have become so dependent upon central government to choose from time to time the representative of this government.

Alexis de Tocqueville concluded:

Increasing despotism in the administrative sphere... they reckon citizens are incompetent ... It is ... difficult to imagine how men who have completely given up the habit of self-government could successfully choose those who should do it for them ...

The vices of those who govern and the ineptitude of those governed would soon bring it to ruin and ... revert to its abasement to one single master.

General Douglas MacArthur warned in a speech to the Salvation Army, Dec. 12, 1951, stating:

History fails to record a single precedent in which nations subject to moral decay have not passed into political and economic decline. There has been either a spiritual awakening to overcome the moral lapse, or a progressive deterioration leading to ultimate national disaster.

After usurping power, Plato wrote in *The Republic* how a tyrant will stay in power:

The tyrant must be always getting up a war ...

He is always stirring up some war or other, in order that the people may require a leader.

James Madison stated at the Constitutional Convention, June 29, 1787 (*Max Farrand's Records of the Federal Convention of 1787*, Vol. I (1911, p. 465):

In time of actual war, great discretionary powers are constantly given to the Executive Magistrate. Constant apprehension of War, has the same tendency to render the head too large for the body.

A standing military force, with an overgrown Executive will not long be safe companions to liberty. The means of defense against foreign danger have been always the instruments of tyranny at home. Among the Romans it was a standing maxim to excite a war, whenever a revolt was apprehended.

Throughout all Europe, the armies kept up under the pretext of defending, have enslaved the people.

Madison wrote in *Federalist No. 47,* Jan. 30, 1788:

The accumulation of all powers, Legislative, Executive, and Judiciary, in the same hands, whether of one, a few, or many, and whether hereditary, self-appointed, or elective, may justly be pronounced the very definition of tyranny.

When those who helped him gain power begin to confront him, the tyrant eliminates them, as Plato wrote:

Then some of those who joined in setting him up, and who are in power, speak their minds to him and to one another, and the more courageous of them cast in his teeth what is being done ...

And the tyrant, if he means to rule, must get rid of them; he cannot stop while he has a friend or an enemy who is good for anything ...

Some he kills and others he banishes.

Machiavelli wrote on the politics of personal destruction:

Men ought either to be indulged or utterly destroyed, for if you merely offend them they take vengeance, but if you injure them greatly they are unable to retaliate, so that the injury done to a man ought to be such that vengeance cannot be feared ...

The new ruler must determine all the injuries that he will need to inflict. He must inflict them once and for all ...

If an injury has to be done to a man it should be so severe that his vengeance need not be feared ...

Men should be either treated generously or destroyed, because they take revenge for slight injuries – for heavy ones they cannot ...

Severities should be dealt out all at once, so that their suddenness may give less offense; benefits ought to be handed ought drop by drop, so that they may be relished the more ...

Whoever conquers a free town and does not demolish it commits a great error and may expect to be ruined himself ...

The wise man does at once what the fool does finally.

Plato described how the tyrant goes from bad to worse:

Must he not either perish at the hands of his enemies, or from being a man become a wolf – that is, a tyrant? ...

He who has tasted the entrails of a single human victim ... is destined to become a wolf.

Suetonius, biographer of Roman Emperor Tiberius, wrote:

The cause of his hesitation was fear of the dangers which threatened him on every hand, and often led him to say that he was "holding a wolf by the ears."

A 1718 edition of *Suetonius's Works* was owned by Jefferson, who wrote from Monticello to Lydia Huntley Sigourney, July 18, 1824:

We have the wolf by the ear and feel the danger of either holding or letting him loose.

Plato wrote:

The lion and serpent element in them disproportionately grows and gains strength.

The tyrant then purges the country of successful people who disagree with him, as Plato described:

And therefore he must look about him and see who is valiant, who is high-minded, who is wise, who is wealthy; happy man, he is the enemy of them all, and must seek occasion against them whether he will or no, until he has made a purgation of the State.

Yes, I said, not the sort of purgation which the physicians make of the body; for they take away the worse and leave the better part, but he does the reverse.

Plato shared how the tyrant will replace his former friends with a devoted mob of convicts and slaves which he freed, and as such, were indebted and loyal to him alone:

And the more detestable his actions are to the citizens the more satellites and the greater devotion in them will he require ...

And who are the devoted band, and where will he procure them? ...

He will rob the citizens of their slaves; he will then set them free and enroll them in his bodyguard ...

To be sure ... he will be able to trust them best of all.

Plato added:

What a blessed creature ... must this tyrant be; he has put to death the others and has these for his trusted friends ...

These are the new citizens whom he has called into existence, who admire him and are his companions, while the good hate and avoid him ...

But they will ... attract mobs, and hire voices fair and loud and persuasive, and draw the cities over to tyrannies.

Plato explained how the tyrant will raid the treasury:

Let us ... inquire how the tyrant will maintain that... ever-changing army of his ...

If, he said, there are sacred treasures in the city, he will confiscate and spend them.

Jefferson wrote in his *Notes on Virginia*, 1782:

Mankind soon learns to make interested uses of every right and power which they possess, or may assume. The public money and public liberty ... will soon be discovered to be sources of wealth and dominion to those who hold them; distinguished, too, by this tempting circumstance, that they are the instrument, as well as the object of acquisition. "With money we will get men," said Caesar, "and with men we will get money."

BREAD & THE CIRCUS – WELFARE STATE

What Plato predicted was seen in 123 BC, when the immensely powerful Roman politician, Gaius Gracchus, began appeasing citizens with a monthly hand-out of free grain, called a "dole." Roman poet Juvenal (c.100 AD) described how this became a means by which emperors controlled the masses. By keeping people obsessed with hand-outs and self-indulgence, they were distracted from the actual conditions of the empire, and less likely to revolt:

> Already long ago, from when we sold our vote to no man, the People have abdicated our duties; for the People who ONCE UPON A TIME handed out military command, high civil office, legions – everything, NOW restrains itself and anxiously hopes for just two things: bread and circuses.

Juvenal continued:

> Tyrants would distribute largess, a bushel of wheat, a gallon of wine, and a sesterce (Roman coin); and everyone would shamelessly cry, "Long live the King"...

> The fools did not realize that they were merely recovering a portion of their own property, and that their ruler could not have given them what they were receiving without having first taken it from them.

Roman consul Marcus Tullius Cicero (106–43 BC) wrote:

> The evil was not in bread and circuses, per se, but in the willingness of the people to sell their rights as free men for full bellies and the excitement of games which would serve to distract them from the other human hungers which bread and circuses can never appease.

The Durants wrote in *The Lessons of History* (p. 92):

> The concentration of population and poverty in great cities may compel a government to choose between ENFEEBLING THE ECONOMY WITH A DOLE or running the risk of riot and revolution.

The Great Ages of Man–Barbarian Europe (NY: Time–Life Books, 1968, p. 39), recorded a Roman as stating:

> Those who live at the expense of the public funds are more numerous than those who provide them.

The tyrant will promote and honor those who do his bidding, as Plato explained:

> Moreover, they are paid for this and receive honor

– the greatest honor, as might be expected, from tyrants.

Actors and artists will praise the tyrant, as Plato wrote:

> Poets ... are the eulogists of tyranny ...

> He also praises tyranny as godlike.

What happens when the public opinion polls show the tyrant losing popularity? Plato wrote:

> But the higher they ascend our constitution hill, the more their reputation fails, and seems unable from shortness of breath to proceed further.

The tyrant will then disarm citizens, as Plato warned:

> By heaven ... the parent will discover what a monster he has been fostering in his bosom; and, when he wants to drive him out, he will find that he is weak and his son strong ...

> Why, you do not mean to say that the tyrant will use violence? What! beat his father if he opposes him? ...

> Yes, he will, having first disarmed him ...

> Then he is a parricide, and a cruel guardian of an aged parent; and this is real tyranny ... as the saying is, the people who would escape the smoke which is the slavery of freemen, has fallen into the fire which is the tyranny of slaves.

Plato concluded:

> Thus liberty, getting out of all order and reason, passes into the harshest and bitterest form of slavery ...

> A tyranny is the wretchedest form of government...

> The longer he lives the more of a tyrant he becomes...

> May we not rightly say that we have sufficiently discussed ... the manner of the transition from democracy to tyranny?

Benjamin Franklin stated in "Dangers of a Salaried Bureaucracy," June 2, 1787:

> Hence, as all history informs us, there has been in every state and kingdom a constant kind of warfare between the governing and the governed; the one

striving to obtain more for its support, and the other to pay less ... Generally ... the ruling power carries its point, and we see the revenues of princes constantly increasing, and we see that they are never satisfied, but always in want of more.

The more the people are discontented with the oppression of taxes, the greater need the prince has of money to distribute among his partisans, and pay the troops that are to suppress all resistance, and enable him to plunder at pleasure.

There is scarce a king in a hundred who would not, if he could, follow the example of Pharaoh—get first all the people's money, then all their lands, and then make them and their children servants forever.

It will be said that we do not propose to establish kings. I know it. But there is a natural inclination in mankind to kingly government. It sometimes relieves them from aristocratic domination. They would rather have one tyrant than five hundred. It gives more of the appearance of equality among citizens; and that they like.

I am apprehensive, therefore—perhaps too apprehensive—that the government of the States may, in future times, end in a monarchy ...

But this catastrophe, I think, may be long delayed, if in our proposed system we do not sow the seeds of contention, faction, and tumult, by making our posts of honor places of profit.

If we do, I fear that, tho we employ at first a number and not a single person, the number will, in time, be set aside; it will only nourish the fetus of a king ... and a king will the sooner be set over us.

Plato believed that avarice was a trait common to man, and therefore democracy would always end in chaos as men inherently do not have virtue.

Men only pretend they are virtuous, but if their life depended on it, they would abandon their virtue to save their life. If there ever were a truly virtuous person born on earth, he would have to die to prove that he would not give up his virtue to save his life.

Plato went on to write, that if a truly virtuous person did in fact live on earth, he would so convict everyone that they would crucify him:

> If a truly just man lived ... let him die as he has lived. I might add ... that the just man will be scourged, racked, bound, will have his eyes put out, and will at last be crucified.

Machiavelli worded it this way:

> The fact is that a man who wants to act virtuously in every way necessarily comes to grief among so many who are not virtuous.

Plato did not think there would ever be a truly virtuous man born on the earth, so he though having a tyrant was inevitable, and the best that could be hoped for was a nice tyrant, which he called a "philosopher–king." Plato wrote:

> When the true philosopher kings are born in a State... they will set in order their own city ... They will ... take possession of the children, who will be unaffected by the habits of their parents; these they will train in their own habits and laws.

Hitler threatened May 1, 1937 (William Shirer, *Rise and Fall of the Third Reich* (NY: Simon & Schuster, 1960, p. 249):

> This new Reich will give its youth to no one, but will itself take youth and give to youth its own education and its own upbringing.

John Dewey wrote in *The Middle Works* (1915, vol. 8, p. 398):

> Education which trains children to docility and obedience, to the careful performance of imposed tasks because they are imposed, regardless of where they lead, is suited to an autocratic society. These are the traits needed in a state where there is one head to plan and care for the lives and institutions of the people.

Plato explained how the philosopher–king teaches children "noble lies," but he thought this was alright, as the lies helped him stay in power, and he was the only one who knew how to run everything, it was alright for him to stay in power. Lord Acton wrote:

> Official truth is not actual truth.

A description of the 'noble lie' was given in the winter 2011 Midstream review of James Glazov's book, *United in Hate: The Left's Romance with Tyranny and Terror*:

> Plato expressed an idea that is related to thought control: he called for **the Noble Lie**, a contradiction in terms if ever there was one. In particular, he said that the people should be taught that Rulers were made with gold, Auxiliaries with silver, and craftsmen with iron and brass.

Jamie Glazov, managing editor of *Frontpage Magazine* and author of *United in Hate: The Left's Romance with Tyranny and Terror*, was cited in George Jochnowitz's article "Why Totalitarians Hate Jews," (*Daily Mailer*, FrontPage, March 11, 2011):

> Hitler, as we have seen, eliminated Jewish musicians and music by composers of Jewish ancestry, but he did not hate music per se. Stalin attacked Prokofiev, Shostakovich, and Khachaturian for composing music that was bourgeois—whatever that means—but he did not hate music per se.
>
> On the other hand, as Glazov informs us, "The Taliban illegalized music completely in Afghanistan, and Ayatollah Khomeini banned most music from Iranian radio and television."
>
> Lenin did not ban music, but he wouldn't listen to it. "It makes you want to say stupid, nice things and stroke the heads of people who could create such beauty while living in this vile hell."
>
> During Chairman Mao's Cultural Revolution, the only musical works that could be performed were eight revolutionary operas selected by Mao's wife, Jiang Qing.
>
> The idea of limiting and censoring music is at least as old as the 4th century B.C.E., when Plato wrote that in *The Republic* he envisioned, the flute and other instruments "capable of modulation into all the

modes" would be banned ...

We don't think of Plato as a totalitarian, but he shared the totalitarian rulers' fear of the power of music to unleash the human spirit.

He continued:

Chairman Mao also divided people into three categories. The first was Mao himself; the second was the Party; the third was the "laobaixing" – the person in the street, the ordinary people (literally the "old 100 surnames").

When I was teaching in China in 1989, during Beijing Spring, passers-by approached me and asked questions, often in Chinese. One man asked me whether, if Plato were alive today, he would consider Chairman Mao an example of the Philosopher King. My Chinese is not very good, but the man was very patient and made sure that I understood his question.

Since I disapprove of the politics of both Plato and Chairman Mao, I said yes.

The question led me to understand that it was no accident that Mao and Plato both wanted to ban certain kinds of music. Plato said that literature should be altered so that people should not fear death:

"The poets must be told to speak well of that other world. The gloomy descriptions they now give must be forbidden, not only as untrue, but as injurious to our future warriors."

We are reminded of the perpetrators of 9/11, who willingly died so that they could kill, even though their dramatic and well-coordinated plan could not in any conceivable way have helped the cause of Islam.

Hitler stated Nov. 6, 1933 (William Shirer, *Rise and Fall of the Third Reich* (NY: Simon & Schuster, 1960, p, 249):

When an opponent declares, "I will not come over to your side," I calmly say, "Your child belongs to us already ... What are you? You will pass on. Your descendants, however, now stand in the new camp. In a short time they will know nothing else but this new community."

Karl Marx stated:

Take away the heritage of a people and they are easily destroyed.

Dale Evans wrote in the article "Sex Education Part of Longterm Social Engineering," March 27, 2015:

The ex-military psychiatrist, Brock Chisholm... became first Director-General of the UN World Health Organization. In the Feb. 1946 issue of Psychiatry, Chisholm wrote,

"To achieve world government, it is necessary to remove from the minds of men their individualism, loyalty to family traditions, national patriotism, and religious dogmas."

He continued: "We have swallowed all manner of poisonous certainties fed us by our parents, our Sunday and day school teachers, our politicians, our priests ... The reinterpretation and eventual eradication of the concept of right and wrong which has been the basis of child training, the substitution of intelligent and rational thinking for faith in the certainties of old people, these are the belated objectives ... for charting the changes in human behavior."

Chisholm was a strong supporter of early childhood sex education: "Children have to be freed from ... religious and other cultural prejudices forced upon them by parents, civil and religious authorities... Sex education should be introduced in the 4th grade, eliminating 'the ways of elders' by force if necessary."

Rep. Fisher Ames, who proposed the wording of the First Amendment, stated:

When the tyranny of the majority leads to chaos, society will submit to rule by the sword.

James Monroe stated in his Inaugural 1817:

When the people become ignorant and corrupt, when they degenerate ... they are incapable of exercising the sovereignty. Usurpation is then an easy attainment, and an usurper soon found.

Harry S Truman stated April 3, 1951:

Without a firm moral foundation, freedom degenerates quickly into selfishness and ... anarchy. Then there will be freedom only for the rapacious and ... more unscrupulous than the rank and file of the people.

Plato wrote:

"It is in education that bad discipline can most easily creep in unobserved," he replied. "Yes," I agreed, "because people don't treat it seriously there, and think no harm can come of it."

"It only does harm," he said, "because it makes itself at home and gradually undermines morals and manners; from them it invades business dealings generally, and then spreads into the laws and constitution without any restraint, until it has made complete havoc of private and public life."

This was echoed by historians Will and Ariel Durant in *The Lessons of History* (NY: Simon & Schuster, 1968):

Civilization is not inherited; it has to be learned and earned by each generation anew, if the transmission should be interrupted ... civilization would die, and we should be savages again.

Plato's disillusionment with democracy was mentioned by Will and Ariel Durant in *The Lessons of History* (p. 74):

By the time of Plato's death, his hostile analysis of Athenian democracy was approaching apparent confirmation by history. Athens recovered wealth, but this was now commercial rather than landed wealth; industrialists, merchants, and bankers were at the top of the reshuffled heap ...

The poor schemed to despoil the rich by legislation, taxation, and revolution; the rich organized themselves for protection against the poor...

The poorer citizens captured control of the Assembly, and began to vote the money of the rich into the coffers of the state, for redistribution among the people through governmental enterprises and subsides. The politicians strained their ingenuity to discover new sources of public revenue.

In *The Story of Civilization* (Vol. 2–The Life of Greece, Simon & Schuster, 1939, p. 554), Will and Ariel Durant described what happened in Athens:

> The class war had turned democracy into a contest in legislative looting.

Jefferson wrote in his *Notes on Virginia*, 1782:

> Mankind soon learns to make interested uses of every right and power which they possess, or may assume. The public money ... will soon be discovered to be sources of wealth and dominion to those who hold them; distinguished, too, by this tempting circumstance, that they are the instrument, as well as the object of acquisition.

Edmund Burke stated in *A Letter to a Member of the National Assembly*, 1791:

> What is liberty without wisdom and without virtue? It is the greatest of all possible evils; for it is folly, vice, and madness, without restraint.

The poor controlling Athens' democracy was described as "empowered envy" by the Durants in *The Lessons of History* (NY: Simon & Schuster, 1968, p. 74):

> The middle classes, as well as the rich, began to distrust democracy as empowered envy, and the poor distrusted it as a sham equality of votes nullified by a gaping inequality of wealth. The rising bitterness of the class war left Greece internally as well as internationally divided when Philip of Macedon pounced down upon it in 338 BC ... Athenian democracy disappeared under Macedonian dictatorship.

TIMELINE 585–509 BC

585 BC – Cyaxares, King of the Median Empire, LARGEST EMPIRE IN THE WORLD AT THIS DATE, SURPASSING ALL PREVIOUS ONES.

c.563 BC – Gautama Buddha born in India.

560 BC – Croesus, King of the Lydian Empire of Anatolia (world's richest man, issuing the first gold coins)

559 BC – Cyrus the Great of the Persia Empire, allowed exiled Jews to return to their homeland, even providing the funds to rebuild their temples.

551 BC – Confucius born during China's Spring and Autumn Period of history.

522 BC – Darius the Great, King of Kings, Persian Achaemenid Empire, LARGEST EMPIRE IN THE WORLD TO THIS DATE, SURPASSING ALL PREVIOUS ONES, ruling an estimated 44 percent of the world's population. The historian Herodotus noted "the most disgraceful thing in the world [the Persians] think, is to tell a lie; the next worst, to owe a debt." On a monument on the road to Kermanushah in the Behistun mountains, is the inscription of Darius the Great:

> I was not a lie-follower, I was not a doer of wrong... According to righteousness I conducted myself. Neither to the weak or to the powerful did I do wrong. The man who cooperated with my house, him I rewarded well; who so did injury, him I punished well.

510 BC – Roman King Tarquin the Proud.

509 BC – ROMAN REPUBLIC

ROMAN REPUBLIC "SPQR"

The Roman Republic existed from 509 BC to 27 BC. It was controlled by 600 Senators. "SPQR" stood for Senatus Populusque Romanus, or Senate & People of Rome. The word "republic" is from the Latin phrase "res publica," which means "a public affair." Yale President Ezra Stiles addressed Connecticut's General Assembly, May 8, 1783:

> The senatorial constitution and consulate of the Roman Empire lasted from Tarquin (510 BC, the Latin King chased out by Romans) to Caesar (44 BC).

A republic is a form of government where representatives are trusted by the people to protect their interests, while the people are busy supporting their families.

Justice James Wilson wrote in *Chisholm v. State of Ga.*, 2 U.S. 419 (1793), 453–466:

> (Roman orator) Cicero says so sublimely, "Nothing, which is exhibited upon our globe, is more acceptable to that divinity which governs the whole universe, than those communities and assemblages of men, which, lawfully associated, are denominated States."

James Wilson stated in his *Lectures on Law* delivered at the College of Philadelphia, 1790–91:

> In the original constitution of Rome, the sovereign power, the dominium eminens, as it is called by the civilians, always resided in the collective body of the people ...

> As to the people, however, in whom the sovereign power resides ... from their authority the constitution originates: for their safety and felicity it is established: in their hands it is as clay in the hands of the potter: they have the right to mold, to preserve, to improve, to refine, and to finish it as they please ...

> In a free country, every citizen forms a part of the sovereign power: he possesses a vote ... The sovereign power residing in the people; they may change their constitution and government whenever they please ... In free states, such as ours, the sovereign or supreme power resides in the people.

James Wilson stated at Pennsylvania's Convention to Ratify the U.S. Constitution, Dec. 1, 1787:

> The sovereignty resides in the people; they have not parted with it.

Yale President Ezra Stiles addressed Connecticut's General Assembly, May 8, 1783:

> They cannot, however, assemble from the territory of an empire, and must, therefore, if they have any share in government, represent themselves by delegation. This constitutes one order in legislature and sovereignty.

The Roman Republic began with the help of Publius

(died 503 BC), who ended the reign of the 7th King of Rome, the brutal Tarquinius Superbus.

King Tarquinius had a son, Sextus, who raped a very virtuous woman named Lucretia, the wife of the Roman Cousul Collatinus. Lucretia gather the Roman leaders together and committed suicide right in front of them. The Roman leaders responded by killing King Tarquinius and making rule that if anybody in Rome ever declared themselves king, anyone could kill that person without any repercussions. This was the beginning of the Roman Republic – a government without a king.

The rape of Lucretia has been referred to in Saint Augustine's *The City of God* (5th century), Geoffrey Chaucer's *The Legend of Good Women* (1385), William Shakespeare's *The Rape of Lucrece* (1593) and Rembrandt's painting *Lucretia* (1664).

When Publius was building a grand mansion, the rumor began to spread that he was considering becoming king. When Publius heard the rumor, he destroyed his own mansion in one night. Publius helped institute several policies in the Roman Republic, such as:

ANYONE attempting to reestablish the monarchy could be executed by any citizen without trial;

ANYONE who seized an office without *popular* vote would suffer execution;

ANY Roman could be a Consul (one of two annually elected chief magistrates);

DECISIONS of the Consuls could be appealed;

NEEDY Romans were exempt from taxation;

PATRICIANS (members of ruling class families) would be punished more severely than plebs (general body of Roman citizens) for disobeying a Consul; and

CONTROL of the treasury was removed from the Consuls to the Temple of Saturn, under administration of quaestors (elected officials).

When the U.S. Constitution was being considered for ratification by the original 13 States, 1787–1788,

Alexander Hamilton, John Jay and James Madison wrote a collection of 85 essays called the *Federalist Papers.* They collectively signed "Publius" in honor of the role Publius played in founding the Roman Republic.

The Roman Republic's constitution had a separation of powers with checks and balances, reflecting the tensions between the aristocracy (patricians) and the common people (plebeians). They eventually had around 600 Senators, who were descendants of founders of the Republic, and two executives, called consuls, who were appointed for one year terms by the Senate. During their respective one year terms of consulship, each consul took turns being head of state, one month on–one month off, thus alternating the office.

E.C. Wines wrote in *Commentaries on the Laws of the Ancient Hebrews, with an Introductory Essay on Civil Society & Government* (NY: Geo. P. Putnam & Co., 1853):

> The old Romans have received the highest praises, because, conscious of the importance of imparting to the rising generation an early knowledge of the laws, they made the twelve tables one of the first elements of public instruction, requiring the youth to commit to memory their entire contents. They were sensible, that what is learned at so early a period is not only likely to be long remembered, but is almost sure to command respect and veneration.

During the period of the Republic, Rome expanded from Italy to controlling the entire Mediterranean, North Africa, the Iberian Peninsula, Greece, Gaul (France) and much of the middle east.

One of the Roman Republic's renown leaders was Cincinnatus (519–438 BC), who twice led Rome's army to victory in battle, then returned to his farm.

In 458 BC, the Aequians, Sabinians and Volscians were attacking in the Alban hills southeast of the city of Rome. The Roman Senate sent messengers to Cincinnatus, who was plowing his field, requesting him to be a temporary dictator and lead the Roman troops. After the victory, Cincinnatus immediately resigned and went back to his farm.

In 439 BC, when the conspiracy of Spurius Maelius threatened Rome, Cincinnatus was again called out of retirement to save Rome, then again return to his farm.

The willingness of Cincinnatus to relinquish absolute authority once the national crisis was over served as an example of civic virtue to not only the Roman Republic, but also early American leaders, including George Washington.

After the victory over the British, a gathering of American officers and soldiers stationed in Newburgh, New York, who had not been paid for years, threatened not to disband, but to march on the capitol, which was then New York City. There was even a suggestion circulating that Washington declare himself king, which would have been supported by many.

Washington arrived at the gathering, March 15, 1783, and urged them to oppose anyone:

> ...who wickedly attempts to open the floodgates of civil discord and deluge our rising empire in blood.

Many were brought to tears as Washington fumbled to put on his new glasses, saying: "Gentlemen, you will permit me to put on my spectacles, for I have not only grown gray but almost blind in the service of my country." Later that year, Washington resigned his commission and returned to his farm.

After serving two terms as President, Washington again returned to his farm. J.R.R. Tolken's novel, *The Lord of the Rings*, tells of man's lust for "the ring of power." George Washington had that power and gave it up, twice.

Every President since has honored his example of only serving two terms until Franklin D. Roosevelt got himself elected four times. This resulted in Congress passing the 22nd Amendment limiting a President to only two terms.

In May of 1783, Major General Henry Knox and Lieutenant Colonel Alexander Hamilton organized the first meeting of the Society of Cincinnati, honoring the example of Roman Dictator Cincinnatus, who resigned to return to farming.

In 1790, a member of the Society, Arthur St. Clair, governor of the Northwest Territory, named the city of Cincinnati, Ohio.

In the early 1780's, while having his portrait painted, King George III asked his American-born painter, Benjamin West, what General Washington would do after winning independence. West replied: "They say he will return to his farm." King George responded:

> If he does that, he will be the greatest man in the world.

In a world where kings killed to get power and kings killed to keep power, George Washington had power and gave it up. President Harry S Truman recorded in a personal memorandum, April 16, 1950:

> There is a lure in power. It can get into a man's blood just as gambling and lust for money have been known to do.

> This is a Republic. The greatest in the history of the world. I want this country to continue as a Republic. Cincinnatus and Washington pointed the way.

> When Rome forgot Cincinnatus, its downfall began. When we forget the examples of such men as Washington, Jefferson and Andrew Jackson, all of whom could have had a continuation in the office, then will we start down the road to dictatorship and ruin.

SUN TZU – *THE ART OF WAR*

481 BC – Sun Tzu (c.544–496 BC) was a Chinese general, strategist and philosopher during China's Warring States Period (481–403 BC). His book, *The Art of War,* is a manual of how to win battles and consolidate control. Tactics include spies, deception, entrapment, plotting and coercion. Sun Tzu has been studied by kings and generals, including:

–Qin Shi Huang (260–210 BC) of the Qin Dynasty, who was the first emperor of unified China

–Japanese generals, beginning in 760 AD, including the samurai, shoguns, daimyos and Japanese Admiral Togo Heihachiro in victory in the Russo–Japanese War;

–French Emperor Napoleon, in his wars in Europe

–Mao Zedong in his Communist victory of China's leader Chiang Kai-shek in 1949

–Ho Chi Minh translated the work into Vietnamese. During the Vietnam War, General Vo Nguyen Giap used it in his battles with French and American forces; Communist guerrilla warfare and insurgencies around the world;

–U.S. Department of the Army, through its Command and General Staff College, has directed all units to maintain libraries within their respective headquarters for the continuing education of personnel in the art of war.

–U.S. Marine Corps Professional Reading Program;

–General Norman Schwarzkopf and General Colin Powell, during the Persian Gulf War in the 1990s, used Sun Tzu's principles of deception, speed, and attacking the enemy's weakness;

–Politicians, who adapted Sun Tzu's tactics to political warfare and subterfuge.

Below are selected excerpts from Sun Tzu's *The Art of War* (translated by Lionel Giles):

I. Laying Plans ...

18. All warfare is based on deception.

19. Hence, when able to attack, we must seem unable; when using our forces, we must seem inactive; when we are near, we must make the enemy believe we are far away; when far away, we must make him believe we are near.

20. Hold out baits to entice the enemy. Feign

disorder, and crush him.

21. If he is secure at all points, be prepared for him. If he is in superior strength, evade him.

22. If your opponent is of choleric temper, seek to irritate him. Pretend to be weak, that he may grow arrogant.

23. If he is taking his ease, give him no rest. If his forces are united, separate them.

24. Attack him where he is unprepared, appear where you are not expected.

25. These military devices, leading to victory, must not be divulged beforehand.

26. Now the general who wins a battle makes many calculations in his temple ere the battle is fought. The general who loses a battle makes but few calculations beforehand. Thus do many calculations lead to victory, and few calculations to defeat: how much more no calculation at all! It is by attention to this point that I can foresee who is likely to win or lose.

II. Waging War ...

2. When you engage in actual fighting, if victory is long in coming, then men's weapons will grow dull and their ardor will be damped. If you lay siege to a town, you will exhaust your strength.

3. Again, if the campaign is protracted, the resources of the State will not be equal to the strain.

4. Now, when your weapons are dulled, your ardor damped, your strength exhausted and your treasure spent, other chieftains will spring up to take advantage of your extremity. Then no man, however wise, will be able to avert the consequences that must ensue.

5. Thus, though we have heard of stupid haste in war, cleverness has never been seen associated with long delays.

6. There is no instance of a country having benefited from prolonged warfare.

7. It is only one who is thoroughly acquainted with the evils of war that can thoroughly understand the profitable way of carrying it on ...

16. Now in order to kill the enemy, our men must be roused to anger; that there may be advantage from defeating the enemy, they must have their rewards ...

19. In war, then, let your great object be victory, not lengthy campaigns.

20. Thus it may be known that the leader of armies is the arbiter of the people's fate, the man on whom it depends whether the nation shall be in peace or in peril.

III. Attack by Stratagem

1. Sun Tzu said: In the practical art of war, the best thing of all is to take the enemy's country whole and intact; to shatter and destroy it is not so good. So, too, it is better to recapture an army entire than to destroy it, to capture a regiment, a detachment or a company entire than to destroy them.

2. Hence to fight and conquer in all your battles is not supreme excellence; supreme excellence consists in breaking the enemy's resistance without fighting.

3. Thus the highest form of generalship is to balk the enemy's plans; the next best is to prevent the junction of the enemy's forces; the next in order is to attack the enemy's army in the field; and the worst policy of all is to besiege walled cities ...

5. The general, unable to control his irritation, will launch his men to the assault like swarming ants, with the result that one-third of his men are slain, while the town still remains untaken. Such are the disastrous effects of a siege.

6. Therefore the skillful leader subdues the enemy's troops without any fighting; he captures their cities without laying siege to them; he overthrows their kingdom without lengthy operations in the field ...

8. It is the rule in war, if our forces are ten to the enemy's one, to surround him; if five to one, to attack him; if twice as numerous, to divide our army into two.

9. If equally matched, we can offer battle; if slightly inferior in numbers, we can avoid the enemy; if quite unequal in every way, we can flee from him...

11. Now the general is the bulwark of the State; if the

bulwark is complete at all points; the State will be strong; if the bulwark is defective, the State will be weak ...

16. But when the army is restless and distrustful, trouble is sure to come from the other feudal princes. This is simply bringing anarchy into the army, and flinging victory away.

17. Thus we may know that there are five essentials for victory:

1) He will win who knows when to fight and when not to fight.

2) He will win who knows how to handle both superior and inferior forces.

3) He will win whose army is animated by the same spirit throughout all its ranks.

4) He will win who, prepared himself, waits to take the enemy unprepared.

5) He will win who has military capacity and is not interfered with by the sovereign.

18. Hence the saying: If you know the enemy and know yourself, you need not fear the result of a hundred battles. If you know yourself but not the enemy, for every victory gained you will also suffer a defeat. If you know neither the enemy nor yourself, you will succumb in every battle.

IV. Tactical Dispositions

1. Sun Tzu said: The good fighters of old first put themselves beyond the possibility of defeat, and then waited for an opportunity of defeating the enemy.

2. To secure ourselves against defeat lies in our own hands, but the opportunity of defeating the enemy is provided by the enemy himself.

3. Thus the good fighter is able to secure himself against defeat, but cannot make certain of defeating the enemy ...

5. Security against defeat implies defensive tactics; ability to defeat the enemy means taking the offensive...

7. The general who is skilled in defense hides

in the most secret recesses of the earth; he who is skilled in attack flashes forth from the topmost heights of heaven. Thus on the one hand we have ability to protect ourselves; on the other, a victory that is complete ...

13. He wins his battles by making no mistakes. Making no mistakes is what establishes the certainty of victory, for it means conquering an enemy that is already defeated.

14. Hence the skillful fighter puts himself into a position which makes defeat impossible, and does not miss the moment for defeating the enemy.

15. Thus it is that in war the victorious strategist only seeks battle after the victory has been won, whereas he who is destined to defeat, first fights and afterwards looks for victory ...

V. Energy ...

4. That the impact of your army may be like a grindstone dashed against an egg – this is effected by the science of weak points and strong.

5. In all fighting, the direct method may be used for joining battle, but indirect methods will be needed in order to secure victory.

6. Indirect tactics, efficiently applied, are inexhaustible ...

10. In battle, there are not more than two methods of attack – the direct and the indirect; yet these two in combination give rise to an endless series of maneuvers.

11. The direct and the indirect lead on to each other in turn. It is like moving in a circle – you never come to an end. Who can exhaust the possibilities of their combination? ...

16. Amid the turmoil and tumult of battle, there may be seeming disorder and yet no real disorder at all; amid confusion and chaos, your array may be without head or tail, yet it will be proof against defeat.

17. Simulated disorder postulates perfect discipline, simulated fear postulates courage; simulated weakness

postulates strength.

18. Hiding order beneath the cloak of disorder is simply a question of subdivision; concealing courage under a show of timidity presupposes a fund of latent energy; masking strength with weakness is to be effected by tactical dispositions.

19. Thus one who is skillful at keeping the enemy on the move maintains deceitful appearances, according to which the enemy will act. He sacrifices something, that the enemy may snatch at it.

VI. Weak Points and Strong ...

9. O divine art of subtlety and secrecy! Through you we learn to be invisible, through you inaudible; and hence we can hold the enemy's fate in our hands...

13. By discovering the enemy's dispositions and remaining invisible ourselves, we can keep our forces concentrated, while the enemy's must be divided ...

16. The spot where we intend to fight must not be made known; for then the enemy will have to prepare against a possible attack at several different points...

25. In making tactical dispositions, the highest pitch you can attain is to conceal them ...

30. So in war, the way is to avoid what is strong and to strike at what is weak ...

VII. Maneuvering ...

4. Thus, to take a long and circuitous route, after enticing the enemy out of the way, and though starting after him, to contrive to reach the goal before him, shows knowledge of the artifice of deviation ...

15. In war, practice dissimulation (feigning, hypocrisy), and you will succeed ...

19. Let your plans be dark and impenetrable as night, and when you move, fall like a thunderbolt ...

33. It is a military axiom not to advance uphill against the enemy, nor to oppose him when he comes downhill...

35. Do not swallow bait offered by the enemy. Do not interfere with an army that is returning home...

VIII. Variation in Tactics ...

12. There are five dangerous faults which may affect a general: (1) Recklessness, which leads to destruction; (2) cowardice, which leads to capture; (3) a hasty temper, which can be provoked by insults; (4) a delicacy of honor which is sensitive to shame; (5) over-solicitude for his men, which exposes him to worry and trouble ...

IX. The Army on the March ...

17. If in the neighborhood of your camp there should be any hilly country, ponds surrounded by aquatic grass, hollow basins filled with reeds, or woods with thick undergrowth, they must be carefully routed out and searched; for these are places where men in ambush or insidious spies are likely to be lurking ...

20. If his place of encampment is easy of access, he is tendering a bait ...

24. Humble words and increased preparations are signs that the enemy is about to advance. Violent language and driving forward as if to the attack are signs that he will retreat ...

26. Peace proposals unaccompanied by a sworn covenant indicate a plot ...

28. When some are seen advancing and some retreating, it is a lure ...

35. The sight of men whispering together in small knots or speaking in subdued tones points to disaffection amongst the rank and file.

36. Too frequent rewards signify that the enemy is at the end of his resources; too many punishments betray a condition of dire distress ...

41. He who exercises no forethought but makes light of his opponents is sure to be captured by them...

X. Terrain ...

7. In a position of this sort, even though the enemy should offer us an attractive bait, it will be advisable not to stir forth, but rather to retreat, thus enticing the enemy in his turn; then, when part of his army has

come out, we may deliver our attack with advantage ...

24. The general who advances without coveting fame and retreats without fearing disgrace, whose only thought is to protect his country and do good service for his sovereign, is the jewel of the kingdom.

25. Regard your soldiers as your children, and they will follow you into the deepest valleys; look upon them as your own beloved sons, and they will stand by you even unto death.

26. If, however, you are indulgent, but unable to make your authority felt; kind-hearted, but unable to enforce your commands; and incapable, moreover, of quelling disorder: then your soldiers must be likened to spoiled children; they are useless for any practical purpose ...

XI. The Nine Situations ...

18. If asked how to cope with a great host of the enemy in orderly array and on the point of marching to the attack, I should say: "Begin by seizing something which your opponent holds dear; then he will be amenable to your will" ...

19. Rapidity is the essence of war: take advantage of the enemy's unreadiness, make your way by unexpected routes, and attack unguarded spots.

20. The following are the principles to be observed by an invading force: The further you penetrate into a country, the greater will be the solidarity of your troops, and thus the defenders will not prevail against you ...

22 ... Keep your army continually on the move, and devise unfathomable plans.

23. Throw your soldiers into positions whence there is no escape, and they will prefer death to flight. If they will face death, there is nothing they may not achieve. Officers and men alike will put forth their uttermost strength.

24. Soldiers when in desperate straits lose the sense of fear. If there is no place of refuge, they will stand firm. If they are in hostile country, they will show a stubborn front. If there is no help for it, they will fight hard ...

29. The skillful tactician may be likened to the shuai-jan. Now the shuai-jan is a snake that is found in the ChUng mountains. Strike at its head, and you will be attacked by its tail; strike at its tail, and you will be attacked by its head; strike at its middle, and you will be attacked by head and tail both.

30. Asked if an army can be made to imitate the shuai-jan, I should answer, Yes. For the men of Wu and the men of Yueh are enemies; yet if they are crossing a river in the same boat and are caught by a storm, they will come to each other's assistance just as the left hand helps the right ...

32. The principle on which to manage an army is to set up one standard of courage which all must reach ...

35. It is the business of a general to be quiet and thus ensure secrecy; upright and just, and thus maintain order.

36. He must be able to mystify his officers and men by false reports and appearances, and thus keep them in total ignorance.

37. By altering his arrangements and changing his plans, he keeps the enemy without definite knowledge. By shifting his camp and taking circuitous routes, he prevents the enemy from anticipating his purpose ...

54. When a warlike prince attacks a powerful state, his generalship shows itself in preventing the concentration of the enemy's forces. He overawes his opponents, and their allies are prevented from joining against him.

55. Hence he does not strive to ally himself with all and sundry, nor does he foster the power of other states. He carries out his own secret designs, keeping his antagonists in awe. Thus he is able to capture their cities and overthrow their kingdoms ...

57. Confront your soldiers with the deed itself; never let them know your design. When the outlook is bright, bring it before their eyes; but tell them nothing when the situation is gloomy.

58. Place your army in deadly peril, and it will survive; plunge it into desperate straits, and it will

come off in safety.

59. For it is precisely when a force has fallen into harm's way that is capable of striking a blow for victory ...

61. By persistently hanging on the enemy's flank, we shall succeed in the long run in killing the commander-in-chief.

62. This is called ability to accomplish a thing by sheer cunning ...

65. If the enemy leaves a door open, you must rush in ...

68. At first, then, exhibit the coyness of a maiden, until the enemy gives you an opening; afterwards emulate the rapidity of a running hare, and it will be too late for the enemy to oppose you.

XII. The Attack by Fire

1. Sun Tzu said: There are five ways of attacking with fire. The first is to burn soldiers in their camp; the second is to burn stores; the third is to burn baggage trains; the fourth is to burn arsenals and magazines; the fifth is to hurl dropping fire amongst the enemy ...

8. (3) When the force of the flames has reached its height, follow it up with an attack, if that is practicable; if not, stay where you are.

17. Move not unless you see an advantage; use not your troops unless there is something to be gained; fight not unless the position is critical.

18. No ruler should put troops into the field merely to gratify his own spleen; no general should fight a battle simply out of pique ...

XIII. The Use of Spies ...

2. Hostile armies may face each other for years, striving for the victory which is decided in a single day. This being so, to remain in ignorance of the enemy's condition simply because one grudges the outlay of a hundred ounces of silver in honors and emoluments, is the height of inhumanity ...

4. Thus, what enables the wise sovereign and the good general to strike and conquer, and achieve things

beyond the reach of ordinary men, is foreknowledge.

5. Now this foreknowledge cannot be elicited from spirits; it cannot be obtained inductively from experience, nor by any deductive calculation.

6. Knowledge of the enemy's dispositions can only be obtained from other men.

7. Hence the use of spies, of whom there are five classes: (1) Local spies; (2) inward spies; (3) converted spies; (4) doomed spies; (5) surviving spies.

8. When these five kinds of spy are all at work, none can discover the secret system. This is called "divine manipulation of the threads." It is the sovereign's most precious faculty.

9. Having local spies means employing the services of the inhabitants of a district.

10. Having inward spies, making use of officials of the enemy.

11. Having converted spies, getting hold of the enemy's spies and using them for our own purposes.

12. Having doomed spies, doing certain things openly for purposes of deception, and allowing our spies to know of them and report them to the enemy.

13. Surviving spies, finally, are those who bring back news from the enemy's camp.

14. Hence it is that which none in the whole army are more intimate relations to be maintained than with spies. None should be more liberally rewarded. In no other business should greater secrecy be preserved.

15. Spies cannot be usefully employed without a certain intuitive sagacity.

16. They cannot be properly managed without benevolence and straightforwardness.

17. Without subtle ingenuity of mind, one cannot make certain of the truth of their reports.

18. Be subtle! Be subtle! and use your spies for every kind of business.

19. If a secret piece of news is divulged by a spy before the time is ripe, he must be put to death together

with the man to whom the secret was told.

20. Whether the object be to crush an army, to storm a city, or to assassinate an individual, it is always necessary to begin by finding out the names of the attendants, the aides-de-camp, and door-keepers and sentries of the general in command. Our spies must be commissioned to ascertain these.

21. The enemy's spies who have come to spy on us must be sought out, tempted with bribes, led away and comfortably housed. Thus they will become converted spies and available for our service.

22. It is through the information brought by the converted spy that we are able to acquire and employ local and inward spies.

23. It is owing to his information, again, that we can cause the doomed spy to carry false tidings to the enemy.

24. Lastly, it is by his information that the surviving spy can be used on appointed occasions.

25. The end and aim of spying in all its five varieties is knowledge of the enemy; and this knowledge can only be derived, in the first instance, from the converted spy. Hence it is essential that the converted spy be treated with the utmost liberality ...

27. Hence it is only the enlightened ruler and the wise general who will use the highest intelligence of the army for purposes of spying and thereby they achieve great results. Spies are a most important element in water, because on them depends an army's ability to move.

The use of deceit was referred to John F. Kennedy addressed the American Newspaper Publishers Association at the Waldorf-Astoria Hotel, New York, April 27, 1961:

The very word "secrecy" is repugnant in a free and open society; and we are as a people inherently and historically opposed to secret societies, to secret oaths and to secret proceedings ...

We are opposed around the world by a monolithic and ruthless conspiracy that relies primarily on covert means for expanding its sphere of influence—on infiltration instead of invasion, on subversion instead of elections, on intimidation instead of free choice, on guerrillas by night instead of armies by day.

It is a system which has conscripted vast human and material resources into the building of a tightly knit, highly efficient machine that combines military, diplomatic, intelligence, economic, scientific and political operations.

Its preparations are concealed, not published. Its mistakes are buried, not headlined. Its dissenters are silenced, not praised. No expenditure is questioned, no rumor is printed, no secret is revealed.

TIMELINE 413–336 BC

413 BC – Shishunaga, King of Northern India's Shishunaga Dynasty of Magadha

400 BC – Agesilaus II, King of Sparta, Eurypontid Dynasty

359 BC – Philip II, King of the Macedonian Empire

336 BC – Alexander the Great, Macedonian Empire, LARGEST EMPIRE IN THE WORLD AT THIS DATE

FALL OF ATHENIAN DEMOCRACY

To the north of Athens was the Macedonian Kingdom, ruled by Philip of Macedon (382–336 BC), whose son was Alexander the Great. Macedonians were looked down upon by the Greeks as uncivilized barbarians.

Philip of Macedon began to seize Greek cities and capture gold and silver mines. With his great wealth, Philip bribed some Greek citizens to betray their city for personal gain. These traitorous citizens would go to the agora marketplace where everyone talked politics and sow seeds of discord. Philip then created a "Macedonian party" of propagandists in every Greek city.

When Philip conquered Thebes, the patriotic citizens of Athens began to call for strengthening their defenses. The paid propagandists, on the other hand, would stand up in the agora marketplace and tell citizens not to jump to conclusions, that Philip was not such a bad guy, and that he was not "conquering" other cities but rather "liberating" them.

The propagandist traitors gathered around themselves simple-minded people that actually believed their lies. These type of people were later referred to by Lenin as "useful idiots"

Thomas Sowell wrote in his article "Degeneration of Democracy" (6/22/2010):

> "Useful idiots" was the term supposedly coined by
> V.I. Lenin to describe similarly unthinking supporters
> of his dictatorship in the Soviet Union.

When Philip finally marched up to the gates of Athens, the city was so confused and disorganized that they threw open the gates and, surrendered. The people of Athens did not get a chance to rule themselves again for over 2,000 years.

After Philip, Athens was under the rule of his son, Alexander the Great, followed by Alexander's General Antigonus and his dynasty, followed by the Romans Emperors, then Byzantine Emperors, then Muslims Sultans, till Greeks won their independence in 1830.

Philip's son, Alexander the Great, conquered Greece, Persia, Egypt, and all the way to the borders of India. By his death in 323 BC, Alexander amassed the largest empire in the world to that date.

The paid propagandists traitors of Greece acted in a role that in later generations might be referred to as paid lobbyists, political operatives, agitators, change agents, community organizers, agent provocateurs, thugs, assassins, spies, moles, and in many cases, agenda driven biased media.

These paid propagandists were later termed "the fifth column," as a typical battle array consisted of two columns and two flanks. The "fifth column" were in essence traitors within a democracy who, for personal gain, spread lies to breed confusion.

The act of fostering dissension causes patriotic citizens to be divided in their opinions, thereby hindering their efforts to rally an adequate defense. Dwight Eisenhower was quoted in *TIME Magazine*, Oct. 13, 1952:

> The Bill of Rights contains no grant of privilege for a group of people to destroy the Bill of Rights. A group ... dedicated to the ultimate destruction of all civil liberties, cannot be allowed to claim civil liberties as its privileged sanctuary from which to carry on subversion of the Government.

Franklin Roosevelt warned Congress, Jan. 3, 1940:

> Doctrines that set group against group, faith against faith, race against race, class against class, fanning the fires of hatred in men too despondent, too desperate to think for themselves, were used as rabble-rousing slogans on which dictators could ride to power. And once in power they could saddle their tyrannies on whole nations.

After the Civil War, Booker T. Washington worked hard to help Blacks become successful despite being surrounded by Southern Democrats who passed Jim Crow Laws, Black Codes, and started the KKK.

He was criticized by Northern racial activists, such as W.E.B. Dubois, who demanded reparations. W.E.B. Dubois later joined the Communist Party and visited China's Communist dictator Mao Zedung.

Booker T. Washington warned in *My Larger Education–Being Chapters from My Experience* (1911, ch. V: The Intellectuals and the Boston Mob, p. 118):

> Some of these people do not want the Negro to lose his grievances, because they do not want to lose their jobs ... There is a certain class of race–problem solvers who do not want the patient to get well, because as long as the disease holds out they have not only an easy means of making a living, but also an easy medium through which to make themselves

prominent before the public.

Martin Luther King, Jr., who attended Booker T. Washington High School in Atlanta, warned, Aug. 28, 1963:

In the process of gaining our rightful place we must not be guilty of wrongful deeds. Let us not seek to satisfy our thirst for freedom by drinking from the cup of bitterness and hatred. We must forever conduct our struggle on the high plane of dignity and discipline. We must not allow our creative protest to degenerate into physical violence ...

New militancy which has engulfed the Negro community must not lead us to a distrust of all white people, for many of our white brothers, as evidenced by their presence here today, have come to realize that their destiny is tied up with our destiny and their freedom is inextricably bound to our freedom. We cannot walk alone.

Booker T. Washington wrote in *Up From Slavery* (1901):

I resolved that I would permit no man, no matter what his color might be, to narrow and degrade my soul by making me hate him. With God's help, I believe that I have completely rid myself of any ill feeling toward the Southern white man for any wrong that he may have inflicted upon my race.

I am made to feel just as happy now when I am rendering service to Southern white men as when the service is rendered to a member of my own race. I pity from the bottom of my heart any individual who is so unfortunate as to get into the habit of holding race prejudice.

Booker T. Washington wrote:

The man is unwise who does not cultivate in every manly way the friendship and goodwill of his next-door neighbor, whether he be black or white.

Booker T. Washington wrote in *Up From Slavery* (1901):

Great men cultivate love ... Only little men cherish a spirit of hatred.

WND.com published the article, May 19, 2015, "Hired

Ferguson protesters demand pay":

> "Black Lives Matter" protesters who were apparently hired to cause a ruckus in Ferguson, Missouri, are angry because, they say, they haven't been paid for their hard work. So they've launched a #CutTheCheck hashtag on Twitter and held a sit-in at the offices of Missourians Organizing for Reform and Empowerment, or MORE – the successor group to the Association of Community Organizations for Reform Now, or ACORN, in Missouri.

> The protesters have received as much as $5,000 a month to generate civil unrest in the troubled suburb of St. Louis, according to FrontPage Mag's Matthew Vadum ... Vadum reported. "MORE and other groups supporting the Black Lives Matter movement have received millions of dollars from billionaire financier George Soros" ...

> OrganizeMO.org, posted a memo on March 30 that announces a "support fund" offering "travel funding for individuals and grassroots groups that are working to advocate for police accountability and Black lives"... A group called Millennial Activists United posted a letter insisting MORE should "cut the checks" to the protesters.

THUG

"Thug" comes from the word "Thuggee" who were originally Muslim tribes and later Hindu followers of Kali. For 600 years, thugs raided caravans traveling across India. Ziya-ud-Din Barani's *History of Firuz Shah* (1356) described how thugs would join an unsuspecting caravan of travelers and pretend to be their friends.

After gaining their victim's trust, thugs would systematically distract them while other thugs would sneak behind and strangle them with a noose or handkerchief. After killing every traveler, thugs were careful to bury all the bodies so the next caravan would not be alerted. The British began eradicating thugs in the 1830s.

ASSASSIN

"Assassin" comes from an 11th century Arabic word "Hashshashin." This was a militant sect of Ismaili Muslims, led by Hassan-i-Sabah (1034–1124), who also called themselves "fedayeen," meaning one who is willing to sacrifice his life for the cause.

As a youth, Hassan-i-Sabah was friends with the Persian poet and mathematician Omar Khayyam (1048–1123), who wrote the Rubaiyat of Omar Khayyam. Hassan-i-Sabah's religious sect specialized in terrorizing their enemies in fearlessly executed, politically motivated killings.

Like an early version of suicide bombers, "hashshashims" would approach their unsuspecting victim in disguise, often in public or in a mosque, and kill them with a dagger. Then they would anxiously wait to be killed so that they would enter paradise and enjoy 72 virgins.

Marco Polo visited the Hashshashim's mountain fortress of Alamut after it was conquered by the Mongols in the 13th century. His was one of the many accounts of how Hassan-i-Sabah recruited assassins.

A future assassin was made to feel he was in danger of being killed, but then, without his knowledge, he was drugged with "hashish" and made to think he had died. In his altered state-of-mind, he would be taken to a garden filled with wine, beautiful women and sumptuous feasting.

Convinced he was in paradise, he would eventually pass out, whereupon he would be carried back to where he had been kidnapped. Upon regaining consciousness, he was told that he had visited paradise and that if he died obeying Hassan-i-Sabah orders to assassinate an enemy, he would return there. "Hashshashim" is the origin of the word "assassin."

PSYCHOLOGICAL PROJECTION

A tactic used in Islamic conquest is psychological projection or "victim–blaming." It is observed on school yards where the bully blames the kid he beats up for provoking him, or, in spousal abuse where a wife-beating husband blames the wife for provoking him. Muslims practice being "offended" at non-Muslims to justify retaliation and elimination of non-Muslim populations.

Mohammed provoked the pagans in Mecca till they chased him out. He claimed to be a victim of the their intolerance, justifying his later retaliation against them.

When his followers were chased out of Mecca, Mohammed allowed them to attack the caravans headed to Mecca.

⊷

AGENT PROVOCATEUR

"Agent provocateur" is a French tern for "inciting agent." This is a person operating undercover to infiltrate a group to entice and provoke them to commit illegal or rash acts which would discredit the group and give an excuse for the government to crush them with overwhelming force.

Undercover law enforcement sometimes infiltrate gangs and encourage them to commit a crime so the government can be justified in arresting them. Lenin and Stalin utilized "agent provocateurs" to infiltrate opposition groups, egging them on to do violence, or at least giving that appearance, so there would be an excuse to crack down on them. In a Fireside Chat, May 26, 1940, Franklin Roosevelt stated:

> Today's threat to our national security is not a matter of military weapons alone. We know of new methods of attack. The Trojan Horse. The Fifth Column that betrays a nation unprepared for treachery. Spies, saboteurs and traitors are the actors in this new strategy.

Franklin Roosevelt stated in a Fireside Chat, Dec. 29, 1940:

Their secret emissaries are active in our own country? They exploit for their own ends our natural abhorrence of war. These trouble-breeders have but one purpose. It is to divide our people into hostile groups and to destroy our unity and shatter our will to defend ourselves.

In the 1980s and 1990s, there was a growing militia movement in America, but when Waco and Oklahoma City bombings were blamed on individuals with tenuous connections to these groups, a "guilt by association" caused the government to vilify and entrap such groups, causing the movement to dry up.

Another potential scenario would be if radical leftists pretended to be conservative in order to infiltrate a right-wing group, then incite them to commit violent acts. The acts would marginalize the group and give a pretense for the government to crack down on the entire movement..

Nazi Minister of Propaganda Joseph Goebbels advised:

The most brilliant propagandist technique will yield no success unless one fundamental principle is borne in mind constantly ... it must confine itself to a few points and repeat them over and over.

Athens' internal problems distracted them from preparing to fight external threats. Will and Ariel Durant wrote in *The Story of Civilization* (Vol. 1, 1935, p. 463):

The bitter lesson that may be drawn from this tragedy is that eternal vigilance is the price of civilization. A nation must love peace, but keep its powder dry.

Once Philip of Macedon won the Battle of Chaeronea in 338 BC, and took control of Athens, the era of Athens as a self-ruling democracy was over.

Following Philip of Macedon, Athens was ruled by Alexander the Great, the Carthaginians, the Romans, the Byzantine Romans, and the Muslim Turks.

Of Rome's conquest of Greece in 168 BC, Will and Ariel

Durant wrote in *The Story of Civilization* (Vol. 2, 1939):

> The essential cause of the Roman conquest of Greece was the disintegration of Greek civilization from within. No great nation is ever conquered until it has destroyed itself.

Greece was not free again until the 19th century AD, but then it came under the control of the Germany's National Socialist Workers Party, then ultimately joined the European Union where its immense debt has nearly led to it relinquishing control over its fate.

MONTESQUIEU'S *THE SPIRIT OF THE LAWS*

As mentioned earlier, Montesquieu wrote the rarity of self-rule in *The Spirit of the Laws*, 1748, Book 3:

> Of a REPUBLICAN GOVERNMENT that ... the COLLECTIVE BODY OF THE PEOPLE ... should be possessed of the supreme power;

> Of a MONARCHY, that the PRINCE should have this power, but in the execution of it should be directed by established LAWS;

> Of a DESPOTIC GOVERNMENT, that a single person should rule according to HIS OWN WILL AND CAPRICE.

> This enables me to discover their three principles; which are thence naturally derived.

Montesquieu continued:

> I shall begin with a REPUBLICAN GOVERNMENT, and in particular with that of DEMOCRACY. Of the Principle of DEMOCRACY.

> There is no great share of probity (virtue) necessary to support a monarchical or despotic government. The force of laws in one, and the prince's arm in the other, are sufficient to direct and maintain the whole.

> But in a *popular* state ("popular" meaning "governed by the people"), one *spring* more is necessary, namely, VIRTUE ...

For it is clear that in a monarchy, where he who commands the execution of the laws generally thinks himself above them, there is less need of virtue than in a *popular* government, where the person entrusted with the execution of the laws is sensible of his being subject to their direction.

Clear is it also that a monarch who, through bad advice or indolence, ceases to enforce the execution of the laws, may easily repair the evil; he has only to follow other advice; or to shake off this indolence.

But when, in a *popular* government, there is a suspension of the laws, as this can proceed only from the corruption of the republic, the state is certainly undone.

Montesquieu went on to describe the English Commonwealth's brief experiment in self-rule:

A very droll spectacle it was in the last century to behold the impotent efforts of the English towards the establishment of democracy. (Oliver Cromwell's English Commonwealth, 1649–1658)

As they who had a share in the direction of public affairs were void of virtue; as their ambition was inflamed by the success of the most daring of their members; as the prevailing parties were successively animated by the spirit of faction, the government was continually changing: the people, amazed at so many revolutions, in vain attempted to erect a commonwealth.

At length, when the country had undergone the most violent shocks, they were obliged to have recourse to the very government (monarchy) which they had so wantonly proscribed (condemned).

Montesquieu continued:

The politic Greeks, who lived under a *popular* government, knew no other support than virtue ... When virtue is banished, ambition invades the minds of those who are disposed to receive it, and avarice possesses the whole community ...

They were free while under the restraint of laws... and as each citizen is like a slave who has run away from his master ... that which was a rule of action he styles constraint ... The members of the commonwealth riot on the public spoils, and its strength is only the power of a few, and the license of many.

Athens was possessed of the same number of forces when she triumphed so gloriously as when with such infamy she was enslaved.

She had twenty thousand citizens when she defended the Greeks against the Persians, when she contended for empire with Sparta, and invaded Sicily. She had twenty thousand when Demetrius Phalereus (ruler of Athens 317–307 BC) numbered them as slaves ...

When Philip attempted to lord it over Greece, and appeared at the gates of Athens she had even then lost nothing but time. We may see in Demosthenes (greatest of Greek orators, 351–341 BC) how difficult it was to awaken her; she dreaded Philip, not as the enemy of her liberty, but of her pleasures.

This famous city, which had withstood so many defeats, and having been so often destroyed had as often risen out of her ashes, was overthrown at the Battle of Chaeronea (338 BC) and at one blow deprived of all hopes of resource.

What does it avail her that Philip sends back her prisoners, if he does not return her men? It was ever after as easy to triumph over the forces of Athens as it had been difficult to subdue her virtue.

Montesquieu went on to describe a MONARCHY:

Virtue is not the Principle of a MONARCHICAL GOVERNMENT. In monarchies, policy effects great things with as little virtue as possible ...

Now in republics private crimes are more public, that is, they attack the constitution more than they do individuals; and in monarchies, public crimes are more private, that is, they are more prejudicial to private people than to the constitution ...

I am not ignorant that virtuous princes are so very rare; but I venture to affirm that in a monarchy it is extremely difficult for the people to be virtuous.

Let us compare what the historians of all ages have asserted concerning the courts of monarchs ... In respect to the wretched character of courtiers... we shall find that these are not airy speculations, but truths confirmed by a sad and melancholy experience.

Ambition in idleness; meanness mixed with pride; a desire of riches without industry; aversion to truth; flattery, perfidy, violation of engagements, contempt of civil duties, fear of the prince's virtue, hope from his weakness, but, above all, a perpetual ridicule cast upon virtue, are, I think, the characteristics by which most courtiers in all ages and countries have been constantly distinguished.

Now, it is exceedingly difficult for the leading men of the nation to be knaves, and the inferior sort to be honest; for the former to be cheats, and the latter to rest satisfied with being only dupes. But if there should chance to be some unlucky honest man among the people.

Cardinal Richelieu, in his political testament, seems to hint that a prince should take care not to employ him. So true is it that virtue is not the *spring* of this government! It is not indeed excluded, but it is not the *spring* of government.

Montesquieu continued regarding a MONARCHY:

Honor, that is, the prejudice of every person and rank, supplies the place of the political virtue ... It is capable of inspiring the most glorious actions, and, joined with the force of laws, may lead us to the end of government ...

Hence, in well-regulated monarchies, they are almost all good subjects, and very few good men ...

Monarchical government supposes ... preeminences and ranks, as likewise a noble descent. Now since it is the nature of honor to aspire to preferments and titles, it is properly placed in this government.

Ambition is pernicious (harmful) in a republic. But in a monarchy it has some good effects; it gives life to the government, and is attended with this advantage, that it is in no way dangerous, because it may be continually checked.

It is with this kind of government as with the system of the universe, in which there is a power that constantly repels all bodies from the center, and a power of gravitation that attracts them to it.

Honor sets all the parts of the body politic in motion, and by its very action connects them; thus each individual advances the public good, while he only thinks of promoting his own interest.

True it is that, philosophically speaking, it is a false honor which moves all the parts of the government; but even this false honor is as useful to the public as true honor could possibly be to private persons.

Is it not very exacting to oblige men to perform the most difficult actions, such as require an extraordinary exertion of fortitude and resolution, without other recompense than that of glory and applause?

Montesquieu described DESPOTIC GOVERNMENT:

Honor is far from being the principle of DESPOTIC GOVERNMENT ...

Mankind being here all upon a level, no one person can prefer himself to another; and as on the other hand they are all slaves, they can give themselves no sort of preference ...

How can despotism abide with honor? The one glories in the contempt of life; and the other is founded on the power of taking it away.

How can honor, on the other hand, bear with despotism? The former has its fixed rules ... but the latter is directed by no rule, and its own caprices are subversive of all others.

Honor, therefore, a thing unknown in arbitrary governments, some of which have not even a proper word to express it.

Montesquieu explained how DESPOTIC GOVERNMENTS work:

Of the Principle of DESPOTIC GOVERNMENT. As VIRTUE is necessary in a republic, and in a monarchy HONOR, so FEAR is necessary in a despotic government: with regard to virtue, there is no occasion for it, and honor would be extremely dangerous.

Here the immense power of the prince devolves entirely upon those whom he is pleased to entrust with the administration.

Persons capable of setting a value upon themselves would be likely to create disturbances.

Fear must therefore depress their spirits, and extinguish even the least sense of ambition.

A moderate government may, whenever it pleases, and without the least danger, relax its *springs*. It supports itself by the laws, and by its own internal strength.

But when a despotic prince ceases for one single moment to uplift his arm, when he cannot instantly demolish those whom he has entrusted with the first employments, all is over: for as fear, the *spring* of this government, no longer subsists, the people are left without a protector.

It is probably in this sense the Cadis (Muslim magistrates) maintained that the Grand Seignior (Sultan of Turkey) was not obliged to keep his word or oath, when he limited thereby his authority.

It is necessary that the people should be judged by laws, and the great men by the caprice of the prince, that the lives of the lowest subject should be safe, and the pasha's head ever in danger.

We cannot mention these monstrous governments without horror. The Sophi of Persia, dethroned in our days (1722) by Mahomet, the son of Miriveis, saw the constitution subverted before this resolution, because he had been too sparing of blood.

History informs us that the horrid cruelties of Domitian (Roman Emperor 81–96 AD) struck such a terror into the governors that the people recovered themselves a little during his reign.

Thus a torrent overflows one side of a country, and on the other leaves fields untouched, where the eye is refreshed by the prospect of fine meadows.

Montesquieu continued:

Obedience in ... Despotic Governments. In despotic states, the nature of government requires the most passive obedience; and when once the prince's will is made known, it ought infallibly to produce its effect.

Here they have no limitations or restrictions, no mediums, terms, equivalents, or remonstrances; no change to propose: man is a creature that blindly submits to the absolute will of the sovereign.

In a country like this they are no more allowed to represent their apprehensions of a future danger than to impute their miscarriage to the capriciousness of fortune.

Man's portion here, like that of beasts, is instinct, compliance, and punishment. Little does it then avail to plead the sentiments of nature, filial respect, conjugal or parental tenderness, the laws of honor, or want of health; the order is given, and, that is sufficient.

In Persia, when the king has condemned a person, it is no longer lawful to mention his name, or to intercede in his favor. Even if the prince were intoxicated, or non compos (Latin: not of sound mind), the decree must be executed; otherwise he would contradict himself, and the law admits of no contradiction.

This has been the way of thinking in that country in all ages; as the order which Ahasuerus gave, to exterminate the Jews, could not be revoked, they were allowed the liberty of defending themselves.

Montesquieu added:

One thing, however, may be sometimes opposed to the prince's will, namely, religion. They will abandon, nay they will slay a parent, if the prince so commands; but he cannot oblige them to drink wine. The laws of religion are of a superior nature, because they bind the sovereign as well as the subject. But with respect to the law of nature, it is otherwise; the prince is no longer supposed to be a man.

In a despotism, subjects fear their despot, and the

despot is always in fear of being assassinated by subjects.

Montesquieu explained that in a monarchy, subjects want to be honored by their monarch, and the monarch also wants to be honor by his subjects:

> In monarchical and moderate states, the power is limited by its very *spring*, I mean by honor, which, like a monarch, reigns over the prince and his people.
>
> They will not allege to their sovereign the laws of religion; a courtier would be apprehensive of rendering himself ridiculous. But the laws of honor will be appealed to on all occasions.
>
> Hence arise the restrictions necessary to obedience; honor is naturally subject to whims, by which the subject's submission will be ever directed.
>
> Though the manner of obeying be different in these two kinds of government, the power is the same. On which side soever the monarch turns, he inclines the scale, and is obeyed.
>
> The whole difference is that in a monarchy the prince receives instruction, at the same time that his ministers have greater abilities, and are more versed in public affairs, than the ministers of a despotic government.

Sir Alexander Fraser Tytler wrote in *Universal History from the Creation of the World to the Beginning of the 18th Century* (Boston: Fetridge & Co., 1834; 1850, ch. VI):

> In most monarchies, the will of the person called the sovereign is limited by certain constitutional restraints which he cannot transgress with safety. In the British government the will of the prince is controlled by a parliament; in other limited monarchies, by a council of state, whose powers are acknowledged and defined... This parliament, or council ... limits the will of the prince ... Thus it is in limited monarchies.

Montesquieu continued:

> Such are the principles of the THREE sorts of government: which does not imply that in a particular republic they actually are, but that they

ought to be, VIRTUOUS; nor does it prove that in a particular monarchy they are actuated by HONOR, or in a particular despotic government by FEAR; but that they ought to be directed by these principles, otherwise the government is imperfect.

In summary, Montesquieu thus divided governments into three categories: Republics, Monarchs and Despots. The "spring" or characteristic necessary for a republic to work is virtue among the people.

The "spring" necessary for a monarchy to work is honor. The "spring" necessary for a despotism to work is fear.

Montesquieu understood that an underlying premise in all political structures is that human nature is selfish. With that being the case, what would motivate someone to restrain themselves from fulfilling their selfish desires?

Two things: Positive and Negative Motivations. Whether dealing with a toddler, a union boss, a corporate executive, or a president, all humans respond to positive and negative motivations. Corresponding to Montesquieu's three types of government, there are three types of positive and negative motivations:

SPIRITUAL motivations;

MENTAL/EMOTIONAL motivations; and

PHYSICAL/SENSUAL motivations.

In examining Montesquieu's three categories, there is a correlation to the motivations on the three aspects of a human being: spirit, mind and body. A Republic works best by appealing to the spiritual side of a human. Virtue is each individual voluntarily exercising internal restraint.

Montesquieu wrote in *The Spirit of the Laws*, 1748:

> That the Catholic Religion is most agreeable to a Monarchy, and the Protestant to a Republic ... and a despotic Government to the Mahommedan."

Montesquieu explained:

> While the Mahommedan princes incessantly

give or receive death, the religion of the Christians renders their princes ... less cruel. The prince confides in his subjects, and the subjects in the prince. How admirable the religion which, while it only seems to have in view the felicity of the other life, continues the happiness of this! ...

The Mahometan religion, which speaks only by the sword, acts still upon men with that destructive spirit with which it was founded.

Sir Alexander Fraser Tytler wrote in *Universal History from the Creation of the World to the Beginning of the 18th Century* (Boston: Fetridge & Co., 1834; 1850, Chapter VI):

In the most despotic governments, that power is lodged in a single person, whose will is subject to no other control than that which arises from the fear of his own deposition. Of this we have an example in the Ottoman government, which approaches the nearest of any monarchy we know to a pure despotism.

Montesquieu wrote in *The Spirit of the Laws,* Book 24:

The Christian religion is a stranger to mere despotic power. The mildness so frequently recommended in the Gospel is incompatible with the despotic rage with which a prince punishes his subjects, and exercises himself in cruelty ...

A moderate Government is most agreeable to the Christian Religion.

Montesquieu added:

The Christian religion, which orders men to love one another, no doubt wants the best political laws and the best civil laws for each people, because those laws are, after (religion), the greatest good that men can give and receive ...

The morality of the Gospel is the noblest gift ever bestowed by God on man. We shall see that we owe to Christianity, in government, a certain political law, and in war a certain law of nations–benefits which human nature can never sufficiently acknowledge ...

The principles of Christianity, deeply engraved on the heart, would be infinitely more powerful than the false honor of monarchies, than the humane virtues of republics, or the servile fear of despotic states ...

It is the Christian religion that, in spite of the extent of empire and the influence of climate, has hindered despotic power from being established in Ethiopia, and has carried into the heart of Africa the manners and laws of Europe ...

When the Christian religion, two centuries ago, became unhappily divided into Catholic and Protestant, the people of the North embraced the Protestant, and those of the south adhered still to the Catholic.

The reason is plain: the people of the north have, and will forever have, a spirit of liberty and independence, which the people of the south have not; and therefore a religion, which has no visible head, is more agreeable to the independency of the climate, than that which has one.

Sir Alexander Fraser Tytler wrote in *Universal History from the Creation of the World to the Beginning of the 18th Century* (Boston: Fetridge & Co., 1834; 1850, ch. 6):

We have now traced Greece from her origin ... to the highest rank among the civilized nations of the earth. We have seen the foundation and rise of her independent states; the vigorous perseverance by which they succeeded in shaking off the yoke of intolerable tyranny, and establishing a *popular* system of government ...

We have remarked the domestic disorders which sprang from the abuse of that freedom which these republics enjoyed; and, finally, that general corruption of manners which, tainting all the *springs* of public virtue, and annihilating patriotism, at length brought this illustrious nation entirely under subjection to a foreign yoke.

Alexander Tytler continued:

The revolutions which in this progress the states of Greece underwent ... that their history is a school of instruction in politics, as there is scarce a doctrine in that important science which may not find an example... from... their history ...

I shall adopt this criterion in laying before my readers a few reflections ... from ... Grecian history.

The miserable oppression which ... the states of Greece sustained under their first governors, a set of tyrants, who owed their elevation to violence, and whose rule was subject to no control from existing laws or constitutional restraints, was assuredly a most justifiable motive on the part of the people for emancipating themselves from that state of servitude, and for abolishing entirely that worst of governments — a pure despotism.

It is therefore with pleasure we remark, in the early history of this nation, the noble exertion by which those states shook off the yoke of their tyrants, and established for themselves a new system of government on the just and rational basis of an equality of rights and privileges in all the members of the commonwealth.

We admit, without scruple, the belief that those new republics were framed by their virtuous legislators in the true spirit of patriotism.

But the intentions of the legislator are no test of the actual merits of the institutions themselves: and it is certain that those boasted republics were very far from exhibiting in practice that perfect system of political freedom which was expected from them in theory.

We seek in vain either in the history of ATHENS or of Lacedaemon (SPARTA), for the beautiful idea on which speculative writers have exercised their fancy of a well-ordered commonwealth.

In treating formerly of the peculiar constitution of those two great and leading states, we endeavored to point out such circumstances as appeared to be defects in the constitution of those political fabrics.

In the republic of SPARTA, Lycurgus (the Lawgiver), by exterminating luxury, by the equal partition of the lands, and by banishing every motive to the ambition of individuals, certainly laid the foundation of that equality among the citizens of his common wealth which is essential to the constitution of a perfect republic.

Yet, under the Spartan government, there were some circumstances which seem totally adverse to this spirit of equality. It was adverse to equality that there should be any citizen invested with the honors and appendages of royalty. The idea of a king possessing rank without power is an absurdity; and if the law denies it him, it will be his constant endeavor to wrest and arrogate it.

The high authority of the Ephori (five leaders elected annually) was likewise adverse to the spirit of equality. There was a perpetual contention for superiority of power between those magistrates and the kings; and the people, dividing themselves into parties, bribed to support those opposite and contending interests, furnished a continual source of faction and disorder.

In the ATHENIAN republic the great defect of the constitution seemed to be ... that it was doubtful where the supreme power was definitively lodged.

The senate was, in theory, a wise institution, for it possessed the sole power of convoking the assemblies of the people, and of preparing all business that was to be the subject of discussion in those assemblies.

But, on the other hand, this senate being annually elected, its members were ever under the necessity of courting that people for their votes, and of flattering their prejudices and passions, by adopting and proposing measures which had no other end than to render themselves popular.

These delegates were therefore the mean dependents on the mob who elected them. The guardians nominally of the people's rights, they were themselves the abject slaves of a corrupted populace.

Tytler added:

There were other radical defects in the constitution of Athens. All the offices of the state were by Solon destined to be filled from the three first classes of the richer citizens.

The fourth or inferior class had, however, an equal right of suffrage (voting) in the public assembly, and being superior in number to all the other three, had it in their power to carry every question against the higher classes.

Thus there was a perpetual source of discord inherent in this constitution; the power and preeminence of office exclusively vested in one division of the people, which they would jealously maintain by every possible means; while, at the same time, the other was furnished with arms sufficient to defeat that power altogether, or, at least, to maintain at all times a violent struggle for superiority.

The best apology that can be made for Solon is, that his intentions were good. He knew that a constitution purely democratic is an absolute chimera (unrealizable dream) in politics.

Kelly O'Connell wrote in "Pagan Government Theory Insures Tyranny Returns to the West":

Both Greece and Rome had representational, democratic assemblies, but the powers of these bodies were controlled by the elites.

Tytler continued:

The detail of the systems of SOLON and LYCURGUS, such as they are described to us by ancient writers, and the history of those rival republics, both in their quarrels with each other, in their foreign wars, and above all in their intestine factions and disorders, afford full conviction that the form of government which they enjoyed was in itself extremely faulty ...

They were perpetually divided into factions, which servilely ranked themselves under the banners of the contending demagogues; and these maintained their influence over their partisans by the most shameful corruption and bribery, of which the means were supplied alone by the plunder of the public money ...

It is not, perhaps, unreasonable to conclude, that a pure and perfect democracy is a thing not attainable by man, constituted as he is of contending elements of vice and virtue, and ever mainly influenced by the predominant principle of self-interest.

Unless citizens have virtue, which is a quality at odds with selfish human nature, democracies and republics cannot stand, as Sir Alexander Tytler wrote further:

> Now how does the matter stand with respect to a republic or democracy? ... It is true they elect their governors ... These governors, it is said, are, in a republic, chosen from the people itself, and therefore will respect its interests ...
>
> That they are chosen from the people affords no pledge that they will either be wiser men, or less influenced by selfish ambition, or the passion of tyrannizing; all experience goes to prove the contrary: and that the will of the many is in truth a mere chimera.

Sir Alexander Tytler continued:

> The author of the "Spirit of Laws," a work which must ever be regarded as the production of a most enlightened mind, has built a great deal of plausible and ingenious reasoning on this general idea, that the three distinct forms of government, the MONARCHICAL, the DESPOTIC, and the REPUBLICAN, are influenced by three separate principles, upon which the whole system in each form is constructed, and on which it must depend for its support.
>
> "The principle of the MONARCHICAL form,' says Montesquieu, 'is HONOR; of the DESPOTICAL, FEAR; and of the REPUBLICAN, VIRTUE."
>
> The ingenious author of an *Essay on the History of Civil Society* (Dr. Adam Ferguson, 1767) thus enlarges on the idea of M. Montesquieu: —
>
> "In democracy," says he, "men must love equality; they must respect the rights of their fellow citizens; they must unite by the common ties of affection to the state. In forming personal pretensions, they must be satisfied with that degree of consideration which they can procure by their abilities fairly measured with those of an opponent.

They must labor for the public without hope of profit. They must reject every attempt to create a personal dependence. Candor, force and elevation of mind, in short, are the props of democracy, and virtue is the principle required to its preservation ... "

Sir Alexander Tytler continued critiquing democracies and republics, that they are destined to fail if void of concept that each person is individually accountable to God to "do unto others as you would have them to unto you" — *The Golden Rule*:

The author plainly intimates his own opinion... descriptive of a state of society that never did, and never could exist; a republic not of men, but of angels.

For where, it may be asked, was that democracy ever found on earth, where, in the words of this description, men loved equality; were satisfied with the degree of consideration they could procure by their abilities fairly measured with those of an opponent, (a circumstance in itself utterly destructive of equality,) labored for the public without hope of profit, and rejected every attempt to create a personal dependence?

Did such a government ever exist, or, while society consists of human beings, is it possible that such ever should exist?

While man is a being instigated by the love of power — a passion visible in an infant, and common to us even with the inferior animals — he will seek personal superiority in preference to every matter of a general concern; or at best, he will employ himself in advancing the public good, as the means of individual distinction and elevation: he will promote the interest of the state from the selfish but most useful passion of making himself considerable in that establishment which he labors to aggrandize ...

The nature of a republican government gives to every member of the state an equal right to cherish views of ambition, and to aspire to the highest offices of the common wealth ... The number of candidates excites rivalships, contentions, and factions ...

In such a state of society, how rare is genuine virtue; how singular the character of a truly disinterested patriot! He appears and he is treated as an imposter; he attempts to serve his country in its councils, or in offices; he is calumniated (maliciously lied about), reviled, and persecuted; he dies in disgrace or in banishment; and the same envy which maligned him living, embalms him dead, and showers encomiums (praises) on his memory ...

Selfish ambition and the desire of rule in the commonwealth came in place of the thirst for national glory ...

At length the enthusiasm for freedom, which was at first the glowing character of the Grecian states, gave place to ... an admiration of the fine arts, a passion for the objects of taste, and all those refinements which are the offspring of luxury.

Patriotism always exists in the greatest degree in rude nations, and in an early period of society. Like all other affections and passions, it operates with the greatest force where it meets with the greatest difficulties.

It seems to be a virtue which grows from opposition; which subsists in its greatest vigor amidst turbulence and dangers; but in a state of ease and safety, as if wanting its appropriate nourishment, it languishes and decays.

We must not then wonder at that difference of patriotic character which distinguished the Greeks in the early ages of their history, from that by which they were known in their more advanced and more luxurious periods.

It is a law of nature to which no experience has ever furnished an exception, that the rising grandeur and opulence of a nation must be balanced by the decline of its heroic virtues.

We find in the latter ages of the Grecian history... no traces of that noble spirit of patriotism which excited our respect and admiration when they were infant ... Such was the situation of Greece, when, extending her conquests and importing both the wealth and the manners of foreign nations, she lost with her ancient poverty her ancient virtue.

Venality (open to bribes) and corruption pervaded every department of her states, and became the *spring* of all public measures, which, instead of tending to the national welfare, had for their only object the gratification of the selfish passions of individuals.

Under these circumstances, it was no wonder that she should become an easy prey to a foreign power, which in fact rather purchased her in the market, than subdued her by force of arms ... Greece, thus degenerate and fallen from the proud eminence she once maintained.

John Adams wrote to his wife, Abigail Adams, July 3, 1776, the day after Congress approved Independence:

You will see in a few days a Declaration setting forth the causes, which have impelled us to this mighty revolution, and the reasons which will justify it in the sight of God and man ...

The people will have unbounded power ... The new governments we are assuming ... will require a purification from our vices and an augmentation of our virtues or they will be no blessings ... The people are extremely addicted to corruption and venality ...

I am not without apprehensions from this quarter, but I must submit all my hopes and fears to an overruling Providence.

Plato asserted society had a hierarchical structure made up of three classes or castes, corresponding to the human soul of appetite, spirit, and reason.

Appetite is represented as the abdomen. These are productive workers: laborers, carpenters, plumbers, masons, merchants, farmers, ranchers, etc.

Spirit is represented as the chest. These are the protective, brave, strong, adventurous warriors or guardians.

Reason is represented as the head. These are the intelligent, rational, self-controlled rulers or philosopher–

kings who "love the sight of truth" (*Republic* 475c).

Though Plato acknowledges that humans ultimately are lacking in virtue, he engages in wishful thinking that someday there would arise a few selfless individuals who loved wisdom and could impartially make beneficial decisions for the community.

These would govern, not with the rhetoric and persuasion necessary in a democracy, but instead with reason and wisdom. (*Republic* 473c-d)

Plato, though, spends much time examining how it is that in this ideal luxurious city, injustice grows. (*Republic* 372e)

According to Plato's *Republic*, book 2, (369c-372d), the "true" and "healthy" city is one of farmers, craftsmen, merchants, and wage-earners, without the guardian class of philosopher–kings, and without their accompanying delicacies of "perfumed oils, incense, prostitutes, and pastries."

Plato's purpose of describing the ideal city was to elaborate on the three qualities of the human soul: appetite, spirit and reason. He was not actually promoting it as a blueprint for government. Unfortunately, dictators and tyrants in the centuries following Plato repeatedly engage in self-delusion, imaging themselves to be the elusive, long-awaited "philosopher–kings."

The Greek experiment of self-rule was referred to by one of America's founders, James Warren, in his anti-federalist writings. Following the hated Stamp Act of 1765, the British committed the Boston Massacre in 1770, firing into a crowd, killing five.

In 1773, James Warren proposed that Samuel Adams form Committees of Correspondence to inform the rest of the nation of injustices being committed in Boston:

> The rights of the colonists, and of this province
> in particular, as men, as Christians, and as subjects;
> to communicate and publish the same to the several
> towns in this province and to the world as the sense
> of this town.

The British increased taxes and in response colonists

had the Boston Tea Party, Dec. 16, 1773. In 1774, the British retaliated by blocking Boston Harbor to starve the city into submission.

In 1775, when President of the Massachusetts Provincial Congress, Dr. Joseph Warren, was killed in the Battle of Bunker Hill, James Warren, who also fought there, was elected the next President.

As President of the Massachusetts Provincial Congress, James Warren approved the Resolution, June 16, 1775:

> It has pleased Almighty GOD in his Providence to suffer the Calamities of an unnatural War to take Place among us ...
>
> And as we have Reason to fear, that unless we become a penitent and reformed People, we shall feel still severer Tokens of his Displeasure.
>
> And as the most effectual Way to escape those desolating Judgments, which so evidently hang over us ... will be – That we repent and return everyone from his Iniquities, unto him that correcteth us ...
>
> Among the prevailing Sins of this Day, which threaten the Destruction of this Land, we have Reason to lament the frequent Prophanation of the Lord's Day, or Christian Sabbath ...
>
> It is therefore RESOLVED ... by this Congress... the People ... throughout this Colony ... pay a religious Regard to that Day, and to the public Worship of God thereon.

James Warren, who died Nov. 28, 1808, was husband of Anti-Federalist author Mercy Otis Warren. She was called "the conscience of the Revolution" for her correspondence with many founding fathers. Other Anti-Federalists were Patrick Henry, Samuel Adams, George Mason, Richard Henry Lee, Robert Yates, James Monroe, George Clinton, Melancton Smith, Arthur Fenner, James Winthrop and Luther Martin.

Anti-Federalists opposed the new U.S. Constitution as they did not think there were enough limits on the Federal Government to prevent it from usurping power and becoming a totalitarian dictatorship. Anti-Federalist pressure is responsible for addition of the Bill of Rights.

James Warren submitted essays to the local newspaper under the name "Helvitius Priscus," which was the name of a Roman republican who resisted the dictator Nero. On Dec. 27, 1787, the *Independent Chronicle* published an article by "Helvitius Priscus" in which James Warren criticized the Constitutional Convention:

> That assembly, who have ambitiously and daringly presumed to annihilate the sovereignties of the thirteen United States; to establish a Draconian Code; and to bind posterity by their secret councils.

James Warren referred to the Lycian League, a thriving confederation of independent Greek city-states which existed from the 8th century BC until conquered by Phillip of Macedon, the father of Alexander the Great, in 338 BC:

> Everyone acquainted with ancient history... turn their thoughts to the miserable fate of the Lycians... a sober, virtuous people, who maintained their independence, and their freedom, for several centuries; and supported their own simple institutions, under twenty-three district sovereignties...
>
> A people bearing a strong resemblance to a party in America had crept in among them, and ... an ambitious Phillip had his emissaries in that body, who by political intrigue, and well-timed plausible speeches, enabled him ... to set himself at the head of the Grecian States; to annihilate their constitutions, and to degrade them to the most abject submission to the will of a despotic tyrant ...
>
> The tyrant alleged the same excuse for his encroachment, that we hear hacknied in the streets of our capitals, for subjugating the Americans.

James Warren added:

> The application ... is left for the consideration of every lover of his country. America has fought for her liberties ... purchased them by the most costly sacrifices ...
>
> And shall ... her freedom be sported away by

the duplicity, and the intrigues of those, who never participated in her sufferings? ... mad ambition of a mind ready to sacrifice ... humanity for its gratification? FORBID IT HEAVEN!

James Warren warned further:

Let the youth of America ... instead of indulging a rapturous admiration for the modern superficial speechifyers in favor of an American monarchy, let them examine the principles of the late glorious revolution ...

and before they embrace the chains of servitude, let them scrutinize ... if their pride ... will suffer them to lick the hand of a despotic master ...

Let him be stigmatized with the odium ... the base betrayer of the rights of his country ... though he may artfully have obtained an election.

James Warren concluded:

Let the old Patriots come forward, and instead of secretly wrapping up their opinions within their own breasts, let them lift up the voice like a trumpet, and show this people their folly and ... impending danger.

TIMELINE 332–322 BC

332 BC – Candance of Meroe, Queen of African Nubian Empire (halted Alexander)

321 BC – Mahapadma, Ruler of India's Nanda Dynasty (halted Alexander)

322 BC – Chandragupta Maurya, unifier of India, Emperor of India's Mauryan Empire, LARGEST EMPIRE IN THE WORLD AT THIS DATE

GOLDEN AGE OF INDIA

After India repulsed Alexander the Great, King Chandragupta Maurya under the direction of his prime minister, Chanakya (350–283 BC), amassed the largest empire in the world in 250 BC, the Mauryan Empire.

Chanakya, who is also called "Kautilya," has been described as India's Machiavelli for writing his work, *Arthashastra*, a work which was lost near the end of the Gupta dynasty (320–550 AD) and not rediscovered until 1915.

Chanakya's *Arthashastra* gives shrewd, brutal instructions on deceit, assassination, statecraft and military strategy to accumulate power.

Using the politics and backstabbing that governed relations between various kings and officials of that time, Chanakya advocated "land reform" where the government confiscated land from private citizens.

He counseled that the king should keep his eyes open through the use of spies. He considered crises, such as people and subjects fighting amongst themselves, to actually help the king consolidate power by their mutual rivalry.

Max Weber wrote in *Politics as a Vocation* (1919), that "compared to Chanakya's *Arthashastra*, Machiavelli's *The Prince* is harmless."

Roger Boesche, who wrote "Kautilya's *Arthashastra* on War and Diplomacy in Ancient India" (*The Journal of Military History*, 2003), described the harsh political pragmatism in the Arthashastra:

> Is there any other book that talks so openly about when using violence is justified? When assassinating an enemy is useful? When killing domestic opponents is wise? How one uses secret agents? When one needs to sacrifice one's own secret agent? How the king can use women and children as spies and even assassins? When a nation should violate a treaty and invade its neighbor?
>
> Kautilya — and to my knowledge only Kautilya — addresses all those questions. In what cases must a king spy on his own people? How should a king test his ministers, even his own family members, to see if they are worthy of trust? When must a king kill a prince, his own son, who is heir to the throne? How does one protect a king from poison?

What precautions must a king take against assassination by one's own wife? When is it appropriate to arrest a troublemaker on suspicion alone? When is torture justified?

At some point, every reader wonders: Is there not one question that Kautilya found immoral, too terrible to ask in a book? No, not one. And this is what brings a frightful chill. But this is also why Kautilya was the first great, unrelenting political realist.

Chanakya's initial advice of a direct attack on the Nanda Empire failed, whereupon he noticed a mother scolding her child for burning himself by eating from the middle of a bowl of porridge rather than the cooler edges.

Chanakya then decided the way to overthrow the Nanda Empire was to slowly chip away at its edges. Chanakya was a master of shrewd diplomacy, and recommended King Chandragupta Maurya use different strategies with neighboring powers:

1) Sanman–Appeasement, treating with equality, non-aggression pact;

2) Danda–Strength, punishment, war;

3) Dana–Gift, bribery, enticement;

4) Bheda–Divide, split, separating opposition, sowing dissension;

5) Maya–Illusion, deceit;

6) Upeksha–Ignoring the enemy;

7) Indrajala–Faking military strength.

∽

TIMELINE 304–222 BC

304 BC – Ptolemy I Soter I, of Egypt's Ptolemaic Dynasty (Alexander's General)

301 BC – Seleucus I Nicator, Ruler of the Seleucid Persian Empire (Alexander's General)

301 BC – Lysimachus, Thrace, Asia Minor (Alexander's General)

301 BC – Cassander, Ruler of Macedonia and Greece (Alexander's General)

297 BC – Pyrrhus, Ruler of the Epirus and Macedon Kingdoms

269 BC – Ashoka the Great of the Maurya Dynasty, one of India's greatest Emperors

222 BC – Antiochus III the Great, Seleucid Persian Empire

∽

CHINA

221 BC – Qin Shi Huang, First Emperor of a unified China, Qin Dynasty. Qin is pronounced 'chin' from which the name 'China' is derived. Emperor Qin Shi Huang centralized rule by destroying the walls that surrounded the lands of the various feudal lords, preventing them from reasserting their independence. Qin Shi Huang is remembered for being buried in an elaborate tomb with 6,000 terracotta warriors.

He replaced these with the Great Wall of China to protect the empire from outside attacks by the Xiongnu people ("hsiong nu," possibly the Huns) in the north.

Qin Shi Huang centralized control, bringing a unification of China under his Qin Dynasty government (221–206 BC). Unfortunately for Qin Shi Huang, his forced conscription of citizens to build the Great Wall, as well as other cruel practices, provoked a rebellion which eventually culminated in the overthrowing of the Qin Dynasty.

The Great Wall was lengthened by subsequent dynasties, and extensively rebuilt by the Ming Dynasty. It was expanded to stretch across a 5,500 mile border, and when the length of all branches are included, it totaled over 13,000 miles.

In 213 BC, to avoid being compared to past kings, Qin Shi Huang ordered almost all books burned. Books were actually thin slats of wood, similar to venetian blinds.

This was an effort to eliminate the history prior to the Qin Dynasty and remove remnants of obsolete writing script. Citizens were punished if they were caught with a book of classic history or a book of songs. The Records of the Grand Historian relay an account of Emperor Qin Shi Huang burying 460 scholars alive for possessing forbidden books.

During China's Qin Dynasty the emperor's chief eunuch was Zhao Gao (died 207 BC). Zhao Gao is included among history's corrupt advisors, along with Chanakya, Machiavelli, Tallyrand, as well as Iago, the fictional character in Shakespeare's play Othello.

The Shiji records that Zhao Gao's parents committed crimes and their punishment included Zhao Gao and his brother being made eunuchs.

Zhao Gao became an expert in law and punishment. Emperor Qin Shi Huang valued Zhao Gao for the negative motivations he could use to control people.

Earlier in his career, Zhao committed a crime and the official Meng Ye sentenced him to death, but Emperor Qin Shi Huang pardoned him and returned to his position.

When Emperor Qin Shi Huang suddenly died, Zhao Gao took revenge on Meng Ye and his sons, Meng Tian and Meng Yi.

Zhao Gao and the Imperial Secretary Li Si conspired to falsify the Emperor's Will, thus causing the Emperor's second son, Fusu, to commit suicide. It stripped Fusu's supporter Meng Tian of his command, even though he was a general commanding over 200,000 troops fighting the Huns.

Zhao Gao's conspired to have a decree issued forcing Meng Tian to commit suicide and having his brother Meng Yi killed. This court manipulation allowed Qin Er Shi to be the next Qin Emperor, who conveniently had been schooled by Zhao Gao.

Zhao Gao had the Imperial Secretary Li Si killed by 'The Five Pains', a method ironically invented by Li Si.

First the victim's nose was cut off, then a hand and a foot were cut off, then castration, then he was cut in two across the waist. Zhao Gao executed all of Li Si's relatives to the third generation.

When rebellions occurred across China in 207 BC, Zhao Gao was afraid the Second Emperor would blame him. Zhao decided to overthrow of the Second Emperor, but was not sure who would side with him. He had a deer brought into the court of the Second Emperor, but called it a horse.

The Second Emperor laughed: "Is the chancellor perhaps mistaken, calling a deer a horse?" When the Second Emperor asked those in the court if it was a deer or a horse, some identified it as a deer, while those wanting to ingratiate themselves to Zhao Gao called it a horse.

Zhao Gao then secretly arranged for false accusations to be brought up against those who identified it as a deer, causing all the rest of the court officials to be terrified of Zhao Gao. (tr. Watson 1993:70)

Zhao Gao forced the Second Emperor to commit suicide, arranging him to be replace with his nephew, Ziying. Finally, Ziying killed Zhao Gao. The internal dissension so weakened the Qin Dynasty that it collapsed less than 20 years after it was founded.

Ling Cangzhou's book, *Dragon Blood, Wolf Smoke* (Workers' Publishing House), examines history from the unification of China under the Qin dynasty in 256 BC to the fall of the Qing dynasty in 1912. In Tang Qiwei's article for RFA's Mandarian service, Ling Cangzhou stated:

> A lot of people in contemporary China right now have a dream that China can return to the glory of the Han and Tang dynasties ... I am telling them that in reality those dynasties were stained with blood and behaved in a despicable manner ... In ancient times, they said hell had 18 levels. Chinese history has been played out all along on the 17th level of hell, that of cruel dictatorships and barbarous conquests.

CARTHAGE

221 BC – Hannibal of the North African Carthage (Phoenician) Empire. Carthage, in present-day Tunisia, was founded amongst North Africa's Berber population by Phoenicians from the city of Tyre (present-day Lebanon).

The legend is that Queen Dido fled from her brother, King Pygmalion of Tyre in 814 BC and founded Carthage, meaning "new city." Its location across from Sicily on the southern Mediterranean coast gave it strategic control of sea traffic. The colony developed its own Punic language and culture.

Carthaginians developed a Republic which was one of the longest-lived and largest states in the ancient Mediterranean world. Carthage became the major rival of the Roman Republic, resulting in three Punic Wars.

After the loss of the First Punic War, 264 to 241 BC, Carthage was forced to pay a large sum to Rome. In the Second Punic War, Hannibal landed his Carthaginian army in Spain 218 BC and marched them over the Alps to attack Italy. For a decade, Hannibal was nearly invincible, decisively winning numerous battles.

The leaders back in Carthage, though, hesitated sending him reinforcements. Then Rome's General Fabian Maximus employed a strategy of avoiding direct confrontations with Hannibal, thus wearing down his forces.

Eventually the Roman General Scipio attacked Carthage and with a successful tactic of confusing Hannibal's war elephants, won the Battle of Zama in 202 BC.

At the end of the Third Punic War in 146 BC, Rome finally destroyed Carthage, along with most of their historical records. Montesquieu wrote of the Republic of Carthage:

> How was it possible for Carthage to maintain her ground? When Hannibal, upon his being made praetor, endeavored to hinder the magistrates from plundering the republic, did not they complain of him to the Romans? Wretches, who would fain be citizens

without a city, and be beholden for their riches to their very destroyers!

Rome soon insisted upon having three hundred of their principal citizens as hostages; she obliged them next to surrender their arms and ships; and then she declared war. From the desperate efforts of this defenseless city, one may judge of what she might have performed in her full vigor, and assisted by virtue.

TIMELINE 209–206 BC

209 BC – Modu Chanyu, Majesty Son of Heaven, Central Asia Xiongnu Tribal Empire

206 BC – Xiang Yu, King of China's Western Chu Dynasty

206 BC – Gaozu, Emperor of China's Han Dynasty. The Han Dynasty ended the practice of burning books and historical records of previous dynasties. Han Emperor Wu (141–87 BC) popularized the teachings of Confucius (c.551–479 BC), who had lived centuries earlier during China's Spring and Autumn Period of history.

TEACHINGS OF CONFUCIUS SPREAD

Confucius was a moral philosopher who taught a social order of behavior for oneself, one's family, the state and the empire. Based on respect and virtue, his axioms were in some respects like Solomon's Book of Proverbs. They were read by many, including Benjamin Franklin, who rendered some in his own style in his *Pennsylvania Gazette* and *Poor Richard's Almanac*.

The teachings of Confucius reaffirmed the idea of the "mandate of heaven" (tianming) and, in this sense, cemented into Chinese culture the hierarchical structure with the Emperor at the top.

One of the Five Confucian Relationships was "Ruler to Ruled." Social order was to be maintained by individuals knowing their place in the hierarchical structure, either as a superior or inferior to others, and acting accordingly. Compiled in *The Analects* are the statements of Confucius:

> There is government, when the prince is prince, and the minister is minister; when the father is father, and the son is son ...

> If, in serving his prince, he can devote his life ...

> The rules of propriety in serving one's prince ...

> A prince should employ his minister according to the rules of propriety; ministers should serve their prince with faithfulness ...

> When the prince's order called him, without waiting for his carriage to be yoked, he went at once ...

> What is called a great minister, is one who serves his prince according to what is right, and when he finds he cannot do so, retires ...

> When a prince's personal conduct is correct, his government is effective without the issuing of orders...

> To be a prince is difficult; to be a minister is not easy ...

> A minister, in serving his prince, reverently discharges his duties, and makes his emolument a secondary consideration ...

> Chi K'ang asked how to cause the people to reverence their ruler, to be faithful to him, and to go on to nerve themselves to virtue. The Master said, "Let him preside over them with gravity; – then they will reverence him. Let him be final and kind to all; – then they will be faithful to him. Let him advance the good and teach the incompetent; – then they will eagerly seek to be virtuous."

In the Confucian system, respect began with the son honoring his father and culminated honoring the emperor as the father of the country.

An interesting side note is that Confucius's family name is Kong Fuzi, and there are 83 recorded father-to-son generations of the Kong family, making it one of the longest extant pedigrees in the world to the present time.

TIMELINE 171–10 BC

171 BC – Mithridates I, Great King of Parthian Arsacid Empire

160 BC – Menander I, North India Indo-Greek Kingdom

150 BC – Bhagabhadra, of India's Sunga Empire of Magadha

141 BC – Wu, Emperor of China's Han Dynasty, one of China's greatest emperors

100 BC – Maues, Ruler of the India-Scythian Saka Kingdom

83 BC – Artaxias, Ruler of the Armenian Empire

50 BC – Dhanadeva, Ruler of India's Kosala Dynasty

45 BC – Julius Caesar, Dictator of the Roman Republic.

37 BC – Herod the Great, King of Judea.

30 BC – Cleopatra VII, last Pharaoh, Egypt's Ptolemaic Dynasty.

27 BC – Augustus Caesar turned the Roman "Republic" into an "Empire" and ordered a census of the whole Roman world. All subsequent emperors ruled as tyrants.

20 BC – Gondophares I, Ruler of the Indo-Parthian Kingdom

10 BC – Kharavela, of India's Maha-Meghavahana Dynasty

∾

END OF ROMAN REPUBLIC

Towards the end of the Roman Republic, leaders forgot the example of Cincinnatus. The political scene was dominated by usurpers intent on exceeding constitutional limitations. Montesquieu wrote:

> When Sylla (Sulla 81 BC) thought of restoring Rome to her liberty, this unhappy city was incapable of receiving that blessing. She had only the feeble remains of virtue, which were continually diminishing.

Instead of being roused from her lethargy by Caesar, Tiberius, Caius Claudius, Nero, and Domitian, she riveted every day her chains; if she struck some blows, her aim was at the tyrant, not at the tyranny.

Comparing America's republic with the Republic of Rome, Fisher Ames wrote in *The New England Palladium* of Boston, 1804 (*Works of Fisher Ames*, compiled by a number of his friends, Boston: T.B. Wait & Co., 1809, p. 272):

We now set out with our experimental project, exactly where Rome failed with hers. We now begin, where she ended.

Kelly O'Connell wrote in "Pagan Government Theory Insures Tyranny Returns to the West" (*Canada Free Press*):

Both Greece and Rome ... there was no argument regarding whether the state or church should be preeminent since church didn't exist ... The general theory animating Greek and Roman government was humanistic, pagan, and superstitious theory over an imperfect yet often effective skeleton of democratic and republican bodies.

Julius Caesar (100–44 BC) was from an aristocratic family that had fallen into great debt. He escaped his debtors by serving in the military. Becoming a successful general, he positioned himself as a champion of the people, called "populares," against the aristocracy, called "optimates."

Realizing that money was the key to Roman politics, Caesar made an informal alliance in 59 BC, called a Triumvirate, with the famed Roman general Pompey the Great, and the immensely rich Crassus, with whose money they could buy supporters to challenge the powerful senatorial elite.

Pompey was a famous general who won battles in North Africa, Spain and the Middle East. He even conquered Jerusalem and went into the holy Temple, after which he told his soldiers to leave it alone. As a result, the Jews respected Pompey.

Crassus's fire brigades: Beginning in 70 BC, Marcus

Licinius Crassus positioned himself to rule Rome. He amassed an enormous amount of wealth through his "fire brigades." Someone's mansion would suspiciously catch on fire. Crassus' slaves would race to the scene, followed by Crassus, who would offer to buy the building for pennies on the dollar. If the owner agreed to sell, Crassus would tell his slaves to put out the fire. If the owner hesitated, Crassus would lower the amount of his offer. The more the building burned, the less Crassus offered. In this way, Crassus became the largest private land owner in Rome. Crassus financed Julius Caesar against Cicero.

Then Rome suffered a crisis. The gladiator-slaves revolted, led by Spartacus. They arranged for pirate ships to carry them away from Italy but Crassus bribed the ships not to show up. With the gladiator-slaves starving, they headed back to Rome. Panic and terror spread through the city.

In the confusion, the citizens of Rome declared Crassus "Praetor" – emergency dictator. Spartacus and the gladiator-slaves were crushed, though the citizens of Rome gave Pompey the credit. Nevertheless, the following year Crassus was elected Consul of Rome, and when the dust settled, the Roman citizens had significantly abdicated their Republican form of government.

Politics became the game of the extreme wealthy, so Julius Caesar sought Crassus' help. This under-the-table agreement with Julius Caesar and a respected old military hero, Pompey was the first Triumvirate.

In an effort to save the Republic, Cicero campaigned against Caesar. The common people in Rome, though, were in debt and had grown dependent on money from the government. Cicero warned the Romans in 55 BC:

> The budget should be balanced, the Treasury should be refilled, public debt should be reduced, the arrogance of officialdom should be tempered and controlled, and the assistance to foreign lands should be curtailed lest Rome become bankrupt. People must again learn to work, instead of living on public assistance.

Julius Caesar wanted to extend citizenship to those living outside of Italy to increase his support base. When Crassus died in 53 BC, contention grew between the two survivors of the First Triumvirate: Caesar and Pompey.

In 49 BC, after being victorious in Gaul, Caesar disobeyed the Senate's order to disband his legions before returning to Rome. Crossing the Rubicon River in Northern Italy on Jan. 10, 49 BC, Caesar uttered his famous saying, "The die is cast," as he began his long civil war against Pompey and the Optimates.

Pompey withdrew from Rome to a defensive position south of the city. Without Crassus' wealth, Caesar's political ambitions were thwarted. Needing money to pay his supporters, Caesar did the unthinkable. He raided the public treasury kept in the Temple of Saturn, availing himself of treasures which had accumulated since the Temple's founding in 497 BC: 15,000 bars of gold, 30,000 bars of silver, and 50 million sesterces of coins.

Lucan wrote in *The Civil War* (3.153–8; 161–2; 167–8):

> Then for the first time was Rome poorer than a Caesar.

This was similar to when the Greek leader Pericles used public money stored in the Delian League's treasury at Delphos, or during the Israelite Republic when Abimelech seized power, described in the Book of Judges 9:4.

Referring to Caesar buying of supporters, Will and Ariel Durant wrote in *The Lessons of History* (1968):

> In Italy ... rival factions competed in the wholesale purchase of ... votes; in 53 BC, one group of voters received ten million sesterces for its support ...

> When money failed, murder was available; citizens who had voted the wrong way were in some instances beaten close to death and their homes were set on fire. Antiquity had never known so rich, so powerful, and so corrupt a government.

Jefferson wrote in his *Notes on Virginia*, 1782:

> The public money ... will soon be discovered to

be sources of wealth and dominion to those who hold them; distinguished, too, by this tempting circumstance, that they are the instrument, as well as the object of acquisition. "With money we will get men," said Caesar, "and with men we will get money."

President William Henry Harrison warned in his Inaugural Address, March 4, 1841:

It is not by the extent of its patronage alone that the Executive department has become dangerous, but by the use which it appears may be made of the appointing power to bring under its control the whole revenues of the country ...

There was wanting no other addition to the powers of our Chief Magistrate to stamp monarchical character on our Government but the control of the public finances ...

The first Roman Emperor, in his attempt to seize the sacred treasure, silenced the opposition of the officer to whose charge it had been committed by a significant allusion to his sword ...

I know the importance ... to the divorce ... the Treasury from the banking institutions ... It was certainly a great error in the framers of the Constitution not to have made ... the head of the Treasury Department entirely independent of the Executive.

Caesar's political strategy was the classic example of "class warfare," seizing power using a populist tactic, namely, be perceived as siding with the people ("populares") against Pompey, who was defending the Republic ruled by an aristocracy of wealthy Senators ("optimates").

Caesar even wanted to extend Roman citizenship to illegal immigrants and those living outside of Italy, causing them to be indebted to him as loyal supporters.

Pompey lost to Caesar at the Battle of Pharsalus and then fled to Egypt, where he was assassinated. As the domestic situation in Rome became more chaotic, Caesar usurped more power. The 600 Senators in the Roman Senate lost control until they functioned simply a rubber stamp of Caesar's agenda.

Julius Caesar had the Senate declare him dictator for life in 44 BC, then deify him, giving him his own cult, with Caesars' General, Mark Anthony, serving as high priest.

Julius Caesar even changed the calendar and named a month after himself – "July." President William Henry Harrison, on March 4, 1841, warned in his Inaugural Address, written with the help of Daniel Webster:

> As long as the love of power is a dominant passion of the human bosom, and as long as the understanding of men can be warped and their affections changed by operations upon their passions and prejudices, so long will the liberties of a people depend on their constant attention to its preservation.

> The danger to all well-established free governments arises from the unwillingness of the people to believe in (the) existence ... of designing men ...

> This is the old trick of those who would usurp the government of their country. In the name of democracy they speak, warning the people against the influence of wealth and the danger of aristocracy. History, ancient and modern, is full of such examples.

> Caesar became the master of the Roman people and the senate under the pretense of supporting the democratic claims of the former against the aristocracy of the latter.

Harrison continued:

> Cromwell, in the character of the protector of the liberties of the people, became the dictator of England, and Bolivar possessed himself of unlimited power with the title of his country's liberator ...

> The tendencies of all such governments in their decline is to monarchy, and the antagonist principle to liberty there is the spirit of faction – a spirit which assumes the character and in times of great excitement imposes itself upon the people as the genuine spirit of freedom,

> and, like the false Christs whose coming was foretold by the Savior, seeks to, and were it possible

would, impose upon the true and most faithful disciples of liberty. It is in periods like this that it behooves the people to be most watchful of those to whom they have entrusted power.

President Harrison added:

The great danger to our institutions does ... appear to me to be ... the accumulation in one of the departments of that which was assigned to others ...

Limited as are the powers which have been granted, still enough have been granted to constitute a despotism if concentrated in one of the departments.., particularly ... the Executive ...

The tendency of power to increase itself, particularly when exercised by a single individual... would terminate in virtual monarchy

Harrison stated further:

Republics can commit no greater error than to ... continue any feature in their ... government which may ... increase the love of power in the bosoms of those to whom necessity obliges them to commit the management of their affairs ...

When this corrupting passion once takes possession of the human mind, like the love of gold it becomes insatiable. It is the never-dying worm in his bosom, grows with his growth and strengthens with the declining years of its victim ...

It is the part of wisdom for a republic to limit the service of that officer ... to whom she has entrusted the management of her foreign relations, the execution of her laws, and the command of her armies and navies to a period so short as to prevent his forgetting that he is the accountable agent, not the principle; the servant, not the master.

Harrison warned further:

The great dread ... seems to have been that the reserved powers of the States would be absorbed by ... the Federal Government and a consolidated power established, leaving to the States the shadow only of that independent action for which they had so zealously contended ...

There is still an undercurrent at work by which, if not seasonally checked, the worst apprehensions of our anti-federal patriots will be realized ...

Not only will the State authorities be overshadowed by the great increase of power in the Executive department ... but the character of that Government, if not its designation, be essentially and radically changed.

This state of things has been in part effected by... the never-failing tendency of political power to increase itself .

Harrison went on to compare "spirit of liberty" with a "spirit of party" faction:

There is at times much difficulty in distinguishing the false from the true spirit, a calm investigation will detect the counterfeit ...

The true spirit of liberty ... is mild and tolerant and scrupulous ... whilst the spirit of party, assuming to be that of liberty, is harsh, vindictive, and intolerant, and totally reckless as to the character of the allies which it brings to the aid of its cause ...

The reign of an intolerant spirit of party amongst a free people seldom fails to result in a dangerous accession to the Executive power introduced and established amidst unusual professions of devotion to democracy.

Lord Acton wrote:

A public man has no right to let his actions be determined by particular interests. He does the same thing as a judge who accepts a bribe. Like a judge he must consider what is right, not what is advantageous to a party or class.

Harrison concluded his Inaugural Address:

I deem the present occasion sufficiently important and solemn to justify me in expressing to my fellow citizens a profound reverence for the Christian religion, and a thorough conviction that sound morals, religious liberty, and a just sense of religious responsibility are essentially connected with all true and lasting happiness.

And to that good Being who has blessed us by the gifts of civil and religious freedom ... let us unite in fervently commending every interest of our beloved country in all future time.

Now being dictator for life, Caesar stacked the Roman Senate, increasing the number of Senators to 900, with the majority being subservient partisans who supported him.

Senators loyal to the Republic realized that Julius Caesar was becoming too powerful. In order to save the Republic, they plotted to assassinate Caesar on the "Ides of March" (March 15) 44 BC.

Rather than save the Republic, this led to further turmoil, as the citizens like Caesar because he had given them lots of money. At Caesar's funeral, instead of smoothing things over, Mark Anthony incited the mob, stirring them up to riot. The Durants wrote in *The Lessons of History* (1968):

> Yet the senate continued to meet in the temple of liberty to talk of the sacredness and beauty of the Commonwealth and gaze at the statues of the elder Brutus and of the Curtii and Decii, and the people assembled in the forum,
>
> not, as in the days of Camillus and the Scipios, to cast their free votes for annual magistrates or pass upon the acts of the senate, but to receive from the hands of the leaders of the respective parties their share of the spoils and to shout for one or the other, as those collected in Gaul or Egypt and the lesser Asia would furnish the larger dividend.

In 43 BC, Mark Anthony formed a military dictatorship, called the Second Triumvirate, with Lepidus, a wealthy patrician who had been Caesar's strongest supporter, and Caesar's 20 year old grandnephew, Octavius.

Their official purpose was to act as sort of constitutional convention, a "three-man commission for restoring the constitution of the republic." In order to accomplish this, they were given power to make or annul law without approval from either the senate or the people, and their judicial decisions could not be appealed.

Octavius forced Lepidus to resign, and the contest for total power in Rome was between Octavius and Mark Anthony. President Harrison stated in his Inaugural Address, 1841:

> In the Roman senate Octavius had a party and Antony a party, but the Commonwealth had none.

Mark Anthony had conquered much of the Middle East, installed Herod as King in Judea, and fell in love with Cleopatra IV of Egypt. The power struggle between Octavius and Mark Anthony ended with the sea Battle of Actium, Sept. 2, 31 BC. Shortly after, Mark Anthony and Cleopatra committed suicide in Egypt, and the Roman Republic was effectively ended.

Octavius Caesar was now the undisputed Emperor of Roman Empire, even taking the divine title of "Augustus." This superior status was embraced by future emperors, as Justice James Wilson wrote in *Lectures on Law*, 1790–91:

> (Roman Emperor) Caligula's reasoning was concise and conclusive. "If I am only a man, my subjects are something less: if they are men, I am something more."

A recap of the end of the Roman Republic was given by the Durants in *The Lessons of History* (1968, p. 76):

> The aristocrats engaged Pompey to maintain their ascendancy; the commoners cast in their lot with Caesar; ordeal of battle replaced the auctioning of victory; Caesar won, and established a popular dictatorship. Aristocrats killed him, but ended by accepting the dictatorship of his grandnephew and stepson Augustus (27 BC).
>
> Democracy ended, monarchy was restored, the Platonic wheel had come full turn. When Mark Anthony spoke at Caesar's funeral, instead of restoring order to the Roman Republic, he stirred the people into a frenzied mob which burned and rioted on the rich Senators.

Will and Ariel Durant wrote in *The Lessons of History*:

> After the breakdown of Roman democracy in the class wars of the Gracchi, Marius, and Caesar, Augustus organized, under what in effect, was monarchical rule.

Augustus Caesar also named a month after himself, "August." The Roman Empire became thoroughly a "patronage" or "bribery" system, where each person was indebted to the next wealthier and more politically connected patron, who was indebted to the next wealthier and more politically connected patron, on up the ladder, till the patron was dependent on a Senator, and ultimately the Emperor's favor.

This state of affairs is present in many countries where the middle class in a society is squeezed out of existence and common people are encumbered with debt. A culture develops where each person is expected to give a bribe to their boss or superior. As Benjamin Franklin warned:

> Place before the eyes of such men a post of honor, that shall, at the same time, be a place of profit, and they will move heaven and earth to obtain it ... And of what kind are the men that will strive for this profitable preeminence, through all the bustle of cabal, the heat of contention, the infinite mutual abuse of parties, tearing to pieces the best of characters?
>
> It will not be the wise and moderate, the lovers of peace and good order, the men fittest for the trust. It will be the bold and the violent, the men of strong passions and indefatigable activity in their selfish pursuits. These will thrust themselves into your government and be your rulers.

Cicero stated:

> A nation can survive its fools, and even the ambitious. But it cannot survive treason from within. An enemy at the gates is less formidable, for he is known and carries his banner openly.
>
> But the traitor moves amongst those within the gate freely, his sly whispers rustling through all the alleys, heard in the very halls of government itself.

For the traitor appears not a traitor; he speaks in accents familiar to his victims, and he wears their face and their arguments, he appeals to the baseness that lies deep in the hearts of all men. He rots the soul of a nation, he works secretly and unknown in the night to undermine the pillars of the city, he infects the body politic so that it can no longer resist. A murderer is less to fear. The traitor is the plague.

Roman historian Livy (59 BC–17 AD) stated:

Here are the questions to which I should like every reader to give his close attention: what life and morals were like; through what men and what policies, in peace and in war, empire was established and enlarged.

Then let him note how, with the gradual relaxation of discipline, morals first subsided, as it were, then sank lower and lower, and finally began the downward plunge which has brought us to our present time, when we can endure neither our vices nor their cure.

Yale President Ezra Stiles addressed Connecticut's General Assembly, May 8, 1783:

That symbol of union, the American flag with it increasing stripes and stars, may have an equally combining efficacy for ages.

The senatorial constitution and consulate of the Roman Empire lasted from Tarquin to Caesar ...

Pragmatic sanction ... secured the imperial succession in the house of Austria for ages.

The Medo-Persian and Alexandrine Empires, and that of Timur Beg, who once reigned from Smyrna to the Indus, were for obvious reasons of short and transitory duration: but that of the Assyrian endured without mutation through a tract of one thousand three hundred years from Semiramis to Sandanapolus.

Nor was the policy of Egypt overthrown for a longer period from the days of Metzraim till the time of Cambyses and Amasis.

Whatever mutations may arise in the United States, perhaps hereditary monarchy and a standing army will be the last.

The Roman Republic ended in 27 BC and officially became an Empire, controlled by Emperor Augustus Caesar.

To count all those whose lives he controlled, August Caesar ordered an empire-wide census, an ancient version of the NSA tracking citizens. This census necessitated Mary and Joseph having to travel to Bethlehem to be counted, resulting in Mary giving birth to Jesus there, as foretold by the prophet Micah, chapter 5:2–4:

> But thou, Bethlehem Ephratah, though thou be little among the thousands of Judah, yet out of thee shall he come forth unto me that is to be ruler in Israel; whose goings forth have been from of old, from everlasting.

∽

"THY KINGDOM COME"

To understand the thinking of America's founders, it is important to study the Christian beliefs they held. When Jesus was tempted in the desert:

> The devil, taking Him up on a high mountain, showed Him ALL THE KINGDOMS OF THE WORLD in a moment of time. And the devil said to Him, "All this authority I will give You, and their glory; for this has been delivered to me, and I give it to whomever I wish. Therefore, if You will worship before me, all will be Yours."

> And Jesus answered and said to him, "Get behind Me, Satan! For it is written, You shall worship the LORD your God, and Him only you shall serve."

In other parts of the Gospels, Jesus mentioned:

> He lifted up his eyes on his disciples, and said, "Blessed be ye poor: for yours is the KINGDOM OF GOD." (Lk. 6:20)

> "How hard is it for them that trust in riches to enter into the KINGDOM OF GOD!" (Mk. 10:24)

> "Heal the sick that are therein, and say unto them, The KINGDOM OF GOD is come nigh unto you."

(Lk. 10:9)

"Except a man be born again, he cannot see the KINGDOM OF GOD." (Jn. 3:3)

And when he was demanded of the Pharisees, when the KINGDOM OF GOD should come, he answered ... "The KINGDOM OF GOD cometh not with observation: Neither shall they say, Lo here! or, lo there! for, behold, the KINGDOM OF GOD is within you." (Lk. 17:20-21)

Jesus answered, "MY KINGDOM is not an earthly kingdom. If it were, my followers would fight to keep me from being handed over to the Jewish leaders. But MY KINGDOM is not of this world." (Jn. 18:36)

"For what is a man profited, If he shall gain THE WHOLE WORLD, and lose his own soul?" (Mat. 16:26)

Jesus taught disciples to pray ... "THY KINGDOM come, Thy will be done on earth as it is in heaven." (Mat. 6:10)

But HOW can "Thy Kingdom come" if it is:

–not of this world (Jn. 18:36);

–not an earthly kingdom (Jn. 18:36);

–cometh not with observation (Lk. 17:21);

–cannot see unless born again (Jn. 3:3);

–is within you (Lk. 17:21).

The colonial founders of New England attempted to answer this question. New England was a rare experiment where pastors and their churches founded communities and set up their local governments:

–Pilgrims–Rev. John Robinson

–Boston, Massachusetts–Rev. John Cotton

–Barnstable, Massachusetts–Rev. John Lothropp

–Providence, Rhode Island–Rev. Roger Williams

–Exeter, New Hampshire–Rev. John Wheelwright

–Hartford, Connecticut–Rev. Thomas Hooker

When settlers inquired how to set up the government, Rev. Thomas Hooker preached a sermon, May 31, 1638, explaining:

> The foundation of authority is laid firstly in the free consent of the people.

This was revolutionary, as most of the world at the time was ruled by kings, emperors, czars, sultans and chieftains.

Rev. Hooker's sermon continued:

> They who have the power to appoint officers and magistrates, it is in their power, also, to set the bounds and limitations of the power and place unto which they call them ...

> The privilege of election ... belongs to the people according to the blessed will and law of God.

Rev. Hooker's sermon became the basis for *The Fundamental Orders of Connecticut,* 1638, which according to historian John Fiske, comprised the first written constitution in history. It was used in Connecticut till 1818, serving as a blueprint for other New England colonies and eventually the United States Constitution.

Fundamental Orders of Connecticut, 1638, stated:

> Where a people are gathered together the word of God requires that to maintain the peace and union ... there should be an orderly and decent Government established according to God ...

> The people ... conjoin ourselves to be as one Public State or Commonwealth ... to maintain and preserve the liberty and purity of the Gospel of our Lord Jesus which we now profess ...

> According to the truth of the said Gospel is now practiced amongst us; as also in our civil affairs to be guided and governed according to such Laws, Rules, Orders and Decrees as shall be made ...

> The Governor ... shall have the power to administer justice according to the Laws here established, and for want thereof, according to the Rule of the Word of God.

Connecticut's General Assembly designated Connecticut "The Constitution State" in 1959. A statue of Rev. Thomas Hooker holding a Bible stands prominently at the Connecticut State Capitol, with the inscription on the base:

Leading his people through the wilderness, he founded Harford in June of 1636. On this site he preached the sermon which inspired the Fundamental Orders. It was the first written Constitution that created a government.

A historical marker in England reads:

Thomas Hooker 1586-1647, Curate of St. Mary's Church, Chelmsford and Town Lecturer 1626-1629, Founder of the State of Connecticut 1636, "Father of American Democracy."

Another marker reads:

Hinckley & Bosworth Borough Council, Thomas Hooker (1586-1647), Puritan Clergyman, Pupil of this School, Reputed Father of "American Democracy."

A plaque in Cambridge, Massachusetts, reads:

Here Stood The Original Meeting House of the First Church in Cambridge. Built in 1632 and the center of the Civic and Religious Life of the Town. Here Ministered 1633–1636 Thomas Hooker–A Peerless Leader of Thought and Life in both Church and State.

President Calvin Coolidge stated at the 150th Anniversary of the Declaration of Independence, Philadelphia, July 5, 1926:

The principles ... which went into the Declaration of Independence ... are found in ... the sermons... of the early colonial clergy who were earnestly undertaking to instruct their congregations in the great mystery of how to live.

They preached equality because they believed in the fatherhood of God and the brotherhood of man.

They justified freedom by the text that we are all created in the divine image ...

Placing every man on a plane where he acknowledged no superiors, where no one possessed any right to rule over him, he must inevitably choose his own rulers through a system of self-government...

In order that they might have freedom to express these thoughts and opportunity to put them into action, WHOLE CONGREGATIONS WITH THEIR PASTORS MIGRATED TO THE COLONIES.

These pastors reasoned that since Jesus never forced anyone to believe in Him, they should not. Contrary to kings, sultans and despots who killed people for not believing what they did, the pastors in New England insisted that governments should never force the consciences of citizens, thus putting into practice Jesus' Sermon on the Mount, "Do unto others as you would have them do unto you."

Believing that the KINGDOM OF GOD could NEVER BE FORCED from the top-down upon people, these pastors reasoned that if the majority of PEOPLE held godly values and voted for REPRESENTATIVES who held those godly values, then LAWS could passed reflecting those values, and values of the KINGDOM OF GOD could be come voluntarily from the bottom-up.

The overarching question they addressed was:

Does Power flow from God > to the King > to the People;

or does Power flow from God > to the People > to the Political Leaders.

WHO IS THE KING IN AMERICA?

Webster's 1828 Dictionary defined "KING" as:

The chief or SOVEREIGN of a nation; a man invested with supreme authority over a nation, tribe or country; a monarch. Kings are absolute.

Romans 13:1

Let everyone be subject to the governing authorities, for there is no authority except that which God has established.

Signer of the Constitution Gouverneur Morris wrote:

This magistrate is not the king. THE PEOPLE are THE KING.

John Jay, the First Chief Justice of the Supreme Court,

wrote in *Chisholm v. Georgia*, 1793:

> THE PEOPLE are the SOVEREIGN of this country.

Signer of Constitution James Wilson stated at the Pennsylvania Convention to ratify the U.S. Constitution:

> SOVEREIGNTY resides in THE PEOPLE; they have not parted with it.

Thomas Jefferson wrote to William Johnson, 1823:

> But the Chief Justice says, "There must be an ULTIMATE ARBITER somewhere." True, there must... The ULTIMATE ARBITER is THE PEOPLE.

James Madison wrote in Federalist No. 46, 1788:

> The ULTIMATE AUTHORITY... resides in THE PEOPLE ALONE.

Abraham Lincoln said in a debate with Stephen Douglas:

> THE PEOPLE of these United States are the rightful MASTERS of both congresses and courts.

President Andrew Jackson wrote to William B. Lewis, Aug. 19, 1841:

> THE PEOPLE are the government, administering it by their agents; they are the government, the SOVEREIGN POWER.

President James K. Polk stated Dec. 7, 1847:

> The PEOPLE are the only SOVEREIGNS recognized by our Constitution ... The success of our admirable system is a conclusive refutation of the theories of those in other countries who maintain that a 'favored few' are born to rule and that the mass of mankind must be governed by force.

President Grover Cleveland stated, July 13, 1887:

> The SOVEREIGNTY OF 60 MILLIONS OF FREE PEOPLE, is ... the working out ... of the divine right of man to govern himself and a manifestation of God's plan concerning the human race.

President Gerald Ford stated at Southern Methodist University, Sept. 13, 1975:

> Never forget that in America our SOVEREIGN is THE CITIZEN ... The state is a servant of the individual. It must never become an anonymous monstrosity that masters everyone.

President Ronald Reagan opened the John Ashbrook Center in 1983, stating of America's founders:

> The Founding Fathers understood that only by making government the servant, not the master, only by positing SOVEREIGNTY in THE PEOPLE and not the state can we hope to protect freedom.

General Omar Bradley stated in his Armistice Day Address, Nov. 10, 1948:

> In the United States it is THE PEOPLE who are SOVEREIGN ... The Government is THEIRS – to speak THEIR voice and to voice THEIR will.

A "republic" is where the will of THE PEOPLE is the law. *The Pledge of Allegiance* is to the Flag of the United States of America and "to the REPUBLIC for which it stands." In a republic, THE PEOPLE rule through individuals they chose to represent them. When someone steps on the Flag, what they are saying is that they no longer want to be the king, they no longer want to rule, they want someone else to determine the fate of their lives.

If the PEOPLE are the KING in America, who are the COUNSELORS to the KING? In 374 AD, the Christian Roman Emperor Theodosius I went to church in Milan, Italy, where the pastor was the Bishop St. Ambrose.

Imagine what it must have been like to be Bishop St. Ambrose with the Emperor sitting in your church pew. Yet that is exactly what occurs in America, with nearly 70 percent of Americans identifying themselves as Christian, according to *The Pew Religious Landscape Survey* (2015). They are mostly in church on Sundays listening to their pastors. **In this sense, pastors are, counselors to the KING.**

In the movie *The Lord of the Rings: The Two Towers* there is a scene where King Theoden's kingdom of Rohan was on the verge of destruction as he had been asleep – under a spell. A wicked counselor to the King was Wormtongue, who whispers in the King's ear to stay asleep even though his kingdom is being overrun. Another counselor to the King is Gandalf, who breaks the evil spell and wakes the king up. King Theodon dramatically comes to his senses and takes his sword.

This scene demonstrates two different kinds of Pastors:

– one kind are those who whisper in the ears of the "KING–PEOPLE" to stay asleep even though their kingdom faces destruction;

– the other kind are those who want the "KING PEOPLE" to wake up and take responsibility to rule – a responsibility for which they will one day be held accountable before God.

If THE PEOPLE are the King, what responsibility do they have? To answer this, imagine traveling through a kingdom to visit a KING, and on the way, you witness the KING's servants committing crime and corruption.

As you enter the KING's chamber, he reluctantly asks you, "Did you see all the crime and corruption as you came in here... I wish someone would fix this mess." You tap the KING on shoulder and remind him that HE is the KING, that it is HIS servants who are creating the problems, and that HE is the one responsible to fix the mess.

This is like someone in America watching television, seeing politicians committing crime and corruption, and saying "I wish someone would fix this mess." A finger should reach through the TV screen and tap the viewer on the shoulder reminding them, "In America, you are the KING. You are responsible to fix this mess."

Voting is not just a right, but a responsibility for which every American will be held accountable to God.

James Wilson wrote in his Lectures on Law, 1790–91:

In a free country, EVERY CITIZEN forms a part of the SOVEREIGN POWER: he possesses a vote.

Sam Adams stated in 1781:

Let each citizen remember at the moment he is offering his vote ... that he is executing one of the most solemn trusts in human society for which he is accountable to God.

Billy Graham stated:

Bad politicians are elected by good people who don't vote.

Rev. Martin Luther King, Jr., stated:

The Church is the conscience of the State.

As explained earlier in this book, one of the very first instances in history of people choosing their leaders was ancient Israel. When they came out of Egypt, Moses' father-in-law Jethro gave advice to Moses.

Exodus 18:21 stated:

Moreover thou shalt provide OUT OF ALL THE PEOPLE able men, such as fear God, men of truth, hating covetousness; and place such over them, to be rulers of thousands, and rulers of hundreds, rulers of fifties, and rulers of tens.

Deuteronomy 1:3–13:

Moses spoke unto the children of Israel ... How can I myself alone bear your ... burden ... TAKE YOU wise men, and understanding, and KNOWN AMONG YOUR TRIBES, and I will make them rulers over you.

Deuteronomy 16:18–19:

Judges and officers SHALT THOU MAKE THEE IN ALL THY GATES which the Lord thy God giveth thee throughout thy tribes.

One of America's first elections occurred in Woburn, Massachusetts, which was founded in 1642 by Captain Edward Johnson, a contemporary of Governor John Winthrop. Captain Edward Johnson described the town's original election in Wonder-Working Providences of Sion's Saviour in New England, 1654:

The number of faithful people of Christ ... gather into a church ... Having fasted and prayed ... they joined together in a holy Covenant with the Lord and with one another ... Those who are chosen to a place in government, must be men truly fearing God, wise and learned in the truths of Christ ... Neither will any Christian of a sound judgment vote for any, but those who earnestly contend for the faith.

Alexis de Tocqueville wrote of elections in Democracy in America, 1835:

If a political character attacks a (religious) sect, this may not prevent even the partisans of that very sect from supporting him; but if he attacks all the sects together, every one abandons him and he remains alone ... Moreover, all the sects of the United States are comprised within the great unity of Christianity

President Calvin Coolidge commented on elections in a Radio Address, Nov. 3, 1924:

I therefore urge upon all the voters of our country, without reference to party, that they assemble...at their respective voting places in the exercise of the high office of American citizenship, that they approach the ballot box in the spirit that they would approach a sacrament, and there, disregarding all appeals to passion and prejudice, dedicate themselves truly and wholly to the welfare of their country ...

When an election is so held, it ... sustains the belief that the voice of the people is the voice of God.

On Sept. 20, 2001, President George W. Bush addressed Congress after the 911 Islamic terrorist attack:

Our enemy is a radical network of terrorists... They hate our freedoms – our freedom of religion, our freedom of speech, OUR FREEDOM TO VOTE.

President Calvin Coolidge stated in 1924:

The history of government on this earth has been almost entirely... rule of force held in the HANDS OF A FEW. Under our Constitution, America committed itself to power in the HANDS OF THE PEOPLE.

John Adams wrote:

Thirteen (State) governments thus founded on the natural authority of THE PEOPLE alone.

President Theodore Roosevelt stated in 1903:

In NO other place and at NO other time has the experiment of government of the PEOPLE, by the PEOPLE, for the PEOPLE, been tried on so vast a scale as here in our own country.

Ronald Reagan stated in 1961:

In this country of ours took place the GREATEST REVOLUTION that has ever taken place IN THE WORLD'S HISTORY ... Every other revolution simply exchanged one set of rulers for another ...

Here for the first time in all the THOUSANDS OF YEARS of man's relation to man ... the founding fathers established the idea that YOU and I had WITHIN OURSELVES the GOD-GIVEN RIGHT and ABILITY TO DETERMINE OUR OWN DESTINY.

Franklin Roosevelt stated in Hyde Park, NY, Nov. 6, 1944:

Tomorrow ... the people of the United States again vote as free men and women, with full freedom of choice – with no secret police watching over your shoulders. And for generations to come Americans will continue to prove their faith in free elections ...

In the midst of fighting ... our soldiers and sailors and airmen will not forget election day back home. Millions of these men have already cast their own ballots, and they will be wondering about the outcome of the election, and what it will mean to them in their future lives ... for the cause of decency and freedom and civilization.

We need strength and wisdom which is greater than is bequeathed to mere mortals. We need Divine help and guidance ... People of America have ever had a deep well of religious strength, far back to the days of the Pilgrim Fathers. You will find it fitting that I read a prayer ...

"Almighty God ... Thou hast gathered our people out of many lands and races into a great Nation. We commend to Thy overruling providence the men and women of our forces by sea, by land, and in the air ... Enable us to guard for the least among us the freedom we covet for ourselves ...

"Preserve our union against all the divisions of race and class which threaten it ... May the blessing of God Almighty rest upon this whole land; May He give us light to guide us, courage to support us, charity to unite us."

Yale President Ezra Stiles addressed Connecticut's General Assembly, May 8, 1783:

Not only the polity, or exterior system of government, but the laws and interior regulations of each state, are already excellent, surpassing the institutions of Lycurgus or Plato; and by the annual appeals to the public a power is reserved to the people to remedy any corruptions or errors in government.

And even if the people should sometimes err, yet each assembly of the states, and the body of the people, always embosom wisdom sufficient to correct themselves; so that a political mischief cannot be durable. Herein we far surpass any states on earth. We can correct ourselves, if in the wrong.

The Belgian states, in their federal capacity, are united by a perfect system, constituted by that great prince, William of Nassau, and the compatriots of that age; but they left the interior government of the judicial tribunals, cities, and provinces, as despotic and arbitrary as they found them.

So the elective monarchical republic of Poland is an excellent constitution for the nobles, but leaves despotism and tyranny, the portion and hard fate of the plebeians, beyond what is to be found in any part of Europe.

Not so the American states; their interior as well as exterior civil and judicial polities are so nearly perfect, that the rights of individuals, even to numerous millions, are guarded and secured.

The crown and glory of our confederacy is the amphictyonic council (league of ancient Greek city-states) of the General Congress, standing on the annual election of the united respective states, and revocable at pleasure.

This lays the foundation of a permanent union in the American Republic, which may at length convince the world that, of all the policies to be found on earth... the most perfect one has been invented and realized in America.

WASHINGTON'S FAREWELL

In the 6,000 year record of human history, kings killed to get power and kings killed to keep power. Only rarely did a leader of a nation voluntarily relinquish power. On Sept. 19, 1796, the world stood in disbelief as President George Washington delivered his Farewell Address:

Of all the dispositions and habits which lead to political prosperity, Religion and Morality are indispensable supports. In vain would that man claim the tribute of Patriotism who should labor to subvert these great Pillars ... Let us with caution indulge the supposition that morality can be maintained without religion.

Washington added:

Reason and experience both forbid us to expect that national morality can prevail in exclusion of religious principle ... Morality is a necessary *spring* of *popular* government ... Who that is a sincere friend to it can look with indifference upon attempts to shake the foundation?

He continued:

And of fatal tendency ... to put, in the place of the delegated will of the Nation, the will of a party; – often a small but artful and enterprising minority ...

They are likely, in the course of time and things, to become potent engines, by which cunning, ambitious, and unprincipled men will be enabled to subvert the Power of the People and to usurp for the themselves the reins of Government; destroying afterwards the very engines which have lifted them to unjust dominion ...

One method of assault may be to effect, in the forms of the Constitution, alterations which will impair the energy of the system, and thus to undermine what cannot be directly overthrown ...

Washington explained further:

I have already intimated to you the danger of Parties in the State ... Let me now take a more comprehensive view, and warn you in the most solemn manner against the baneful effects of the spirit of Party, generally. This spirit, unfortunately, is inseparable from our nature, having its roots in the strongest passions of the human mind.

It exists under different shapes in all Governments, more of less stifled, controlled, or repressed; but, in those of the *popular* form it is seen in its greatest rankness and is truly their worst enemy ...

Domination of one faction over another, sharpened by the spirit of revenge natural to party dissension, which in different ages and countries has perpetrated the most horrid enormities, is itself a frightful despotism.

He continued:

But this leads at length to a more formal and permanent despotism. The disorders and miseries, which result, gradually incline the minds of men to seek security and repose in the absolute power of an Individual ... [who] turns this disposition to the purposes of his own elevation, on the ruins of Public Liberty ...

Ill-founded jealousies and false alarms, kindles the animosity of one part against another, foments occasionally riot and insurrection.

It opens the doors to foreign influence and corruption, which find a facilitated access to the Government itself through the channels of party passions. Thus the policy and the will of one country, are subjected to the policy and will of another ...

Washington added:

It is important, likewise, that the habits of thinking in a free Country should inspire caution in those entrusted with its administration, to confine themselves within their respective Constitutional spheres; avoiding in the exercise of the Powers of one department to encroach upon another.

The spirit of encroachment tends to consolidate the powers of all the departments in one, and thus to create, whatever the form of government, a real despotism.

A just estimate of that love of power, and proneness to abuse it, which predominates the human heart is sufficient to satisfy us of the truth of this position.

The necessity of reciprocal checks in the exercise of political power; by dividing and distributing it into different depositories, and constituting each the Guardian of the Public Weal [common good] against invasions by the others, has been evinced by experiments ancient and modern; some of them in our country and under our own eyes. To preserve them must be as necessary as to institute them.

Washington warned against usurpation:

If in the opinion of the People, the distribution or modification of the Constitutional powers be in any way particular wrong, let it be corrected by an amendment in the way which the Constitution designates.

But let there be no change by usurpation; for though this, in one instance, may be the instrument of good, it is the customary weapon by which free governments are destroyed. The precedent must always greatly overbalance in permanent evil any partial or transient benefit which the use can at any time yield ...

Washington continued:

Avoiding likewise the accumulation of debt, not only by shunning occasions of expense, but by vigorous exertions in time of Peace to discharge the Debts which unavoidable wars may have occasioned, not ungenerously throwing upon posterity the burden which we ourselves ought to bear ... .

In the execution of such a plan nothing is more essential than that permanent ... attachments for other [countries] should be excluded ... It gives to ambitious, corrupted, or deluded citizens ... facility to betray, or sacrifice the interests of their own country, without odium, sometimes even with popularity: gilding with the appearances of a virtuous sense of obligation, a commendable deference for public opinion, or a laudable zeal for public good, the base or foolish compliances of ambition, corruption or infatuation.

As avenues to foreign influence in innumerable ways, such attachments are particularly alarming to the truly enlightened and independent Patriot. How many opportunities do they afford to tamper with domestic factions, to practice the arts of seduction, to mislead public opinion, to influence or awe the public Councils!

Such attachments of a small or weak, towards a great and powerful Nation, dooms the former to be the satellite of the latter.

Against the insidious wiles of foreign influence, (I conjure you to believe me fellow citizens) the jealously of a free people to be constantly awake; since history and experience prove that foreign influence is one of the most baneful foes of Republican Government.

Washington concluded:

Real Patriots, who may resist the intrigues of the favorite, are liable to become suspected and odious; while its tools and dupes usurp the applause and confidence of the people, to surrender their interests...

'Tis folly in one Nation to look for disinterested favors from another ... it must pay with a portion of its Independence for whatever it may accept ... There can be no greater error than to expect, or calculate upon real favors from Nation to Nation.

'Tis an illusion which experience must cure, which a just pride ought to discard ...

In offering to you, my Countrymen these counsels of an old and affectionate friend, I dare not hope they will make the strong and lasting impression, I could wish ... to warn against the mischiefs of foreign Intrigue.

Fisher Ames sat in the pew next to George Washington at the service in New York's St. Paul's Chapel following Washington's Inauguration. Ames helped ratify the U.S.

Constitution. He was a Congressman from Massachusetts where, on Aug. 20, 1789, he proposed as the wording of the First Amendment (*Annals of Congress*, 1:766):

> Congress shall make no law establishing religion, or to prevent the free exercise thereof, or to infringe the rights of conscience.

Fisher Ames compared monarchy to a republic (Ralph Waldo Emerson, *Essays*, 2nd Series, chapter 7–"Politics," 1844, p. 97; *Library of America*, 1983):

> Monarchy is a merchantman (cargo ship), which sails well, but will sometimes strike on a rock, and go to the bottom; whilst a republic is a raft, which would never sink, but then your feet are always in water.

Warning against the temptation to increase government, Fisher Ames stated in "Speeches on Mr. Madison's Resolutions" (*Works of Fisher Ames, compiled by a number of his friends*, Boston: T.B. Wait & Co., 1809, p. 48):

> To control trade by law, instead of leaving it to the better management of the merchants ... (is) to play the tyrant in the counting house, and in directing the private expenses of our citizens, are employments equally unworthy of discussion.

At the Massachusetts Convention, Jan. 15, 1788, Fisher Ames warned that democracy without morals would reduce the nation to the basest of human passions, swallowing freedom:

> A democracy is a volcano which conceals the fiery materials of its own destruction.

Fisher Ames commented in "The Dangers of American Liberty," 1805 (published in *Works of Fisher Ames: with a selection from his speeches and correspondence*, Boston: Little, Brown & Co., 1854, pp. 349):

> The known propensity of a democracy is to licentiousness (sexual depravity), which the ambitious call, and the ignorant believe to be, liberty.

Russell Kirk described Fisher Ames in *The Conservative Mind: From Burke to Eliot* (Washington D.C.: Regnery Publishing, Inc., 2001, chapter 3, p. 81–85):

As time runs on, Ames grows more intense. Democracy cannot last ... When property is snatched from hand to hand ... then society submits cravenly to the immorality of rule by the sword ... Of all the terrors of democracy, the worst is its destruction of moral habits.

"A democratic society will soon find its morals... the surly companion of its licentious joys" ...

Is there no check upon these excesses? ... The press supplies an endless stimulus to popular imagination and passion; the press lives upon heat and coarse drama and incessant restlessness.

"It has inspired ignorance with presumption" ... "Constitutions," says Ames, "are but paper; society is the substratum of government" ...

Like Samuel Johnson, (Ames) finds the key to political decency in private morality.

Aaron McLeod wrote in "Great Conservative Minds: A Condensation of Russell Kirk's *The Conservative Mind*" (Oct. 2005, Alabama Policy Inst., Birmingham, AL, ch. 3, p. 9):

Ames was pessimistic about the American experiment because he doubted there were sufficient numbers of men with the moral courage and charisma to preserve the country from the passions of the multitudes and the demagogues who master them.

He was convinced that the people as a body cannot reason and are easily swayed by clever speakers and political agents. In his words, "few can reason, all can feel" ...

"Democracy could not last," Ames thundered ... "for despotism lies at the door; when the tyranny of the majority leads to chaos, society will submit to rule by the sword."

Aaron McLeod continued:

To Ames, what doomed the American experiment was the democratic destruction of morals ...

Ames believed that justice and morality in America would fail, and *popular* rule cannot support justice, without which moral habits fall away.

Neither the free press nor paper constitutions could safe-guard order from these excesses, for the first is merely a stimulus to popular passion and imagination, while the other is a thin bulwark against corruption.

When old prescription and tradition are dismissed, only naked force matters.

John Adams wrote to Rev. Zabdiel Adams, June 21, 1776:

Statesmen, my dear Sir, may plan and speculate for liberty, but it is religion and morality alone, which can establish the principles upon which freedom can securely stand. The only foundation of a free Constitution is pure virtue, and if this cannot be inspired into our people in a greater measure, than they have it now, they may change their rulers and the forms of Government, but they will not obtain a lasting liberty.

After George Washington's death, Dec. 14, 1799, Fisher Ames delivered a eulogy "An Oration on the Sublime Virtues of General George Washington," Feb. 8, 1800, at Boston's Old South Meeting-House, before the Lieutenant Governor, the Council, and both branches of the Massachusetts Legislature (Boston: Young & Minns, 1800):

Our liberty depends on our education, our laws, and habits ... It is founded on morals and religion, whose authority reigns in the heart, and on the influence all these produce on public opinion before that opinion governs rulers.

Fisher Ames was elected Harvard's president, but he declined due to an illness. On July 4, 1808, exactly 32 years to the day after America declared its Independence, Fisher Ames died at the age of 50. Fisher Ames wrote in *The Mercury and New-England Palladium of Boston* (Vol. XVII, No. 2,8, Tuesday, Jan. 27, 1801, p. 1; John Thornton Kirkland, *Works of Fisher Ames*, 1809, p. 134–35):

It has been the custom of late years to put a number of little books into the hands of children, containing fables and moral lessons ... Many books for children are ... injudiciously compiled ... the moral is drawn from the fable they know not why ...

Some of the most admired works of this kind abound with a frothy sort of sentiment ... the chief merit of which consists in shedding tears and giving away money ...

Why then, if these books for children must be retained ... should not the Bible regain the place it once held as a school book? Its morals are pure, its examples captivating and noble. The reverence for the Sacred Book, that is thus early impressed, lasts long – and probably, if not impressed in infancy never takes firm hold of the mind.

One consideration more is important: In no book is there so good English, so pure and so elegant – and by teaching all the same book they will speak alike, and the Bible will justly remain the standard of language as well as of faith.

D. James Kennedy summarized Fisher Ames words in "The Great Deception" (Fort Lauderdale, FL: Coral Ridge Ministries, 1989; 1993, p. 3; The Great Deception–a speech delivered Dec. 1, 1992, Ottawa, IL):

We have a dangerous trend beginning to take place in our education. We're starting to put more and more textbooks into our schools. We've become accustomed of late of putting little books into the hands of children, containing fables and moral lessons.

We're spending less time in the classroom on the Bible, which should be the principal text in our schools. The Bible states these great moral lessons better than any other man-made book.

PLANS OF CENTRALIZATION

President Calvin Coolidge stated:

No plan of centralization has ever been adopted which did not result in bureaucracy, tyranny, inflexibility, reaction, and decline.

Of all forms of government, those administered by bureaus are about the least satisfactory to an enlightened and progressive people. Being irresponsible they become autocratic.

Unless bureaucracy is constantly resisted it breaks down representative government and overwhelms democracy. It sets up the pretense of having authority over everybody and being responsible to nobody.

Plans of centralization of power in ancient history include:

*Ancient Civilizations at war

*Israel under Saul (c.1079 BC–1007 BC)

*Plato (429–347 BC)

*Sun Tzu (c.544–496 BC)

*Chanakya (350–283 BC)

*Julius Caesar (100–44 BC).

Further plans of centralization of power were carried out by leaders, philosophers and big-government policies:

*Mohammed (570–632AD)

*Machiavelli (1469–1527)

*Cromwell (1599–1658)

*Robespierre (1758–1794)

*Talleyrand (1754–1838)

*Napoleon (1769–1821)

*Bolívar (1783–1830)

*Santa Anna (1794–1876)

*Hegel (1770–1831)

*Marx (1818–1883)

*Engels (1820–1895)

*Gramsci (1891–1937)

*Lenin (1870–1924)

*Stalin (1878–1953)

*Hitler (1889–1945)

*Mao Zedung (1893–1976)

*Pol Pot (1925–1998)

*Ho Chi Minh (1890–1969)

*Saul Alinsky (1909–1972)

*Fidel Castro (b.1926)

*Idi Amin (1925–2003)
*Hugo Chavez (1954-2013)
*Second Bank of the United States (1816-1841)
*New House Chamber changed Congressional Ratio
*Bank failures & creation Federal Reserve Bank
*Income Tax (1913)
*17th Amendment election of Senators (1913)
*Federal Court usurpation-legislating from the bench
*Election manipulation, voter fraud, hacking
*Czars appointed by the President
*Executive Orders, Memos & Directives
*Government-run Healthcare
*Cloward-Piven: Marxism via Financial Bankruptcy

Addressing Karl Marx's centralization policies, "the seeds of Leninism, Stalinism, revolution, and the Cold War," John F. Kennedy told the American Newspaper Publishers Association, Waldorf-Astoria Hotel, NY, April 27, 1961:

You may remember that in 1851 the *New York Herald Tribune*, under the sponsorship and publishing of Horace Greeley, employed as its London correspondent an obscure journalist by the name of Karl Marx.

We are told that foreign correspondent Marx, stone broke, and with a family ill and undernourished, constantly appealed to Greeley and Managing Editor Charles Dana for an increase in his munificent salary of $5 per installment, a salary which he and Engels ungratefully labeled as the "lousiest petty bourgeois cheating."

But when all his financial appeals were refused, Marx looked around for other means of livelihood and fame, eventually terminating his relationship with the *Tribune* and devoting his talents full time to the cause that would bequeath to the world **the seeds of Leninism, Stalinism, revolution and the Cold War**... If only Marx had remained a foreign correspondent, history might have been different.

Kelly O'Connell wrote in "Pagan Government Theory Insures

Tyranny Returns to the West" (*Canada Free Press*, 2012):

Contrast this divine model to ... humanistic philosophy ... which forms the outline of Marxism—or any other kind of leftist ideology—such as the Humanist Manifesto. Why should one humanistic rule be preferred over any other, except personal taste? In such a setting humans are highly at risk ...

According to P.H. Vigor in *A Guide To Marxism*, any act is acceptable to a Marxist given the right circumstances: For ethics or morality, the fundamental point for a Marxist is that there is no such thing as an absolute Right and Wrong, being relative for a Marxist. A thing wrong at one time, and in one set of circumstances, will be right in another.

It is therefore simply not possible to settle an argument with them by reference to ethical principles—by saying, for instance, that the consequence of a particular policy would be murder, and you cannot commit murder. From a Marxist standpoint, you can—in certain circumstances ...

Marx was excited to read Darwin's works and believed himself providing an economic explanation of Darwin's biological principles, according to Roger Trigg in *Ideas of Human Nature, An Historical Introduction*. This gave Marx an unsentimental, pseudo-scientific manner of describing others, not seeing individuals but..."the personification of economic-categories, the bearers of particular class-relations and interests."

As an atheistic Darwinian materialist, Marx believed in no religion, but felt people's "human nature" can be changed, and for the better, in the right social conditions. Overall, Marx—like all socialist writers, believed salvation was a concept to apply only to the enlightened group, not individuals—since there was no afterlife to be saved into, anyway. If only the group matters, then "human rights" are an unnecessary fiction ...

It is a simple fact that no leftism, whether Marxism, socialism, or any other garden variety liberalism, contains the seeds of human liberty.

Whether by genius or luck, **it is the biblical theory of government which carries the potential to defend men and women from unjust state actions.**

For these reasons alone, it is crucial modern man does not abandon the West's unique perspective on government and accept leftism's pagan practices. These afford no people anywhere real safety from mindless tyrants.

Instead we are at risk from bombastic, bureaucratic simpletons, drunk in their cruel quest for power, who move as zombie-like followers of their long-dead, failed general – Karl Marx.

At a reception for his 80th birthday in West Branch, IA, Aug. 10, 1954, former President Herbert Hoover stated:

I have witnessed on the ground in 20 nations the workings of the philosophy of that anti-Christ, Karl Marx ... I want to say something ... not in the tones of Jeremiah but in the spirit of Saint Paul ...

Our Founding Fathers did not invent the priceless boon of individual freedom and respect for the dignity of men. That great gift to mankind sprang from the Creator and not from governments ...

Today the Socialist virus and poison gas generated by Karl Marx and Friedreich Engels have spread into every nation on the earth ... Their dogma is absolute materialism which defies truth and religious faith ...

A nation is strong or weak, it thrives or perishes upon what it believes to be true. If our youth are rightly instructed in the faith of our fathers ... then our power will be stronger.

To this whole gamut of Socialist infections, I say to you ... God has blessed us with ... heritage. The great documents of that heritage are not from Karl Marx. They are from the Bible, the Declaration of Independence and the Constitution of the United States. Within them alone can the safeguards of freedom survive.

President Coolidge stated, laying the cornerstone of the Jewish Community Center, Washington, D.C., May 3, 1925:

Our country, and every country based on the principle of popular government, must learn ... the patriots who laid the foundation of this Republic drew their faith from the Bible ...

We cannot escape the conclusion that if American democracy is to remain the greatest hope of humanity, it must continue abundantly in the faith of the Bible.

John Jay, as President of the Continental Congress, approved the "Circular Letter from the Congress of the United States of America to their Constituents," Sept. 13, 1779:

The rulers of the state are the servants of the people, and not the masters ... The ungrateful despotism and inordinate lust of domination, which marked the unnatural designs of the British king ... to enslave the people of America, reduced you to the necessity of either asserting your rights by arms, or ingloriously passing under the yoke ...

Remember we are contending against a kingdom... without public virtue ... betrayed by their own representatives; against a Prince governed by his passions; ... against a government by the most impious violations of the rights of religion, justice, humanity and mankind, courting the vengeance of Heaven.

John Jay, as Chief Justice of New York, charged the Grand Jury of Ulster County, Sept. 8, 1777:

The Americans are the first people whom Heaven has favored with an opportunity of ... choosing the forms of government under which they should live. All other constitutions have derived their existence from violence or accidental circumstances ...

Your lives, your liberties, your property, will be at the disposal only of your Creator and yourselves. You will know no power but such as you will create; no authority unless derived from your grant; no laws but such as acquire all their obligation from your consent.

PATRICK HENRY'S WARNING

Virginia's State Seal has a female figure personifying *Virtus,* the Roman Republic's attribute of virtue, with her foot crushing the neck of a tyrant. The Seal's Latin motto *Sic semper tyrannis,* means "Thus always to tyrants." Patrick Henry, the five-time Governor of Virginia, renown for stating: "Give me liberty or give me death," warned at Virginia's Ratifying Convention, June 5, 1788:

> Examples are to be found in ancient Greece and ancient Rome ... of the people losing their liberty by their carelessness and the ambition of a few ...

> We are told that we need not fear; because those in power, being our Representatives, will not abuse the power we put in their hands: I am not well versed in history, but I will submit to your recollection, whether liberty has been destroyed ... by the tyranny of rulers? ...

> Those nations, who, omitting to resist their oppressors, or negligently suffering their liberty to be wrested from them, have groaned under intolerable despotism. Most of the human race are now in this deplorable condition ...

> My great objection to this Government is, that it does not leave us the means of defending our rights, or of waging war against tyrants ...

> Let my beloved Americans guard against that fatal lethargy ... I would recur to the American spirit to defend us ... to that illustrious spirit I address my most fervent prayer, to prevent our adopting a system destructive to liberty ...

> Oh, Sir, we should have fine times indeed, if to punish tyrants ... Your arms wherewith you could defend yourselves, are gone ... Did you ever read of any revolution in a nation, brought about by the punishment of those in power, inflicted by those who had no power at all? ...

> A few neighbors cannot assemble without the risk of being shot by a hired soldiery, the engines of despotism. We may see such an act in America. A standing army we shall have also, to execute the

execrable commands of tyranny:

And how are you to punish them? ... What resistance could be made? The attempt would be madness ... You cannot force them to receive their punishment: Of what service would militia be to you, when most probably you will not have a single musket in the State ...

Can the annals of mankind exhibit one single example, where rulers overcharged with power willingly let go the oppressed ... A willing relinquishment of power is one of those things which human nature never was, nor ever will be capable of ...

When the American spirit was in its youth ... liberty, Sir, was then the primary object ... We drew the spirit of liberty from our British ancestors; by that spirit we have triumphed over every difficulty:

But now, Sir, the American spirit, assisted by the ropes and chains of consolidation, is about to convert this country to a powerful and mighty empire ... If you make the citizens of this country agree to become the subjects of one great consolidated empire of America... such a government is incompatible with the genius of republicanism. There will be no checks, no real balances, in this government ...

Suppose it should prove oppressive, how can it be altered? ... Is it not, therefore, a consolidated government? ... There is to be a great and mighty President, with very extensive powers – the powers of a king.

Patrick Henry concluded:

This Constitution is said to have beautiful features; but when I come tof examine these features, sir, they appear to me horribly frightful ... It squints towards monarchy ... Your President may easily become king ...

If your American chief be a man of ambition and abilities, how easy is it for him to render himself absolute! The army is in his hands, and if he be a man of address, it will be attached to him, and it will be the subject of long meditation with him to seize the first auspicious moment to accomplish his design; and, sir, will the American spirit solely relieve you when this happens?...

The President, in the field, at the head of his army, can prescribe the terms on which he shall reign master, so far that it will puzzle any American ever to get his neck from under the galling yoke ...

If ever he violates the laws, one of two things will happen: he will come at the head of his army, to carry every thing before him; or he will give bail, or do what Mr. Chief Justice will order him.

If he be guilty, will not the recollection of his crimes teach him to make one bold push for the American throne? Will not the immense difference between being master of every thing, and being ignominiously tried and punished, powerfully excite him to make this bold push?

But, sir, where is the existing force to punish him? Can he not, at the head of his army, beat down every opposition? Away with your President! we shall have a king: the army will salute him monarch... What will then become of you and your rights? Will not absolute despotism ensue? ...

My great objection to the Constitution ... that the preservation of our liberty depends on the single chance of men being virtuous enough to make laws to punish themselves.

America is drifting toward more oversight of its citizens, with politicians advocating for socialism, to the applause of some college students. Those wanting to preserve liberty must remind the next generation of Vladimir Lenin's statement:

The goal of socialism is communism.

Franklin Roosevelt basically described socialism as simply a monarchy makeover:

The Soviet Union ... is run by a dictatorship as absolute as any other dictatorship in the world.

Is history repeating itself? After reviewing the rise and fall of great republics, kings and tyrants, and gleaning profound insights from notable philosophers, statesmen and historians, it is hoped that a renewed appreciation will be gained for America's uniqueness in world history and a desire to make America great again.

Justice John Jay received an invitation from the City of New York to a celebration of America's 50th anniversary. Jay, age 82, replied June 29, 1826, recommending:

> A general and public return of praise to Him from whose goodness these blessings descend ... The most effectual means of securing the continuance of our civil and religious liberties is, always to remember with reverence and gratitude the Source from which they flow.

Lincoln stated at Edwardsville, IL, Sept. 11, 1858:

> What constitutes the bulwark of our own liberty?... Our reliance is in the love of liberty which God has planted in us ...
>
> Destroy this spirit and you have planted the seeds of despotism at your own doors ... You have lost the genius of your own independence and become the fit subjects of the first cunning tyrant who rises among you.

John Jay stated Sept. 13, 1779:

> Can there be any reason to apprehend that the Divine Disposer of human events, after having separated us from the house of bondage, and led us safe through a sea of blood, towards the land of liberty and promise will leave the work of our political redemption unfinished ... or suffer us to be carried back in **chains** to that country of oppression from whose tyranny He hath mercifully delivered us?

William Penn is attributed with the statement:

> Those who will not be governed by God will be ruled by tyrants.

Patrick Henry warned:

> It is when a people forget God that tyrants forge their **chains**.

CPSIA information can be obtained
at www.ICGtesting.com
Printed in the USA
FSOW03n0929111016
25888FS